Exploring the Multitude of Muslims in Europe

Muslim Minorities

Editorial Board

Aminah McCloud (*DePaul University, Chicago*)

VOLUME 27

The titles published in this series are listed at *brill.com/mumi*

Exploring the Multitude of Muslims in Europe

Essays in Honour of Jørgen S. Nielsen

Edited by

Niels Valdemar Vinding
Egdūnas Račius
Jörn Thielmann

BRILL

LEIDEN | BOSTON

Photo of Jørgen S. Nielsen by Leif Tuxen.

The Library of Congress Cataloging-in-Publication Data is available online at http://catalog.loc.gov
LC record available at http://lccn.loc.gov/2017058914

Typeface for the Latin, Greek, and Cyrillic scripts: "Brill". See and download: brill.com/brill-typeface.

ISSN 1570-7571
ISBN 978-90-04-36249-9 (hardback)
ISBN 978-90-04-36252-9 (e-book)

Copyright 2018 by Koninklijke Brill NV, Leiden, The Netherlands.
Koninklijke Brill NV incorporates the imprints Brill, Brill Hes & De Graaf, Brill Nijhoff, Brill Rodopi,
Brill Sense and Hotei Publishing.
All rights reserved. No part of this publication may be reproduced, translated, stored in a retrieval system,
or transmitted in any form or by any means, electronic, mechanical, photocopying, recording or otherwise,
without prior written permission from the publisher.
Authorization to photocopy items for internal or personal use is granted by Koninklijke Brill NV provided
that the appropriate fees are paid directly to The Copyright Clearance Center, 222 Rosewood Drive, Suite
910, Danvers, MA 01923, USA. Fees are subject to change.

This book is printed on acid-free paper and produced in a sustainable manner.

Contents

Publisher's Preface   IX
Editors' Introduction   XI
Note from Aminah B. McCloud   XXV
List of Contributors   XXVI
Bibliography of Jørgen S. Nielsen   XXX

PART 1
Conceptualising Islam and Muslims

1   Between Islam as a Generic Category and Muslim Exceptionalism   3
Thijl Sunier

2   European Muslims as Skilled Kite Flyers   20
Werner Menski

3   Does European Islam Think?   35
Mohammed Hashas

4   Churchification of Islam in Europe   50
Niels Valdemar Vinding

5   "Perpetual First Generation": Religiosity and Territoriality in Belonging
Strategies of Turks of France   67
Samim Akgönül

PART 2
Producing Islam and Muslims in Europe

6   Alternative Dispute Resolution among Muslims in Germany and
the Debate on "Parallel Justice"   91
Mathias Rohe

7   Islamic Law in Lithuania? Its Institutionalisation, Limits and
Prospects for Application   109
Egdūnas Račius

8   The King, the Boy, the Monk and the Magician: Jihadi Ideological
Entrepreneurship between the UK and Denmark   128
Jakob Skovgaard-Petersen

9   "ALLAH IS IGNORANCE": An Essay on the Poetic Praxis of Yahya
Hassan and the Critique of Liberal Islam   141
Thomas Hoffmann

PART 3
Multitudes of Muslims in Europe

10   Human First – To be Witnesses to Each Other's Life: Twenty-one Years
of Struggle for Equal Human Dignity   157
Naveed Baig, Lissi Rasmussen and Hans Raun Iversen

11   Muslims Accused of Apostasy: An Ahmadi Refutation   172
Göran Larsson

12   Marginalised Islam: Christianity's Role in the Sufi Order of
Bektashism   183
Emil B.H. Saggau

13   Islamic Literature in Bosnian Language 1990–2012: Production and
Dissemination of Islamic Knowledge at the Periphery   198
Ahmet Alibašić

14   European Islam in the Light of the Bosnian Experience   212
Safet Bektovic

Index   225

Publisher's Preface

At the time of Jørgen S. Nielsen's first book publication with Brill nobody knew that this would be the start of a very fruitful collaboration, resulting in a rapidly expanding number of publications on Muslims in Europe and elsewhere under his careful and dedicated editorship. The publication in question was *Muslim Networks and Transnational Communities in and across Europe* (2002), which Jørgen edited with Stefano Allievi. Its publication would mark the beginning of a long list of Brill publications that involve Jørgen in one capacity or another.

As one of the founding editors of our *Muslim Minorities* book series, Jørgen has supervised the publication of no less than 28 academic books in the series to date (not including the present volume), both edited volumes and monographs, discussing Muslims as a minority all over Europe, and as far away as New Zealand.

In 2007, Jørgen and Brill first exchanged ideas about developing an annual publication on the situation of Muslims in Europe. This new and unparalleled reference work would include a country-by-country summary of essential data, offering basic statistics on Muslims in Europe, surveys of legal status and arrangements, existing Muslim organizations, as well as an analysis and research articles of current issues and themes affecting Muslims in Europe and a book review section of published works of significance. Never one to shy away from a significant challenge, Jørgen supported these ambitious ideas and became the project's editor-in-chief. In its early days, the *Yearbook* was supported by five institutions across Europe, all recruited from Jørgen's large network of colleagues, peers and friends. Together with a dedicated editorial board, Jørgen succeeded in bringing together 52 different contributors to write on Muslims in 37 European different countries. This number would expand to 46 countries and even more contributors in the following years.

The first volume of the *Yearbook of Muslims in Europe* appeared in September 2009, only two years after the initial exchange of ideas between Brill and Jørgen had started. This is certainly no small accomplishment, because, as Jørgen himself once shared with me, "working with academics is a bit like herding cats." Of course, he did not consider himself to be an exception to this rule. I will neither confirm nor deny whether this is true, but the fact that Jørgen succeeded in getting this project off the ground in such a short amount of time certainly attests to his professionalism, dedication, hard work and enthusiasm.

YME 1 turned out as a hefty volume of 575 pages, followed by volume 2 consisting of more than 700 pages in 2010, and growing even further to an impressive 768 pages in 2011. Now covering 46 European countries, the *Yearbook* is in its 9th volume year and is still going strong on the foundations laid by Jørgen. On top of that, volume 1 was translated into Bosnian in 2011.

Next to his work for the *Muslim Minorities* book series and the *Yearbook*, Jørgen also found time to serve as the first editor-in-chief of the *Journal of Muslims in Europe* from 2012–2015. This journal started in 2012 as a spin-off from the analysis section of the *Yearbook of Muslims in Europe* when that section became too large for the *Yearbook* itself. Under his dedicated editorship this new journal quickly proved very successful, filling a gap in the existing literature. Recognition of its success showed in its almost immediate inclusion in one of the largest and selective abstracting and indexing services in the world: SCOPUS.

Jørgen is currently working on a series on legal documents on Islam in Europe. The *Annotated Legal Documents on Islam in Europe* consist of an annotated collection of currently valid legal documents affecting the status of Islam and Muslims in Europe. The project will cover the 28 member states of the European Union (including Croatia), Norway and Switzerland, the European Union and the European Court of Justice, and the European Court of Human Rights. To date 15 volumes have been published: Poland, Cyprus, Bulgaria, The Netherlands, Estonia, Croatia, Belgium, Latvia, Italy, France, Greece, Switzerland, Finland, Lithuania, and Sweden. The project will culminate in an online database, creating the only database and reference work of its kind on this topic.

Of course, Jørgen's contributions to academia in general, and the study of Muslims in Europe in particular, extend far beyond Brill's publication programme. One only has to throw a quick glance at his long list of publications in this volume to see the extent of his research. His numerous publications have not only shaped Brill's publishing programme, but have also defined the research field on Muslims in Europe.

I want to congratulate the editors of the present volume, and Niels in particular, for taking the initiative of putting this well-deserved volume together in Jørgen's honour. It has been a pleasure and a privilege working with Jørgen over the past 8 years and I look forward to working together for many more years to come.

Nicolette van der Hoek
Acquisitions Editor, BRILL

Editors' Introduction

Though the history of Islam and Muslim influence in Europe is both long and complex with periods of interreligious coexistence as well as periods when Muslims ruled over or were majorities in certain parts of the Old Continent, the presence of Muslims in Europe seems to the vast majority of Europeans today to be a novel phenomenon. To many this presence is marked by uncertainty and met with fear, invariably reducing Muslims in Europe to the single issue of security. However, long before "the Muslim question" became so overstressed and securitized, the complexity of the increasing presence of a multitude of Muslims in Europe was recognised by a few pioneering scholars in the emerging field of the studies of Islam and Muslims in contemporary Europe. Jørgen S. Nielsen was a part of this nascent development. As he wrote in the foreword to the first edition of his *Muslims in Western Europe* in 1992, "[only] a few academics began to see valid research possibilities in the issues arising out of the Muslim presence in Europe ..." In the recently updated fourth edition co-written with Jonas Otterbeck, he elaborates that "... it was not until the mid-1980s that a recognition of the Islamic dimension of community and ethnic relations began to spread beyond small specialist cadres,"[1] but stressing also that this was echoed by emerging research amongst sociologists and anthropologists in France, Germany, Britain and Scandinavia. Jørgen S. Nielsen, of course, did not write this to point to the fact that he was a pioneer in this field, but rather was able to write so because he has been at the heart of the development of research on Muslims and Islam in Europe since the late 1970s.

In September 2016, Jørgen S. Nielsen celebrated his 70th birthday. The articles in the present volume are collected in expectation of that joyous occasion. As often is in academia, it is only now that we have been able to gather and publish all the contributions from friends and colleagues. As will be evident in the following, 2017 also marks a number of jubilees in Jørgen S. Nielsen's life and career. In this editors' introduction we give an overview of his biography, a selection of the themes in his work, and return to look at the impact and timeliness of his contribution to the study of Islam and Muslims. Looking through his biography here, readers might want to cross-reference with the highlighted bibliography printed in this volume to see how his production corresponds with the stages and positions of his career. These articles collected in this volume are introduced and we see how they indeed echo the themes and

---

1 Nielsen, J.S. with Jonas Otterbeck, *Muslims in Western Europe*, The New Edinburgh Islamic Surveys. Edinburgh University Press. 2015, 174.

curiosity in Jørgen S. Nielsen's own exploration of the multitude of Muslims in Europe.

Life and Career[2]

Jørgen Schøler Nielsen was born 18 September 1946, in Frederiksberg, Copenhagen, to Marie Schøler Nielsen and Erik W. Nielsen. His father was a trained theologian, ordained Lutheran Minister, and in the years after the Second World War – from 1950 – he was working in London as Research Secretary with the International Missionary Council. Jørgen S. Nielsen had his first few years of schooling in England, but in 1959 the family moved back to Denmark as his father was appointed General Secretary to the Danish Missionary Society, and Jørgen S. Nielsen did his secondary schooling at Sankt Annæ Gymnasium in Denmark. In 1965, the family would return to London as Erik W. Nielsen had the previous year been appointed Director in the Theological Education Fund associated with the World Council of Churches. By then Jørgen S. Nielsen had completed his Danish schooling and moved with them. In London, he did his A-levels in German and History in order to qualify for university.

His father's work and travels in Asia, Africa and the Middle East were inspirations for Jørgen S. Nielsen and he shared in many of the interests and discussions on religion, theology and dialogue.[3] While his father's focus was on the education and capacity building in the churches, the challenges they faced were marked by the political, social and cultural disruption in the wake of the decolonisation after Second World War. These global trends would also have an impact on Jørgen S. Nielsen and he reflects on them in one of his first publications, which was an edited collection of travel letters from his father, titled *A World on the Way to Freedom?* (1974)[4]

Consulting his father, they agreed that language was key to understanding a new and changing world. The choice was between Arabic or Chinese, and of the two, Arabic covered more of the surface of the globe. A further dimension to this choice was the question of how the Christian communities, which his

---

2 We owe many thanks to Meline Nielsen for sharing with us her thoughts on Jørgen S. Nielsen's life and work.

3 For a full account of Erik W. Nielsen's life, work and travels, see his biography by Harald Nielsen, *Erik W. Nielsen - og hans bidrag til efterkrigstidens danske missionsteologi*, Copenhagen: Dansk Missionsråd, 2012.

4 Jørgen S. Nielsen (ed.), *En verden paa vej mod frihed?* edited travel letters of Erik W. Nielsen, Copenhagen: DMS-forlag, 1974.

EDITORS' INTRODUCTION XIII

father knew well, interacted and were in dialogue with Islam, which became a future perspective in Jørgen S. Nielsen's career and academic life.

Jørgen S. Nielsen chose Arabic Language and Literature as his BA at University of London's School of Oriental and African Studies, which was followed by an MA in Middle East Area Studies with a focus on Islamic law in 1970. He then applied to go to Cambridge University to study theology, and he was accepted. Before going, however, he took a year out to travel, and he chose Lebanon. Through his father's contacts, he volunteered as an English teacher at a Maronite Secondary School in a village in southern Lebanon, almost on the border to Israel. He was very fond of it and got along with the people there, and ended up staying for a year.

During that year, in 1971, his father died. This was a tragic loss, not just for Jørgen S. Nielsen, but for the whole family. Following that and as a result of his growing affection for Lebanon, Jørgen S. Nielsen wanted to stay in Lebanon and applied for a doctorate in Arab History at the American University of Beirut, effectively abandoning the idea of theology. He drew very much on his MA in Islamic law, and wrote on the 12th and 13th century administration of law in Mamluk Egypt. Under the supervision of Constantin Zureiq, Kamal Salibi and Tarif Khalidi, he defended his thesis on "Mazalim under the Bahri Mamluks 622/1264 – 789/1387" for a PhD in Arab History, which he obtained in 1978.

During the early years of his doctorate, Jørgen S. Nielsen met his future wife, Meline, in Beirut as he was boarding at the Near East School of Theology, and Meline was employed as Assistant Librarian at the library. Jørgen S. Nielsen was teaching and had a position as a Graduate Assistant teaching world history, and was aspiring to a position at AUB with the History Department.

In 1975, however, the Lebanese civil war started. Jørgen S. Nielsen was finalising his research, and in 1977, his first son, Mikael, was born, and that same spring he submitted his dissertation. By then Jørgen S. Nielsen was looking to Europe, to Denmark and the United Kingdom, for positions in order to get out of wartime Beirut. While Copenhagen did not provide any opportunities for Jørgen S. Nielsen, the newly established Centre for the Study of Islam and Christian-Muslim Relations at Selly Oak Colleges in Birmingham hired Jørgen in January 1978 as Lecturer in Islam and Christian-Muslim Relations. The initial contract was for three years, and by then the family hoped to be able to return to Beirut as, surely, the war would have ended by then. Meline did post graduate studies in library studies and later joined the Library there. With this position, his focus would move into the contemporary scene and very much also address the situation of Muslims in Europe and in the United Kingdom.

As the war in Lebanon continued, the family expanded by a second son, Philip, and Birmingham became home. Jørgen S. Nielsen engaged himself further in the challenges of the job. While he started as Lecturer, he would become senior lecturer and then principal lecturer, and in 1988, he was appointed director of the Centre for the Study of *Islam and Christian-Muslim Relations*. While at the Centre, Jørgen would edit the *Series of Research Papers on Muslims in Europe* from 1979 to 1989, and for a greater part of the 1990s, he would edit the journal Islam and Christian-Muslim Relations together with John Esposito from 1996 onwards. In 1996 Jørgen S. Nielsen was appointed Professor of Islamic Studies, at the Department of Theology of the University of Birmingham, and in 1999, he helped bring about the merger of the Centre for the Study of Islam and Christian-Muslim Relations with that Department. From 2001 to 2004 he served as Director for the Graduate Institute for Theology and Religion and as Deputy Head of the Department.

Throughout the 1980s and the 1990s, with the growth of Islam in Europe as a research field and the rise in academic interest in the subject, Jørgen S. Nielsen not only built up the Centre, recruiting students and strengthening the interdisciplinary and cross-departmental academics, but he also established a vast array of contacts and connections around Europe and the Middle East. Jørgen S. Nielsen consulted for governments and NGO's across the both Europe and the Islamic world, joining expert committees, working groups, and expert councils in addition to regular teaching, dozens of PhD examinations and appointment committees in academia. Throughout these almost forty years, Jørgen S. Nielsen wrote thirty monographs and edited books – many of which were co-authored and co-edited with contributors to this volume – he published more than hundred articles and have had more than several hundred speaking appointments and invitations to give key notes, literally around the world.[5]

When the Danish Institute in Damascus was looking for a new director, it would prove an opportunity to have a break from university life in Birmingham and to return to the Middle East once more, which he did in that position from October 2005. The very day he travelled there was the day the infamous Mohammed Cartoons were published in Denmark, and while the crisis did not break until early 2006, Jørgen S. Nielsen found himself very much in the middle of it. As the crisis roared, his excellent relations with the Syrian religious leadership, the government and civil society representatives helped Danish diplomacy to calm things down. And while the time in Damascus was overall peaceful, he would again need to assist with evacuations and Danish diplomacy during the 2006 Israel–Hezbollah War in Lebanon.

---

5   See the bibliography of Jørgen S. Nielsen in this volume.

EDITORS' INTRODUCTION

In the wake of the Danish Cartoon Crisis, the priority research area "Religion in the 21st Century" at University of Copenhagen, under the direction of Hans Raun Iversen, had been working towards a wider and more inclusive study of Islam across the faculties of the university. With Iversen and Danish colleagues at the Faculty of Theology, Jørgen S. Nielsen applied to the Danish National Research Foundation, which won him the Danish National Research Professorship and a grant to set up the Centre for European Islamic Thought in Copenhagen in October 2007. Not only did Jørgen S. Nielsen launch the *Yearbook of Muslims in Europe* project and subsequently the *Journal of Muslims in Europe*, but also one of the major successes was the participation, with Jørgen S. Nielsen as Deputy Director of the RELIGARE project. Financed by the 7th Framework Programme of the European Commission as a conglomerate of twelve European research institutions, RELIGARE was a three-year investigation into religious diversity and secular models in Europe, running from 2010 to 2013. It examined the current socio-legal realities, including the legal rules protecting or limiting the experiences of religious or other faith-based communities across Europe. Its purpose was to explore adequate policy responses to the realities and expectations of both religious and political communities in Europe and the protection of human rights in terms of equality and freedom of thought, conscience and religion.[6]

While Jørgen S. Nielsen officially retired from the Faculty of Theology in 2013, he remains Honorary Professor at University of Copenhagen and to this day he remains deeply engaged in the academic work and networks on Islam and Muslims. He is still busy with writing and editing, and when the University of Birmingham offered him a part-time position in 2016, he became Professor of Contemporary European Islam there.

Impact and Timeliness

One of the interesting things in reading back into Jørgen S. Nielsen's life and work is to see how for the Arabist and historian, religion was always present – both as the subject of study, but also in context. This is true for Islam, of course, but also for Christianity. The assumptions of the secular which were dominating in the study of sociology of religion and related fields, never had any hold over Jørgen S. Nielsen's thought. This, perhaps, is in part due to his upbringing and education, where a very global Christian humanist world view prevailed with his father's international work. However, in part it is also due to the fact

---

6   Read more about RELIGARE on www.religareproject.eu, accessed 10 August 2017.

that Jørgen S. Nielsen brought a view of the complex of religions intertwined and intermingling in society back to the United Kingdom after years in the Middle East, most significantly of course Lebanon before the war. Secularism had never taken hold there, and the religious dimension was present in almost all interactions of society. Trained as a historian and receiving his PhD at the American University of Beirut, he brought this particular scope for the complexities of Muslim-Christian relations in the Middle East back to the United Kingdom in the early 1980s. And as things would have it, this became highly relevant to the research needed for the next 30 years or more.

Jørgen S. Nielsen's work and research seems not only timely, but as suggested above, even ahead of its time. Reviewing the many paths and observations in his publications, it seems that at the end of his writing he often makes extensive observations on the very conditions of Muslim life within the complex of European states churches and international society. As in February 2008, in his inaugural lecture for the Danish National Research Foundation professorship, he reveals not only his own position in the developments during his career, but – rather controversially – also gives his understanding of the responsibility of the scholar of contemporary Islam:

> ... a core dimension of what we are engaged in is the fact of rapid and complex change. This must have an impact on how we understand and interpret what we record and engage with. The academic researcher obviously focuses on what has been and what is, after all that is where our data are to be found. Ironically, the polemicist does the same but in a more blatantly selective manner and with an agenda focused on selected current political or religious priorities. But I would suggest that the scholar of contemporary Islam needs also to include a focus on potential. This is not the same as prediction, although I am sure we shall often be asked to predict. It is, rather, an understanding of the possibilities that the intellectual tradition has accumulated and an acknowledgment that the social, economic, cultural and political changes of our times influence, and will continue to influence, the intellectual routes which Muslim thinkers globally, and particularly in Europe, are developing and will continue to develop. It is also an acknowledgment that, whether we like it or not, western scholars of Islam are participants in this process.[7]

---

7   Nielsen, J.S., *Islam in Europe: retrenchment and renewal*. Originally presented as Inaugural Lecture, Faculty of Theology, University of Copenhagen, 8 February 2008.

EDITORS' INTRODUCTION   XVII

This position was not new, for in 1997, Jørgen S. Nielsen had already understatedly observed:

> Muslims in the late twentieth century seem paradoxically to be trumpeting the traditional much-vaunted tolerance of the Islamic state and of Muslim history while simultaneously complaining of the intolerance of western governments and European society and apparently ignoring the abuse of political power in many of their own states. The paradox depends on where you stand.[8]

Thirty years ago, in 1987, writing on *Islamic Law and its Significance for the Situation of Muslim Minorities in Europe,* Jørgen S. Nielsen observed about exactly the legal, social and religious integration of Muslims into a new, European context that:

> At a time when economic recession, social unrest, and doubts about the supremacy of European models of society and politics have set in, the response of reinforcement of tradition and rejection of all things alien merely serves to underline the essential strangeness of Muslims in Europe. Part of this response includes a renewed emphasis in some quarters on the Christian essence of European cultures and national identities, thus further drawing attention to a perceived fundamental incompatibility between Islam and European Christendom.[9]

To observers of Islam and Muslims in Europe and followers of Jørgen S. Nielsen's work, it should come as no surprise that observations from ten, twenty and thirty year ago are entirely applicable to today's situation. Part of the explanation is the cyclical nature to many of the debates on Muslims in Europe; major debates on headscarves, halal slaughter, sharia and Muslim personal law, and so on, seem to be in their third, fourth, if not fifth iteration. However, an equally significant part of the explanation is that as a historian looking at the present, Jørgen S. Nielsen's observations are of an unquestionable clarity and quality in both his diagnosis of the situation and peril of Muslims in Europe and of his understanding of the European context's history, culture and religion.

---

8 Nielsen, J.S., "Muslims in Europe into the Next Millenium," in: *Islam in Europe: The Politics of Religion and Community*, Vertovic, S., and Ceri Perch (eds.), here as cited from Nielsen, J.S, *Towards a European Islam*, MacMillan Press 1999, 133.

9 Nielsen, J.S, *Islamic Law and its significance for the situation of Muslim minorities in Europe*, Brussels: CCME, 33 1987.

XVIII EDITORS' INTRODUCTION

The observation that perhaps resonates most clear with today's predicament, is the following from a time before the terrorist attacks September 11, 2001, the repeated terrorist attacks in Europe and the rise the Islamic State in Iraq and Syria.

> The current negative European perception of Islam [...] must be modified in the context of the historical perspective behind it. The threat to the democratic traditions of Europe comes not, in the first instance, from Islam and Muslims but from our own fear of that which is perceived to threaten the *modus vivendi* achieved in the nineteenth-century nation state. By resisting, and even attacking, Muslim self-assertion as anything other than an assertion of the right to dignity, self-respect, and democratic participation, we risk forcing Muslim movements, and articulate young Muslims in Europe, to resort to attack as the best form of self-defence.[10]

Contributions to the Volume

The title of this volume in Jørgen S. Nielsen's honour, *Exploring the Multitude of Muslims in Europe*, echoes his academic life and work as much as it characterises the contributions within. Looking through his publications and editorships it becomes apparent that there is hardly a group of Muslims in Europe that has not drawn his scholarly attention. He has worked on Muslims in almost every part and country in Europe. This is clear not only from his editorship of the *Muslim Minorities* series, the *Yearbook of Muslims in Europe* and the *Journal of Muslims in Europe*, but also in his *Muslims in Western Europe* (4th ed., with Jonas Otterbeck) and *Muslims in the Enlarged Europe* (with Dassetto, Allievi & Marechal) as well as a large number of subsequent articles and papers. Thematically the same is true, as there is hardly a perspective or challenge concerning Muslims in Europe, which he has not considered. Historically immigration, Christian-Muslim dialogue, and the former Ottoman space is explored. Adding to that a number of methodological and thematic approaches; theology and sociology of Muslims as minorities; Islamic law and secular legal systems of Europe; history of Muslims both in Europe and the Middle East; Christian and Muslim relations; polemics and dialogue; sharia understood as discourse; questions of method, ethnicity, diversity and pluralism; Muslim political participation; and the future of law and politics in secular Europe. All these key words echo titles of monographs and edited volumes by Jørgen S. Nielsen, in

---

10 Op. cit., Nielsen 1999, 137–138.

EDITORS' INTRODUCTION   XIX

which many of the contributors to this volume were involved. More than most
Jørgen S. Nielsen has identified and demonstrated the need for an interdisciplinary study of Muslims in their variety throughout Europe and beyond.

A number of aspects of this is explored in the articles of the present volume.
There are 14 contributions from scholars from 11 different countries working
on such diverse Muslim groups as Bektashis, Bosnians, Turks, Ahmadis, Tatars,
jihadis and a Muslim poet critical of liberal Muslims.

In the first of three parts in the volume, we have collected contributions
conceptualising Islam and Muslims. Thus, the first article is by Thijl Sunier
(Vrije Universiteit Amsterdam), who takes us back to the dawning realisation that Muslims in Europe were not just labour migrants or refugees settling
eventually to be absorbed into the host societies along the well-known trajectories of civic integration. In the light of the Iranian Revolution, the three Gulf
Wars, the issues of headscarves and the Rushdie affair, it dawned on policy
makers that Muslims were part of a global community. In the 1990s and 2000s,
the question of how to fit Islam into national frameworks became a key issue
in national debates on the position of Muslims, but it also promoted the role
of nation states as cultural agents. Taking the Netherlands as his case study,
Sunier guides us through three decades of religious integration, considering
the genesis of Muslims as a policy category with its own specific epistemology
developed for policy interventions and characterised by reductionism, alienation and "cheap solutions." Invoking the example of Jørgen S. Nielsen, Sunier
reasserts the need for broader perspectives on the complex situation of 21st
Century European religious integration.

Using his dynamic model of the metaphorical kite conjoined in a cross-
section of values, social norms, state and international law, Werner Menski
(School of Oriental and African Studies, University of London) observes how
skilful many Muslims have become over time in navigating and balancing
competing expectations in Europe. Continuously, they risk accusations of illegality, because they do not start their decision-making processes from a state-
centric position of citizens, but think and act first as Muslim individuals and
members of communities. In conversation with Jørgen S. Nielsen's scholarly
work, Menski revisits many of his contributions and connects the work in legal pluralism theory to explore the complex socio-normativities of living as a
Muslim in Europe.

By posing the question "Does European Islam Think?" Mohammed Hashas
(LUISS Guido Carli University) engages in a critical reading and discussion of
Jørgen S. Nielsen and Olivier Roy on the question of how Muslims in Europe
articulate European Islam. Hashas contraposes his deduction of Roy's writing that there is no theological thinking taking place among Muslims in Europe with Jørgen S. Nielsen, who in turn has argued that European Islam does

indeed think. Through Jørgen S. Nielsen's writings since the early 1970s and on-wards, Hashas demonstrates that a European Islamic theology is forming that brings together the dynamic potentials of the Islamic tradition and European modern realities. In his conclusion Hashas underlines that Muslim thinkers in Europe are very much aware of the challenges that Europe and its modernity pose, and also that European Muslims can influence the debate over Islam and modernity in the Islamic classical centres.

Taking his cue from a key observation of Jørgen S. Nielsen's, Niels Valde-mar Vinding (University of Copenhagen) sets out to explore the concept of churchification in relation to Islam in Europe. Through examples from Jørgen S. Nielsen's research and a number of additional and similar usages across Eu-rope, churchification is discussed as a pedagogical or rhetorical device, as a tool of normativisation, as an expression of institutionalisation, and finally as both a deliberate strategy and a counter-strategy of Muslims in Europe.

One of Jørgen S. Nielsen's long-time colleagues and co-authors, Samim Akgönül (University of Strasbourg) explores and discusses the "perpetual first generation strategy" amongst Turks – the largest ethnic group amongst Muslims in Europe. In a specific French context, where laicism is undergoing change French Islam is evolving alongside. Faced with a choice to change or resist, Turks in France apply a strategy that enables them to retain close ties with Turkey, the Turkish language, and the Muslim religion as worshipped in Turkey. The generations born in France do lose their command of Turkish, but this shortcoming is compensated for by religion, customs, and loyalty to "the motherland" and the cultural accumulation of the parents who had originally emigrated from Turkey. As Akgönül sees it, multiple loyalties are indeed expe-rienced, but often expressly rejected.

The second part of this volume takes us through legal aspects, institution-alisation, ideological entrepreneurship and critical producing of Islam and Muslims in Europe. The director of the Erlangen Centre for Islam and Law in Europe, (Friedrich-Alexander-Universität Erlangen-Nürnberg) Mathias Rohe, opens this section of the volume with the question of legal accom-modation of Muslims by looking at alternative dispute resolution among Muslims in Germany within the existing legal framework and the public de-bate. Muslim alternative dispute resolution is generally encouraged in many strong European states. He is arguing for unity in diversity under one legal order by granting far-reaching internal dispositions instead of establishing par-allel legal systems – of course under the enforcement of law by state institutions. However, and this is true for Germany as for many other European countries, the public climate has become unfavourable even to academic debate on this

EDITORS' INTRODUCTION

important topic, demonstrating a widespread lack of knowledge regarding the complexity of sharia as well as of the basics of the rule of law in European states. By outlining the state of research, emphasising the empirical evidence and arguing the specific legal cases, Rohe argues for the vast benefits to both Muslims and society as a whole in making the law a living experience for the overwhelming majority of Muslims, who wish to live self-determined lives with the efficient protection of the state for those in need for it.

Keeping with the theme of Islamic law, Egdūnas Račius (Vytautas Magnus University) investigates the possibility of inclusion of Islamic law into the legal system in Lithuania. His analysis begins with the legal needs of the Muslim community and from there searches for the place of Islamic law. Račius concludes that there is nominally comparatively much legal space for the application of the Islamic law in Lithuania, but it has not been unfolded. This is because of low demand from the Muslim side and limited feasibility, but should that ever change, there is a high likelihood that the Lithuanian legal regulations and the social attitudes will become less accepting of such a direction.

In his article intriguingly titled "The King, the Boy, the Monk and the Magician. Jihadi Ideological Entrepreneurship between the UK and Denmark," Jakob Skovgaard-Petersen (University of Copenhagen) presents his analysis of a jihadist treatise written by the radical ideologist Abu Qatada in London and published by the "bookseller" Said Mansour in Copenhagen. The treatise is a lengthy exegesis of a hadith found in the Sahih Muslim collection. This hadith tells the story of a boy as a paragon of piety who peacefully defies a tyrant king – much in the vein of early Christian hagiography. The jihadist treatise, however, transforms the victimhood of the boy into a legitimisation of suicide operations. It is thus a good example of the need for a legitimising ideological text – and for creating one if it does not exist.

Thomas Hoffmann (University of Copenhagen) explores the provocative phenomenon of Yahya Hassan, a young Danish poet, whose significant style, international fame and cometlike career made headlines beyond the newspaper culture sections and spurred a fierce debate. Hassan is an anarchistic and transgressive voice from the fringes of contemporary Islam. As a Qur'anic scholar, Hoffmann unfolds the multiple layers in Hassan's poetry and reading style that shares important features with traditional Qur'anic recitation. Through Hoffmann's analysis, Hassan's radical praxis is shown to indirectly expose the liberal and moderate Islam as a new orthodoxy, thus echoing calls for a more critical approach to liberal Islam.

The third section of this volume further explores the multitudes of Muslims in Europe. Long-time friends and colleagues of Jørgen S. Nielsen's, Naveed Baig,

Lissi Rasmussen and Hans Raun Iversen, investigate the spheres between activism and scholarly work that Jørgen S. Nielsen has been personally engaged in for more than twenty years. Ethnically homogenous Denmark has been at the forefront in the recent development of nationalism and Islamophobia in Europe. Baig's, Rasmussen's and Iversen's contribution emphasises the importance of two of the present work areas of the Copenhagen-based Islamic-Christian Study Centre (IKS) for equal treatment of all Danish citizens. The first example is providing spiritual care needed by patients with ethnic minority background in Danish hospitals and thus young Muslims' quest for education in Islamic spiritual care. The other example is providing a parental environment for youngsters – primarily with Muslim backgrounds – in prisons of Copenhagen and after their release. The experiences of IKS have shown that the continuous effort to create relationships, unity, and trust over time provides better conditions for coexistence in society: diapraxis provides an even better way to mutual human understanding than religious dialogue alone.

Göran Larsson (University of Gothenburg) explores the key role the Ahmadiyya movement played in the early history, establishment and spread of Islam in Europe. Giving his readers a brief outline of the history and theology through the example of key Ahmadiyya texts, Larsson explores conflicts over how to define who is and who is not a Muslim, effectively showing that the definition of a Muslim is not a static or self-evident category. Authority over interpretation and the laying down of categories and typologies is always related to issues of power, very much informing how and why Ahmadis have been labelled as heretics by many Muslim groups.

Travelling with Jørgen S. Nielsen, Emil Saggau (University of Copenhagen) takes the reader into the cross-roads of the Bektashi Sufi order in between text and lived custom with its syncretic blending of Christian and Islamic traditions. By analysing two central holy Bektashi texts, known as the Velayetname and the Makalat, Saggau explores the role of Christianity in the unique combination and dialectic between social-geographical, religious and historical factors. Both texts bear resemblance to biblical texts and reuse their themes, but were written specifically for a Muslim audience. Saggau links this rewriting and binding together of the tradition with the transition from a charismatic to an established and traditional order, making this pragmatic religiosity a central trait in the Bektashi order and to a great extent the "trademark" of its religious practice.

In the context of a Bosnian experience, Ahmet Alibašic (University of Sarajevo) refers to two recent developments in Islamic literature. The one is the awakening of local Islamic identities in the wake of global outreach of Salafi and Reformist groups, the other is the securitisation of all things Islamic.

These observations are the basis for a qualitative, quantitative and thematic exploration of Islamic literature from a Bosnian context. Due to an increasing demand for Islamic knowledge from European Muslims and non-Muslims, Alibašic concludes that there is a significant opportunity in the production of Islamic literature. Bosnian Islamic scholars may even be able to bridge a Middle Eastern and Arab world to the European languages – as they have done so often before.

The final contribution in the volume is by Safet Bektovic (University of Oslo). Debates about the Muslim presence in Western Europe and the possibility of developing a European form of Islam have been very topical in many European countries. Muslims react very differently to the idea of a uniquely European Islam, as they comprise mainly immigrants or those with an immigrant background, many of whom have an uncertain relationship with Europe and view the idea of a European Islam sceptically, considering it a political project of secularisation of Islam from the outside. In his article Bektovic explores the Balkan Muslims and particularly Bosnian Muslims' different understandings of Europe and different experiences with secular society. Here, Bektovic argues that a deeper reflection on their religious identities could prove to be fruitful for the general discussion on European Islam. He aims to shed light on the theological, historical, and cultural aspects of what it means to be a Muslim "the Bosnian way" and concludes that neither Bosnian nor European Islam are homogeneous and ready-made categories.

A Note of Conclusion

There are many reasons for Jørgen S. Nielsen's success. Profound academic knowledge, exceptional personal skills, tireless networking, and very solid work of unquestionable quality. However, friends and colleagues recognise Jørgen S. Nielsen by how his personal enthusiasm pours into the work, and how he meets everyone and every challenge with interest, curiosity and humility. Jørgen S. Nielsen seeks to make people more aware whenever he educates students or assists journalists and the public. As for politicians and religious leaders, the objective has always been to make sure they have better information to draw conclusions from. Everyone who might be as lucky as to count themselves among Jørgen S. Nielsen's colleagues and friends are the happy beneficiaries of his time, knowledge and loyalty.

On a personal note, I would like to thank Jørgen for the opportunity to pursue an academic life of my own. Jørgen not only helped this along as my advisor from 2009 till 2013, but he keeps guiding and engaging himself in the questions

I pursue. As his recent PhD candidate, I suggested the idea of Festschrift for his 70th birthday. Together with Egdūnas Račius and Jörn Thielmann, it has been our pleasure to collect, subsequently edit and publish this volume. We owe many thanks to Brill Publishers, especially Nicolette van der Hoek and Nienke Brienen-Moolenaar, for supporting the idea of honouring Jørgen S. Nielsen's life and work through the publication of this volume.

On behalf of the Editors,
Niels Valdemar Vinding

Note from Aminah B. McCloud

This is just a note to add to the many accolades in this text for Professor Jørgen S. Nielsen. While the contributors are European, I just wanted to add a word to attest to the fact that his work and his mentoring reach across the Atlantic. I first met him as a graduate student and immediately began to derive benefit from his guidance. As a student and later as a professor myself, I have met him out in the world and still remain awed by his knowledge and insight into both Islam and Muslims from various cultures. For those who had the honor to study directly under him, I envy you. This text shows some of the scope of his rigorous research methodologies and his influence on how to look at communities which are and are not your own. I am forever indebted to him for the people he has introduced me to and especially the quick responses to any questions I still may have.

Aminah B. McCloud
al-Deen Chicago, Illinois, 2018

List of Contributors

Samim Akgönül
PhD (2001), Historian and Political scientist. Professor at Strasbourg University and researcher at the French National Centre for Scientific Research. He also teaches also Political Science at Syracuse University. He studies the evolution of minority concepts as well as the religious minorities in Eastern and Western Europe, especially non-Muslim minorities in Turkey, Muslim minorities in the Balkans and new minorities in Western Europe. He is one of the Co-editors of *Yearbook of Muslims in Europe and Journal of Muslims in Europe* (Brill). Recent publication is *La Turquie « nouvelle »: du rêve d'Europe au cauchemar du Proche Orient*, Paris, Lignes de Repères, 2017.

Ahmet Alibašić
is an Associate Professor at the Faculty of Islamic Studies, University of Sarajevo, teaching Islamic culture and civilization courses. He has authored a book on Islamic opposition in the Arab world, several articles and edited books dealing with Islam in Europe, human rights in Islam, and church-state relations. Most recently he is one of the editors of *Yearbook of Muslims in Europe* (Brill, 2009–2017) and *Journal of Muslims in Europe*.

Naveed Baig
(b. 1975), MA in pastoral care (Faculty of Theology, Copenhagen University) and theologian and hospital chaplain at Rigshospitalet, Copenhagen. Vice-chair of the Centre for Co-existence – Islamic Christian Study Centre. Coordinator of Ethnic Resource Team since 2005, a volunteer corps working in Copenhagen hospitals. Author of various anthologies and articles on the topic of interfaith, healthcare issues in intercultural settings and spiritual care.

Safet Bektovic
is associate professor of Islamic Studies at the Faculty of Theology, University of Oslo. He is teaching Islamic philosophy, Sufism, Social ethics and aesthetics, and his research area also includes philosophy of religion, Søren Kierkegaard, Interreligious theology, Christian-Muslim dialogue, and Balkan Muslims. Among his publications are *Islamisk filosofi* (2012) and *Kulturmøder og religion* (2004), and he has contributed to a number of anthologies and books.

Mohammed Hashas
(b. 1984) is a Postdoctoral Research Fellow at LUISS Guido Carli University of Rome. In 2017 he was a Visiting Research Fellow at Oxford Center for Islamic

Studies, and a Guest Scholar at Leibniz-ZMO Zentrum Moderner Orient in Berlin. Besides various journal articles, Hashas has co-edited *Islam, State and Modernity: Mohamed Abed Al Jabri and the Future of the Arab World* (2017), *Imams in Western Europe: Developments, transformation, and institutional challenges* (forthcoming, 2018), and authored *Intercultural Geopoetics in Kenneth White's Open World* (2017).

Thomas Hoffmann

(b. 1970) holds an MA in comparative religion from the University of Copenhagen and received his PhD in literary studies in 2005 for the dissertation *The Poetic Qur'ân. Studies on Qur'ânic Poeticity* (published by Harrassowitz Verlag). Subsequently he held various postdoctoral scholarships in Islamic studies and worked together with professor Jørgen S. Nielsen at the newly established Center for European Islamic Thought (CEIT). He is currently professor (with special responsibilities) in Qur'anic and Islamic Studies at the Faculty of Theology, University of Copenhagen.

Hans Raun Iversen

(b. 1948), Associate Professor, cand. theol. (1979), dr. theol. h.c. (2012), Director of Centre for Church Research, Faculty of Theology, University of Copenhagen, Denmark. Hans Raun Iversen has dedicated the last 35 years to historical, empirical and theological studies in church and religion, primarily in Denmark, but also in Tanzania, England and the Nordic countries. He is the author of 10 books and 200 scientific articles, as well as several hundred articles in popular media. He has also published 20 books as editor or co-editor.

Göran Larsson

is Full Professor in Religious Studies and Deputy Dean for the Faculty of Arts at the University of Gothenburg. While his research is focused primarily on the study of Islam and Muslims in Europe, he has also written about Islamic theology, Qur'anic studies and issues related to religion and the media. He has published a large number of books and articles in publications like *Journal of Muslims in Europe, Islam and Christian-Muslim Relations, Journal of Religion, Method & Theory for the Study of Religions*.

Werner Menski

(b. 1949) is Emeritus Professor of South Asian Laws at SOAS, where he taught Hindu law, Muslim law and also focused on enriching the coverage of comparative law at a global level. In addition, he developed the study of ethnic minority laws, connected to family law, immigration laws and various aspects of discrimination laws. He remains editor of *South Asia Research* (http://sar

.sagepub.com) and continues to be involved in publishing, as well as mentoring younger scholars.

Egdūnas Račius

(b. 1973), PhD 2004 from University of Helsinki, is Professor of Islamic and Middle Eastern Studies at Vytautas Magnus University in Kaunas, Lithuania. Račius is a member of the editorial boards of the *Yearbook of Muslims in Europe* and the *Journal of Muslims in Europe* (both published by Brill). He has published several dozen articles on Muslims in Europe and the monograph *Muslims in Eastern Europe* (Edinburgh University Press, 2018).

Lissi Rasmussen

(b. 1953), dr.theol., Diocese and prison pastor for ethnic minorities in Copenhagen, director of the Centre for Co-existence – Islamic Christian Study Centre. Lissi Rasmussen has for several years been lecturing and doing research at the University of Aarhus and Copenhagen and has almost 40 years of practical and academic experience with Christian-Muslim relations – in Africa, Europe and Denmark. She has worked with Jørgen S. Nielsen in Birmingham as well as in Copenhagen. The recent years she has been focusing her work on ethnic minority prisoners, about which she has published the book, *Personal Narratives and Crime* (2010).

Mathias Rohe

studies in Law and Islamic Sciences in Tuebingen and Damascus, full professor for Civil Law, Private International Law and Comparative Law at the University of Erlangen-Nuremberg in Germany since 1997, founding director of the Erlangen Centre for Islam and the Law in Europe at this university; numerous publications on Islam and European legal orders and on Islamic law.

Emil B.H. Saggau

holds a Master's degree in Theology from University of Copenhagen, Denmark (2014). Currently, he is working on his doctoral thesis on modern religious historiography in Southeast Europe as a doctoral student at University of Copenhagen. He has been employed as centre secretary at Centre for European Islamic Thought, University of Copenhagen, from 2011–2013 under direction of Jørgen S. Nielsen.

Jakob Skovgaard-Petersen

(b. 1963), dr. Phil, Professor of Islamic and Arabic studies, University of Copenhagen. His field of research is contemporary Islam. His focus is on the establishment of a modern Muslim public sphere, and the role of the Muslim *ulama* in modern Arab states. Lately, his research has primarily focused on the role of Islam in the new pan-Arab television networks. Key publications include, *Defining Islam for the Egyptian State – Muftis and Fatwas of the Dār al-Iftā* (Leiden: Brill, 1997), *Global Mufti. The Phenomenon of Yusuf al-Qaradawi* (co-edited with Bettina Gräf) (London, New York: Hurst/Columbia UP, 2009) and *Arab Media Moguls* (co-edited with Donatella della Ratta and Naomi Sakr). (London: I.B.Tauris, April 2015).

Thijl Sunier
is Full Professor of Cultural Anthropology and holds the chair of 'Islam in European Societies' (VU Amsterdam). Currently he conducts a research project on Islamic authority and leadership in Europe. He is Chairman of the board of the Netherlands Inter-University School for Islamic Studies (NISIS) and Executive Editor of the *Journal of Muslims in Europe* (JOME/Brill). Recent publication (with Nico Landman): *Transnational Turkish Islam. Shifting Geographies of religious Activism and Community Building in Turkey and Europe* (Palgrave Macmillan, 2015).

Jörn Thielmann
(b. 1966), managing director Erlangen Centre for Islam and Law EZIRE, Friedrich-Alexander-University Erlangen-Nuremberg. Series Editor (with Jørgen S. Nielsen and Aminah McCloud) of "Muslim Minorities," and editor of "Journal of Muslims in Europe." He has published (with Ala al-Hamarneh), *Islam and Muslims in Germany* (Brill 2008).

Niels Valdemar Vinding
(b. 1982) is Assistant Professor at the Department of Cross-Cultural and Regional Studies at the University of Copenhagen, with a specific focus on Islam in Europe and European Muslim institutions. His current research is on "Imams of the West" funded from 2014 to 2017 by Carlsberg Research Foundation. His PhD (2013) was on *Muslim Positions in the Religio-Organisational Fields of Denmark, Germany and England.*

Bibliography of Jørgen S. Nielsen

Monographs and Edited Volumes

Belief, Law and Politics: What Future for a Secular Europe?, ed. with Marie-Claire Foblets, Katayoun Alidadi and Zeynep Yanasmayan, Farnham: Ashgate, 2014, 290 pp.

Everyday Lived Islam in Europe, ed. with Nathal M. Dessing, Nadia Jeldtoft and Linda Woodhead, Farnham: Ashgate, 2013, 183 pp.

Muslim Political Participation in Europe, ed., Edinburgh: Edinburgh University Press, 2013, 347 pp.

Interpreting Divorce Laws in Islam, ed. with Rubya Mehdi and Werner Menski, Copenhagen: DJØF, 2012, 317 pp.

Religion, Ethnicity and Contested Nationhood in the Former Ottoman Space, ed., Leiden: Brill, 2012, 293 pp.

Islam in Denmark: The Challenge of Diversity, ed., Lanham MD: Lexington, 2012, 261 pp.

"Methods in the study of non-organised Muslim minorities," ed. with Nadia Jeldtoft, thematic issue of *Ethnic and Racial Studies*, vol. 34, no.7 (July 2011); republished with additional material as *Methods and Contexts in the Study of Muslim Minorities: Visible and Invisible Muslims*, London: Routledge, 2012, 242 pp.

Embedding Mahr in the European Legal System, ed. with Rubya Mehdi, Copenhagen: DJØF Publishing, 2011, 299 pp.

Shari'a as Discourse: Legal Traditions and the Encounter with Europe, ed. with Lisbet Christoffersen, Aldershot: Ashgate, 2010, 267 pp.

Muslims in the enlarged Europe, ed. with F. Dassetto, S. Allievi and B. Marechal, Leiden: Brill, 2003, 602 pp.

European identity and cultural pluralism: Judaism, Christianity and Islam in European curricula, Recommendations and *Supplement: Country reports*, ed. with Lisa Kaul-Seidman and M. Vinzent, Bad Homburg: Herbert-Quandt Stiftung, 2003, 2 vols, 90+190 pp.

Muslim networks and transnational communities in and across Europe, ed. with Stefano Allievi, Leiden: Brill, 2002, 332 pp.

Summary Report on Islamophobia in the EU after 11 September 2001, with Christopher Allen, Vienna: European Monitoring Centre on Racism and Xenophobia, 2002, 56 pp.

Convergences musulmanes: aspects contemporains de l'Islam dans l'Europe élargies, joint ed. with Felice Dassetto and Brigitte Maréchal, Louvains-la-Neuve: Academia Bruylant, 2001, 174 pp.

Ethnology of Sufi orders: theory and practice, ed. with A. Zhelyazkova, Sofia: IMIR, 2001, 628 pp.

BIBLIOGRAPHY OF JØRGEN S. NIELSEN

Towards a European Islam, London: Macmillan, 1999. 156 pp.

Arabs and the West: Mutual images, ed. with Sami Khasawnih, Amman: University of Jordan, 1998. 321 pp.

The Christian-Muslim frontier, ed. London: I.B.Tauris, 1998. 150 pp.

Study, Group of Consultants on Religious and Cultural Aspects of Equality of Opportunities for Immigrants, chair, Strasbourg: Council of Europe, doc. MG-S-REL(95)3, 25 January 1996. 59 pp.

Relations of Compatibility and Incompatibility between Christians and Muslims in Bulgaria, ed. with Antonina Zhelyazkova and Gilles Kepel, Sofia: IMIR, 1996. 395 pp.

Christian Arabic apologetics during the Abbasid period, 750–1258, ed. with Samir Khalil, Leiden: E.J. Brill, 1994. 250 pp.

Muslims in Western Europe, Edinburgh: Edinburgh University Press, 1992, 186 pp. 2nd ed. 1995, 190 pp, German translation *Islam in Westeuropa*, Hamburg: EBV-Rissen, 1995; 3rd edition, 2004, 195 pp., Arabic translation *Al-Muslimun fi Urubba*, Beirut: Saqi, 2006, 301pp; 4th ed. 2015 with Jonas Otterbeck, 215 pp.

Religion and citizenship in Europe and the Arab world, ed. London: Grey Seal, 1992. 129 pp.

Islamic law and its significance for the situation of Muslim minorities in Europe, Brussels: CCME, 1987 (also in German and French). 58 pp.

Muslims in Britain: An annotated bibliography (with Daniele Joly), Bibliographies in Ethnic Relations, no.6, Coventry: University of Warwick, Centre for Research in Ethnic Relations, 1985, 35 pp.

Secular justice in an Islamic state: Mazalim under the Bahri Mamluks, 662/1264–789/1387, Leiden: Netherlands Institute for the Near East, 1985, 227 pp.

"The training of teachers of the children of migrant workers: Cultural values and education in a multicultural society," Report of the 13th European Teachers' Seminar, Council of Europe doc. no. DECS/EGT(81)4; Strasbourg: Council for Cultural Cooperation, 1982. 70 pp.

Muhammads folk (Muhammad's people), Copenhagen: Nyt nordisk Forlag, 1976, 45 pp.

En verden paa vej mod frihed? (A world on the way to freedom?), edited travel letters of Erik W. Nielsen, Hellerup: DMS-forlag, 1974, 122 pp.

Articles, Essays and Papers

"Trends in the management of immigration and diversity across Europe," in *IEMed Mediterranean Yearbook 2016* (Barcelona: European Institute of the Mediterranean, 2016), pp. 141–145.

"The current situation of Christian-Muslim relations: emerging challenges, signs of hope," in Douglas Pratt, Jon Hoover, John Davies and John Chesworth (eds.),

The Character of Christian-Muslim Encounter: Essays in Honour of David Thomas (Leiden: Brill, 2015), pp. 415–427.

"Citizenship Education in Multicultural Societies," in Ednan Aslan and Marcia Hermansen (eds.), *Islam and Citizenship Education*, Wiesbaden: Springer, 2015, pp. 57–66.

"Researching Islam in Europe: The missing contexts," book review article in *International Journal of Turkish Studies*, 20:1/2 (fall 2014), pp. 103–109.

"Western Europe, Islamic Religious Training in" in *Oxford Islamic Studies Online*, http://www.oxfordislamicstudies.com/article/opr/t343/e0133 (accessed Jul 31, 2014).

"Denmark, Islam in," "Islamic Foundation" *Encyclopedia of Islam*, 3rd ed. Leiden: Brill, 2014.

Articles "Great Britain" and "Islam and politics in Europe," *Oxford Encyclopedia of Islam and Politics*, New York: Oxford University Press, 2014.

"The emerging space of European Islam: Germany, Balkans and Turkey," Akademie der Diözese Rottenburg-Stuttgart, 15–16 Nov. 2013, http://downloads.akademie-rs.de/interreligioeser-dialog/131115_nielsen_european-islam.pdf.

"Concluding reflection: Everyday lived Islam and the future of Islamic studies," in Nathal M. Dessing, Nadia Jeldtoft, Jørgen S. Nielsen, and Linda Woodhead (eds.), *Everyday Lived Islam in Europe*, Farnham: Ashgate, 2013, pp. 163–177.

"Religion im Vereinigten Königreich vom britischen Empire zum Commonwealth," in Karlies Abmeier, Michael Borchard and Matthias Riemenschneider (eds.), *Religion im öffentlichen Raum*, Paderborn: Ferdinand Schöningh, 2013, pp. 205–214.

"The new Muslim Europe," in Jeffrey T. Kenney and Ebrahim Moosa (eds.), *Islam in the Modern World*, London: Routledge, 2013, pp. 335–349.

"An early discussion on Islamic family law in the English jurisdiction," in Maurits S. Berger (ed.), *Applying Shari'a in the West: Facts, Fears and the Future of Islamic Rules on Family Relations in the West*, Leiden: Leiden University Press, 2013, pp. 79–96.

"Islam and secular values in Europe: from canon to chaos?," in Peter Cumper and Tom Lewis (eds.), *Religion, Rights and Secular Society: European Perspectives*, Cheltenham: Edward Elgar, 2012, pp. 271–292.

"Reflections on the role and training of imams and Islamic teachers for Europe," in Ednan Aslan and Zsofia Windisch (eds,), *The Training of Imams and Teachers for Islamic Education in Europe*, Frankfurt a/M: Peter Lang, 2012, pp. 91–101.

"Islamiske religion/stat modeller i nutiden" (Contemporary Islamic religion-state models), in Lisbet Christoffersen, Hans Raun Iversen, Niels Kjægaard and Margit Warburg (eds.), *Fremtidens danske religionsmodel* (The future model of state/religion relations in Denmark), Frederiksberg: Anis, 2012, pp. 121–134.

"From Immigrant to Muslim: Changing Perceptions of Muslims in Europe," *Youngstown Papers in Islamic Religion, History and Culture*, Youngstown State University, Center for Islamic Studies, 2012, 27 pp.

"Danish cartoons and Christian-Muslim relations in Denmark," *Exchange*, 39 (2010), pp. 217–235.

"Islam and law in the Nordic countries in the 21st century: Challenges and new perspectives," with Rubya Mehdi, in Lisbet Christoffersen, Kjell Å. Modéer and Svend Andersen (eds), *Law and religion in the 21st century – Nordic perspectives*, Copenhagen: DJØF Publishing, 2010, pp. 505–524.

"The development of the cartoons crisis – a Danish perspective," in Arnim Heinemann, Olfa Lamloum and Anne F. Weber (eds), *The Middle East in the Media: Conflict, censorship and public opinion*, London: Saqi, 2010, pp. 17–34.

"Shari'a between renewal and tradition," in Jorgen S. Nielsen and Lisbet Christoffersen (eds.), *Shari'a as Discourse: Legal Traditions and the Encounter with Europe*, Aldershot: Ashgate, 2010, pp. 1–14.

"Islamin nousu Euroopassa" (The rise of Islam in Europe), in Tuomas Martikainen and Tuula Sakaranho (eds.), *Mitä muslimit tarkoittavat?*, Turku: Savukeidas, Kustannus, 2010, pp. 11–30.

"The participation of Christians and Jews in the Ayyubid and Mamluk state: A historiographical reflection," in Mahmoud Haddad, Arnim Heinemann, John L. Meloy and Souad Slim (eds.), *Towards a Cultural History of the Mamluk Era*, Beirut and Würzburg: Ergon Verlag, 2010, 3–12.

"Religion, Muslims and the state in Britain and France: from Westphalia to 9/11," in Abdulkader Sinno (ed.), *Muslims in western politics*, Bloomington: Indiana University Press, 2009, pp. 50–66.

"Europe and the Arab world in the 20th century: behind the myths of the 'West' and 'Islam,'" in Stephen Goodwin ed., *World Christianity in Muslim encounter: essays in memory of David A. Kerr*, vol. 2, London: Continuum, 2009, pp. 145–159.

"Islam and Europe," book review article, *Middle East Journal*, 62, 2008, pp. 144–148.

"Uddannelse og Islam i en plural verden," *Kritisk forum for praktisk teologi*, no. 110, December 2007, pp. 58–70.

"Udviklingen i *shari'a* og pluralistiske samfund," in Rubya Mehdi (ed.), *Integration & retsudvikling*; Copenhagen: Jurist- og Økonomforbundets Forlag, 2007, pp. 207–216.

"The question of Euro-Islam: restriction or opportunity?" in Aziz al-Azmeh and Effie Fokas (eds.), *Islam in Europe: diversity, identity and influence*, Cambridge: Cambridge University Press, 2007, pp. 34–48.

"The discourse of 'terrorism' between violence, justice and international order," in T. Abbas (ed.), *Islamic political radicalism: a European perspective*, Edinburgh: Edinburgh University Press, 2007, pp. 15–24.

"Religion, religionspolitik, ytringsfrihed og islam i Mellemøsten og Europa," Lisbet Christoffersen (red.), *Gudebilleder – Ytringsfrihed og religion i en globaliseret verden*, Copenhagen: Tiderne Skifter, 2006, pp. 165–180.

(with M. Draper and G. Yemelianova) "Transnational Sufism: The Haqqaniya," in J. Hinnells (ed.), *Sufism in the West*, London: Routledge, 2006, pp. 103–114.

"Western civilisation: myth or reality? A debate about power," in Irfan A. Omar (ed.), *Islam and other religions: Pathways to dialogue. Essays in honour of Mahmoud Mustafa Ayoub*, London: Routledge, 2006, pp. 181–191.

"Islamophobia in Europe and its impact on the push for democratisation in the Arab world," in Birgitte Rahbek (ed.), *Democratisation in the Middle East: Dilemmas and Perspectives*, Århus: Aarhus University Press, 2005, pp. 151–163.

"Muslims and Christians in Europe – from immigration to dialogue," in Beate Schmidt-Belau (ed.), *Building bridges for dialogue and understanding*, Bonn: German Adult Education Association, 2005, pp. 18–23.

"Kalim Siddiqui (1933–1996)," art. in *New Dictionary of National Biography*, Oxford: Oxford University Press, 2004.

"Athar al-islam fi Urubba al-gharbiyya al-mu'asira" (The impact of Islam in contemorary western Europe), in Nadia Mustafa (ed.), *Masarat wa-khabarat fi hiwar al-hadarat*, Cairo: Cairo University, 2004, pp. 205–220.

"Los musulmanes, el Estado y el ámbito público en Gran Bretagna," in Maria-Angèls Roque (ed.), *El Islam Plural*, Barcelona: Icaria, 2004, pp. 263–278.

"Religious dialogue and the academy: a contradiction?" in K. Hock (ed.), *The interface between research and dialogue: Christian-Muslim relations in Africa*, Münster: LIT-Verlag, 2004, pp. 165–176.

"Judentum, Christentum und Islam in europäischen Lehrplänen," *Aus Politik und Zeitgeschichte*, no. 7–8/2004 (16 Feb. 2004), pp. 16–22.

Arts. "Europe, Islam in," and "European culture and Islam," in Richard C. Martin (ed.), *Encyclopedia of Islam and the Muslim World*, 2 vols. New York: Macmillan Reference, 2004.

"Is there an escape from the history of Christian-Muslim relations?" in D. Thomas and C. Amos (eds.), *A Faithful Presence: Essays for Kenneth Cragg*, London: Melisende, 2003, pp. 350–361.

"New centres and peripheries in European Islam?" in *Mediterranean Politics*, vol. 7, no. 3 (autumn 2002), pp. 64–81, repr. in B. Roberson (ed.), *Shaping the current Islamic reformation*, London: Frank Cass, 2003, pp. 64–81.

"Contemporary discussions on religious minorities in Islam," *Brigham Young University Law Review*, vol. 2002, no. 2, pp. 353–369; repr. in *Islam and Christian-Muslim Relations*, vol.14, no.3 (July 2003), pp. 325–335.

"God in a multicultural society," in N. Barfoed and A. Jerichow (eds.), *The wrath of the damned* (Copenhagen: Danish PEN, 2003), pp. 157–173.

"Transnational Islam and the integration of Islam in Europe," in S. Allievi and J.S. Nielsen, *Muslim networks and transnational communities in and across Europe* (Leiden: Brill, 2003), pp. 28–51.

BIBLIOGRAPHY OF JØRGEN S. NIELSEN

"The contribution of interfaith dialogue towards a culture of peace," *American Journal of Islamic Social Sciences*, 19, 2 (Spring 2002), pp. 103–108.

"Les musulmans en Europe deviennent-ils européens?" special issue ed. Albin Michel, "Pour un Islam de paix," *Question de...*, no. 126 (December 2001), pp. 117–126.

"Postscript: tensions between the local and the global in Islamic revival," in A. Zhelyazkova and J. Nielsen (eds.), *Ethnology of Sufi orders: theory and practice* (Sofia: IMIR, 2001), pp. 622–628.

"Orientalism and anti-Orientalism: is there a middle way?" in A. Zhelyazkova and J. Nielsen (eds.), *Ethnology of Sufi orders: theory and practice* (Sofia: IMIR, 2001), pp. 337–351; www.imir-bg.org/imir/books/Sufism1.zip.

"The Mamluk period" (in Arabic), Middle East Council of Churches, *Christianity throughout its history in the Middle East,* Beirut: MECC, 2001, 597–604; English edition, Beirut: MECC, 2005.

Introduction (pp. 7–9) of *Muslimer og kristne ansigt til ansigt*, Copenhagen: Islamisk-Kristent Studiecenter, 2001.

"Muslims, the state and the public domain in Britain," in R. Bonney, F. Bosbach and T. Brockmann (eds.), *Religion and politics in Britain and Germany* (Munich: K.G. Saur, 2001), pp. 145–154.

"'Mapping' Muslim organisations in Britain 1998," in L. Toso (ed), *Europe, its borders and the others* (Naples: Edizioni Scientifiche Italiane, 2000), pp. 513–524.

"Fluid identities: Muslims and Western Europe's nation states," *Cambridge Review of International Affairs*, 13, 2 (spring/summer 2000), 212–227; amended version published in Dutch as "Flexibele identiteiten: moslims en de natiestaten van West-Europa," in D. Douwes (ed.), *Naar en europese islam? Essays* (Amsterdam: Mets & Schilt, 2001), pp. 21–49.

"Muslims in Britain: ethnic minority, community or Ummah?" in H. Coward et al (eds), *The South Asian Diaspora in Britain, Canada, and the United States* (Albany: State University of New York Press, 2000), pp. 109–125.

"Muslims and European education systems," in G.M. Munoz (ed.), *Islam, Modernism and the West: Cultural and Political Relations at the End of the Millennium* (London: I.B.Tauris, 1999), pp. 224–236.

"Muslims in Europe or European Muslims: The Western experience," *Encounters: Journal of Inter-Cultural Perspectives*, 4,2 (Sept. 1998), pp. 205–216.

"Muslim immigrant communities and foreign policy in western Europe," in J.S. Nielsen (ed.), *The Christian-Muslim Frontier* (London: I.B. Tauris, 1998), pp. 129–142.

"Islam and Europe," in V. Melander (ed.), *Culture Confrontation and Local Mobilization: Essays in Honour of Sigbert Axelson* (Uppsala: Swedish Institute of Missionary Research, 1997), 81–90.

"Muslims in Europe: History Revisited or a Way Forward," *Islam and Christian-Muslim Relations*, 8,2 (July 1997), pp. 135–143.

"Muslims in Europe into the next millennium," in S. Vertovec and C. Peach (eds), *Islam in Europe: The Politics of Religion and Community* (London: Macmillan, 1997), pp. 263–272.

"Shurta," *Encyclopaedia of Islam*, 2nd ed., vol. 11, Leiden: E.J. Brill, 1997, p. 510.

"Great Britain" (with S. Vertovec), in F. Dassetto and Y. Conrad (eds.), *Muslims in Western Europe: An Annotated Bibliography* (Paris: L'Harmattan, 1996), pp. 67–94.

"Islam and Europe," in T. Lunden et al (eds), *The second conference on Euro-Islam* (Stockholm: The Swedish Institute, 1996), 72–73.

"Organisation et intégration dans la vie associative," in R. Bistolfi and F. Zabbal (eds.), *Islams d'Europe: Intégration ou insertion communautaire?* (Paris: Editions de l'aube, 1995), pp. 146–149, with report of group debate pp. 154–171.

Arts. "Great Britain," "Islamic Foundation" and "UK Islamic Mission," *Encyclopaedia of the Modern Islamic World*, New York, Oxford University Press, 1995.

"Christian-Muslim relations in Western Europe," *Islamochristiana*, 21 (1995), pp. 121–131.

"Muslims in Europe in the late twentieth century," in Y.Y. Haddad and W.Z. Haddad (eds.), *Christian-Muslim Encounters* (Gainesville: University Press of Florida, 1995), pp. 314–327.

"Europe, Islam in," *A New Dictionary of Religions*, ed. John R. Hinnells, (Oxford: Blackwell. 1995), pp. 159–160.

"Islam and Europe," in R. Hoff and H. Mulder (eds.), *Islamic Revival and the West: Common Values, Common Goals* (The Hague: International Dialogues Foundation, 1995), 21–26.

"Shari'a, change and plural societies," in T. Mitri (ed.), *Religion, law and society* (Geneva: World Council of Churches, 1995), 27–32.

"Islam and Europe," *CSIC Papers: Europe*, no.13 (December 1994), pp. 1–5.

"Human rights in the West," *Al-Nur*, no. 42 (November 1994), pp. 42–46 (in Arabic).

"Will religious fundamentalism become increasingly violent?" *International Journal on Group Rights*, 2 (1994), 197–209.

"Muslims, pluralism and the European nation state," *European Journal of Intercultural Studies*, 5, 1 (1994), pp. 18–22.

"Muslimer i Storbritannien," in I. Svanberg and D. Westerlund (eds.), *Majoritetens Islam: Om muslimer utanför arabvärlden* (Stockholm: Arena, 1994), pp. 359–372.

"National ties today: problems and challenges. A Christian viewpoint," in *Nationalism Today: Problems and Challenges. Acts of a Muslim-Christian colloquium organized jointly by the Pontifical Council for Interreligious Dialogue (Vatican City) and the Royal Academy for Islamic Civilization Research Al Albait Foundation (Amman), 18–20 January 1994*, Rome: n.p. (Pontifical Council for Interreligious Dialogue), 1994, pp. 47–61.

"Religious tolerance: individual, community and state," Strasbourg: Council of Europe Parliamentary Assembly, Committee on Culture and Education, doc. no. AS/

Cult(43)43, 2 March 1992; reproduced in *Religious tolerance in democratic society*, Report of the Committee on Culture and Education (Rapporteur: Mrs Fischer, Germany, CDU/CSU) and related documents, Strasbourg: Council of Europe, Parliamentary Assembly Doc. 6732, 1993, pp. 48–49.

"Il diritto familiare nelle rivendicazioni dell'inserimento nei paesi europei," in J. Waardenburg (ed.), *I musulmani nella societa europea* (Turin: Fondazione Giovanni Agnelli, 1994), pp. 79–89. English version published as "Emerging claims of Muslim populations in matters of family law in Europe," *CSIC Papers: Europe*, no.10 (Nov. 1993).

"State, religion and laicite: The western European experience," in G. Speelman et al (eds.), *Muslims and Christians in Europe: Breaking new ground* (Essays in honour of Jan Slomp), Kampen: Kok, 1993, pp. 90–99. Reprinted in Tarek Mitri (ed.), *Religion, Law and Society* (Geneva: World Council of Churches, 1995), pp. 100–110.

"Islam and Islamic law in the United Kingdom," *Recht van de Islam*, 10 (1992), pp. 92–99.

"Migrant Muslims in Europe," sect.2 of art. "Muslimun," *Encyclopaedia of Islam*, 2nd ed., vol. 7 (Leiden: E.J.Brill, 1992), pp. 699–702.

"History of Muslim organisations in the UK," *Proceedings: Religious Archives Conference, 16 September 1992* (London, 1992), pp. 2–6.

"Musulman et Européen: La tension créatrice," Brussels: Quaker Council for European Affairs, 1992 (paper abridged and translated by David Forbes).

"Christendom and Islam post-Gulf: Return to the Middle Ages or a way forward?" *European Vision*, no. 16, 1991, 28–32. (Also in German and French.)

"Muslim organisations in Europe: Integration or isolation?" in W.A.R. Shadid and P.S. van Koningsveld (eds.), *The integration of Islam and Hinduism in western Europe*, Kampen: Kok Pharos, 1991, 43–61.

"The interfaith network (UK) and interfaith relations," *Islam and Christian-Muslim Relations*, 2,1 (1991), pp. 106–121.

"A Muslim agenda for Britain: Some reflections," *New Community*, 17,3 (April 1991), 467–475.

"Arabische Identität und Islam in der Golfkrise," *Der Überblick*, 26, 4 (December 1990), 41–43.

"Between Arab and Turk: Aleppo from the 11th till the 13th centuries," *Byzantinische Forschungen*, 16 (1990), 323–340.

"Mazalim," *Encyclopaedia of Islam*, 2nd ed., vol. 6, Leiden: E.J.Brill, 1990, pp. 933–935

"The Islamic communities in Britain," in P. Badham (ed.), *Religion and society in modern Britain*, Lampeter: The Edwin Mellen Press, 1989), 225–242.

"Lebanon," in Stuart Mews (ed.), *Religion in politics: A world guide*, London: Longman, 1989, 161–167.

"Muslims in English schools," *Journal: Institute of Muslim Minority Affairs*, 10, 1 (Jan. 1989), 223–245.

"Muslims in Britain and local authority responses," in T. Gerholm and Y.G. Lithman (eds.), *The new Islamic presence in Europe*, London: Mansell, 1988, 53–77; fully documented version in *RPME*, 30/31 (June–Sept. 1986).

"La chari'a," *Vivant univers*, 374 (March–April 1988), 30–32.

"The political geography and administration of Bahri Mamluk Palestine," in H. Nashabe (ed.), *Studia Palaestina: Studies in honor of Constantine K. Zurayk*, Beirut: Institute for Palestine Studies, 1988, 114–135.

"En ny erfaring," *Bibel, dialog og mission*, Hellerup: DMS-forlag, 1987, 96–102.

"Religionsundervisning i et multikulturelt samfund – situationen i Storbritannien" (RE in a multicultural society – the British situation), in A. Olesen (ed.), *Islam og undervisning i Danmark*, Århus: Statens humanistiske forskningsråd, 1987, 160–172.

"Muslims in Europe," *Renaissance and modern studies*, 31 (1987), 58–73.

"Muslims in Britain: Searching for an identity?", *New Community*, 13, 3 (spring 1987), 384–394.

"Other religions," *Reviews of UK statistical sources: Religion*, London: Pergamon Press for the Economic and Social Research Council and the Royal Statistical Society, 1987, 563–617.

"Zusammenleben verschiedener Kulturen – Erfahrungen in Europa," in J. Lahnemann (ed.), *Erziehung zur Kulturbegegnung*, Hamburg: EBV-Rissen, 1986, 135–147; English transl. *Newsletter* CSIC, 16 (Nov. 1986), 18–28.

Review article, "Bat Ye'or, *The Dhimmi*," *Newsletter* CSIC, 15 (May 1986), 26–32.

"Dialog, Mission und Muslime in Europa," in *Islam im Aufbruch: EMW-Informationen*, 68((24 March 1986), Danish transl. *Nordisk Missionstidsskrift*, 97, 3 (1986), 123–135.

"L'immigration et l'installation des musulmans en Grande Bretagne," in Magali Morsy (ed.), *L'Islam en Europe a l'epoque moderne*, Paris: Editions Sindbad, 1985, 365–399.

"Kulturkonflikten og strafferetten" (Cultural conflict and criminal law) (with H. Viltoft), in *Kulturkonflikten* (Copenhagen: Komiteen til forståelse mellem danske og indvandrere, 1985), 35–45.

"Islamisk familieret" (Islamic family law), *Samspil*, 2, 1 (Jan. 1985), 9–11

"Islam og muslimske indvandrerfamilier i England" (Islam and Muslim immigrant families in England), *Islam: Familie og samfund*, Aarhus: Statens humanistiske forskningsraad, 1984, 68–90.

"Islam and mixed marriages," *RPME*, 20(Dec.1983); Spanish transl. *Encuentro*, 143(March 1984); German transl. *CIBEDO-Texte*, May 1984; Dutch transl. *Begrip*, 71(Sept–Oct. 1984).

"Juridical problems facing Muslims in western society," *On the Move* (Vatican), 41 (May 1984), 135–146.

"Sultan Baybars and the appointment of four chief *qadi*s, 663/1265," *Studia Islamica*, 60 (1984), 167–176.

BIBLIOGRAPHY OF JØRGEN S. NIELSEN

"Islam-centret i Selly Oak og dets forhold til muslimer" (The Islam Centre in Selly Oak and its relations with Muslims), *Nordisk Missionstidsskrift*, 95, 1 (1984), 19–26.

"Muslim desires relating to school," *Newsletter* CSIC, 10 (Nov. 1983), 16–20.

"Muslims in Europe's schools," *RPME*, 17 (March 1983); Dutch transl. *Begrip*,66 (Sept.–Oct. 1983), 2–10.

"Mellemøst konflikten" (The Middle East conflict), *Svensk Missionstidskrift*, 71, 3 (1983), 42–50.

"Special focus: Lebanon," *Newsletter* CSIC, 10 (Nov. 1982), 15–20.

"Den nyere Islam" (Modern Islam), *Håndbog i verdens religioner*, 5th ed. Copenhagen: Politikens Forlag, 1982, 356–368.

"Secular and conservative trends in Egypt, 1925–1939," *Alserat*, 8, 1 (April 1982), 15–33.

"The resurgence of Islam," *IDOC International Bulletin*, Jan–Feb. 1982, 1–3.

"Muslims and Christians in Europe – a general survey," in Conference of European Churches, *The churches and Islam in Europe, II*, Geneva: CEC, 1982, 15–20.

"Muslims in Europe – an overview," *RPME*, 12 (Dec. 1981); French transl. *Hommes et migrations*, June 1982.

"Islams status i Mellemøsten" (The status of Islam in the Middle East), *Nordisk Missionstidsskrift*, 92 (1981), 124–132.

"Muslim education at home and abroad," *British Journal of Religious Education*, 3 (1980–81), 94–99.

"A note on the origin of the turra in early Mamluk chancery practice," *Der Islam*, 57 (1980), 288–292.

"Forms and problems of legal recognition for Muslims in Europe," *Research Papers: Muslims in Europe (RPME)*, 2 (June 1979); German transl. *CIBEDO-Dokumentation*, 4(Sept.1979).

"Islam i nutidens politik" (Islam in current politics), *Religionslæreren*, 75, 2 (March 1979), 7–11

"Islam mellem åndelig vækkelse og politisk selvrespekt" (Islam between spiritual revival and political self-respect), *Dansk Kirkeliv*, Aarhus: Aros, 1979, 55–67.

"Kommunismen i Mellemøsten" (Communism in the Middle East), *Nyt Synspunkt*, no. 3, Hellerup: DMS-forlag, 1976, 5–27.

"Mazalim and Dar al-'Adl under the early Mamluks," *The Muslim World*, 66 (1976), 114–132.

"Determining the Lebanon-Palestine border, 1918–1920" (in Arabic), *Shu'un Filastini-yya*, Dec.1975, 85–93.

"Fra den gamle verden til en ny" (From the old world to a new), in J.H. Jensen and E.W. Pedersen (eds.), *Møde med Islam*, Hellerup: DMS-forlag, 1973, 34–40.

PART 1

Conceptualising Islam and Muslims

∵

CHAPTER 1

Between Islam as a Generic Category and Muslim Exceptionalism

Thijl Sunier

Introduction

With his book *Muslims in Western Europe*, first published in 1992, but reprinted and reedited several times, Jørgen S. Nielsen set a standard for the study of Islam in Europe. Not only did he pave the way for the development of Islam in Europe as a scholarly field in its own right with its own dynamics and contextual specificities, he also critically commented on the apparent paradigmatic dichotomy in the study of Islam in Europe. There was a scholarship that considered the study of Islam in Europe simply as part of the larger general field of the study of Islam anywhere. Other scholarship by contrast simply ignored the religious dimensions of the presence of Muslims in Europe and subsumed Muslims under the general category of migrants, using the adjective "Islamic" only generically. Nielsen argued that a proper understanding of how Islam takes shape under new circumstances should take both dimensions into consideration and make it part of the analysis. In other words, we have to take into account the origins and backgrounds of Muslims in Europe as well as the new contexts and circumstances. In hindsight, the book appeared at an important historical turning point and marked the beginning of the development of Islam in Europe as a scholarly field.

At the time Nielsen published the first version of the book in 1992, two pressing issues had largely shaped the image of Islam around the turn of the decade: the Rushdie Affair and the Gulf War. In 1989, the spiritual leader of Iran Ayatollah Khomeini issued a fatwa against the British-Indian author Salman Rushdie in which he condemned him to death and called on Muslims everywhere in the world to kill Rushdie for committing blasphemy. In 1988, Rushdie published his book *The Satanic Verses* in which he allegedly offended the Prophet Mohammed. The book caused a worldwide protest of Muslims and Rushdie had to hide. Also in Europe Muslims organised demonstrations against Rushdie. For many people this came as a shock. Muslims were generally depicted as passive immigrants who were in Europe to accumulate wealth and eventually return to their home countries. Their anger and their support for

© KONINKLIJKE BRILL NV, LEIDEN, 2018 | DOI 10.1163/9789004362529_002

the fatwa against Rushdie shattered the image of Muslims in Europe as an isolated, backward migrant population from rural backgrounds and not in any way connected to the world around them.

The Gulf War broke out in August 1990 after the Iraqi dictator Saddam Hussein invaded Kuwait. The Iraqi goal was to support its ally Saudi Arabia and to liberate Kuwait. In the course of the war it became clear how concerned, connected and divided Muslims in Europe were.

Even without the massive coverage of the events by modern mass media as we witness today, the two events grew into front-page issues (see Sunier, 2011). This contributed to the awareness that Muslims in Europe were part of a global community. It also caused a shock among policy makers. Until then there was a general consensus that Muslims would eventually entirely be absorbed into the host societies along general trajectories of civic integration. Whether that would be accomplished through French secular citizenship or through British multiculturalism and anti-discrimination programs, or any other national format of integration, Muslims would in the end become part of the receiving societies as individual citizens. The dominant assumption was that there was no special attention needed for Islam because Muslims were basically considered immigrants with just a specific cultural background.

The image of a smooth absorption into host societies was shattered and the events, particularly the Rushdie affair, paved the way for the development of national Islam programs and for the "Muslim exceptionalism" that took shape in the 1990s and 2000s. The question of how to fit Islam into national frameworks became a key issue in national debates on the position of Muslims, but it also contributed to the stepping up of the role of nation states as cultural agents. Today, European countries are not afraid to violate the separation of religion and state and even often strongly interfere in the very content of religious thinking if in their eyes developments necessitate that. They promote a "national," domesticated Islam cut off from its origins and consider any foreign influence undesirable, contra-productive and even dangerous (Sunier, 2012). Domesticating Islam became a form of governmentality. One of the consequences was the gradual reduction of the categories "Islam" and "Muslim" to characteristics that were considered policy relevant. This implied that very diverse communities were lumped together, thereby ignoring important cultural and other differences. This also shaped research agendas and programs (Sunier, 2014). In this article, I analyse this shift and the ways in which the concept of "Muslim" developed into a policy category in the Netherlands over the past three decades. Then I return to the work of Jørgen S. Nielsen to evaluate his contribution to the field.

Dimensions of Religious Integration

Apart from the general principles of freedom of religion, there are three dimensions from which the place of Islam in Dutch society should be assessed. These dimensions are crucial to understand how Islam was incorporated in society. The first is the constitutional principle of religious equality. The Dutch Constitution of 1983 stipulates that all religious denominations are equal. Although this principle of equality actually dates back to the liberal Constitution of 1848, the idea was reinforced and reformulated in 1983 by severing all the financial and other ties between churches and the state. An important aspect of the equality principle is that the Dutch system, unlike that in Belgium or Germany, does not apply the principle of religious recognition and registration. Thus there are no religious denominations in the Netherlands that have formally more privileges than others. Equality means equal treatment in similar situations. Although there actually is much inequality between established denominations like the Reformed and Catholic churches and "new" religions like Islam and Hinduism, this principle of equality has indeed offered Islamic leaders a legal and political leverage to demand equal treatment and, in some cases, extra provisions in order to be able to catch up with established denominations. But equality has also been interpreted as a ground for doing nothing and to ignore demands by Muslims.

The second dimension concerns the organisation of Dutch society in much of the 20th century. Dutch society consisted of so-called "pillars," corporate religious communities or blocks that dominated the political landscape. Between the 1920s and 1960s there were two confessional pillars – a Catholic one and a Protestant one. In addition, there was a socialist movement and a so-called liberal sphere. The two confessional pillars comprised more than 50% of the Dutch population and ran through all social classes. They had their own political parties, trade unions, schools, universities, media and all kinds of other associations. The churches were at the heart of these pillars. The socialist movement, though not a pillar in the literal sense, was actually organised as one, although it had its political base mainly in the working class. These three blocks were organised from top to bottom and exerted a great influence on their rank-and-file. The ruling elite of the liberal sphere was economically the strongest faction in society, but from a social-organisational point of view it was the weakest. It was mostly composed of people who were not affiliated with one of the three other blocks and it adhered to the principles of the liberal Constitution of 1848.

Although the societal forces that sustained the pillarisation process have almost completely been replaced by the centralising mechanisms of the emerging modern welfare state after the Second World War, the juridical remnants of the system do still play a role in some crucial areas. The most important is the Dutch school system. Other areas that are organised on the basis of juridical provisions originating in the pillar system are the broadcasting system and pastoral welfare work in hospitals and prisons. Although secularisation took place even at many confessional schools, the system is still one of the most delicate issues in Dutch politics. Muslims can make use of these provisions and since the end of the 1980s a little over thirty state-financed Islamic primary schools and one secondary school have been founded (ISEO, 2001).[1] Even more important than these formal and legal remnants of the era of pillarisation is the fact that pillarisation can be found at the heart of a typical Dutch discourse or even myth about tolerance and mutual respect between the religio-cultural segments of society. It also largely explains the relatively easy way with which minorities are defined along religious lines and the idea that members of religious denominations constitute religious communities that are organised as a pillar in the Dutch (historical) sense.

The third dimension concerns Dutch integration policies. Muslims were migrants and as such they were subject to the specific requirements and aims of the Dutch integration policies that have been set up and developed since the early 1980s. The parameters of these policies, including the important shifts that have taken place since the early 1980s, indicate the trajectories towards a domestication of Islam. Islam has rendered the status of "immigrant religion," its features and characteristics are part and parcel of the cultural background of immigrants – people from outside the Dutch nation-state. Policies are designed to make these people members of Dutch society, not as members of a religious denomination but as individual immigrants (Rath *et al.*, 1996). It is important to note that Dutch integration policies do not deal with religious diversity as such. For example, it is, strictly speaking, incorrect to consider Islamic schools as part of these integration policies. In practice, however, the integration debate is highly relevant for the development of the school issue. These fields are discursively and politically connected.

Key terms of the Dutch integration policies were permanent residence and the participation of migrants in Dutch society together with a (limited) recognition of cultural diversity. Thus, according to the constitutional principle of freedom of religion, Muslims have the right to set up their own religious infrastructure. They can also make use of the juridical provisions that enable them to found their own schools, provided this should in no way hamper the integration process of migrants. The shifting and ever-changing interplay

---

1 Website Central Statistical Office (CBS): https://www.cbs.nl/nl-nl/cijfers.

between these constitutive factors over the past decades have rendered meaning to the typical Dutch notion of citizenship. Thus in the early 1980s there was a strong tendency to treat religious accommodation set up by Muslims as an intermediary between immigrants and the host society. This resulted in a heated debate about the extent to which the Dutch government should support the institutionalisation of Islam as a tool of the integration policies. The paradox that emerged here was that material support may have unintended consequences of stabilising religious accommodation while the integration policies aimed at assimilation of immigrants.

Muslims as a Policy Category

Until the end of the 1970s the government and society considered the presence of Muslims to be a temporary issue. Islam had arrived in the Netherlands as "cultural baggage" of labour migrants who would soon return to their home countries. The cultural and religious background of migrants did not play any significant role in debates about their position in society. Migrants were defined in terms of ethnic origin, but this had no political consequences. Officially, the Netherlands did not yet see itself as an immigration country. Migrants were primarily seen as members of a temporary labor force who would return to their countries of origin. Policies were based on this idea of temporariness. The creation of religious facilities was therefore seen to be something that should be left solely to private initiative. No special policies were needed; it was believed to be a self-regulating process (Sunier, 1996).

Towards the end of the 1970s when family reunion was well on its way, the need for religious facilities increased, especially the need for qualified religious personnel (Landman, 1992). At the same time organisational structures improved and activities increased. Many mosque organisations developed into real cultural centres for migrants. There were teahouses, shops and other facilities. Also in this period for the first time attempts were made by various local Muslim associations to work together, to improve communication and to coordinate activities. The number of religious organisations grew steadily. It was, however, a development that hardly caught the attention of the wider Dutch society.

1980s

In the beginning of the 1980s the government acknowledged that the idea of temporariness was unrealistic. The majority of the migrants were set to stay here permanently. In 1983 the government issued a report in which the outline of a new policy was formulated. It was at this point that the concept of "integration with the preservation of identity" (*integratie met behoud van identiteit*) was introduced (Ministry of Interior [BiZa], 1983, 38–42; Werkgroep-Waardenburg, 1983). Migrants were granted basic rights to live according to their own cultural background, while at the same time they were expected to integrate into society. This became the typical Dutch trajectory to full citizenship. "Integration" was narrowed down to "participation" in the central sectors of society: labour, housing and education (Engbersen & Gabriëls, 1995). Along with this concept of integration the term *achterstand* (best translated as "deprivation") made its way into the discourse. A lack of integration was equated with *achterstand* and vice versa. Equality, a central concept in integration policies in the early 1980s, should be understood here as equal opportunities (of migrants and the indigenous population). It did not refer to an idea of cultural equality. The misconception of these terms and the policy implications are the reason why the Netherlands of the 1980s is still seen as a country with multicultural policies (Sunier, 2010).

During the 1980s, the government adopted a lenient attitude towards cultural and religious diversity. In the first place, there was the general notion of culture and religion as basic properties of human beings. Thus, the relevance of cultural background for a person's wellbeing should be acknowledged (BiZa, 1983). On the pathway to full citizenship the relevance of culture and religion for the people concerned was recognised as a psychological outlet. Immigrants should have time to adapt to the new circumstances and this could best be accomplished in "their own circles." Organisations of migrants would therefore function as a bridge between the individual migrant and society in order to ensure a smooth integration of migrants into society. As such, they gained more significance in the integration process. They were politically and ideologically incorporated into the government's policies (Rath & Sunier, 1993). Islamic organisations were considered important organisations of migrants, and their activities were judged on their functions in the process of integration. It was expected that once integration had succeeded, these organisations would gradually disappear. Organisations could now apply for subsidies to develop activities for their rank-and-file, provided these activities sustained the integration process. This is fundamentally different from granting basic cultural rights as "would-be" pillars. I have described this discursive process as the "migrantisation" of Islamic organisations (Sunier, 1996). One of the consequences of this was that the number of organisations grew significantly in the course of the 1980s.

Some critics of Dutch integration policies of the 1980s have contended that the principle of "integration with the preservation of identity," so typical for Dutch minority policies, originated in the pillarisation history – a sort of multiculturalism *avant-la-lettre*. This is not true. Instead of characterising these

BETWEEN ISLAM AS A GENERIC CATEGORY AND MUSLIM EXCEPTIONALISM 9

policies as multiculturalist, as has been done in debates during the course of the 1980s and 1990s, they should be traced back to the American assimilationist perspective as developed in sociology in the 1950s and 1960s (Sunier, 2010). This perspective has been introduced and elaborated for the Dutch situation by Van Amersfoort (1974). His view on integration became the basis for Dutch minority policies in the 1980s. An important aspect of this new policy was that a relation was constructed between integration on the one hand and cultural background on the other. "Guest workers" were renamed as "ethnic minorities," "cultural minorities," or "ethnic groups." In other words, a shift in the definition of the situation took place. Migrants were moved from an economic category to a cultural one. Cultural background became relevant in integration policies. This is one of the most complicated aspects of Dutch integration and citizenship policies.

Whatever their origin, the policies adopted in the 1980s were as a whole certainly not unfavourable for Islamic organisations (*as migrant organisations*). At the same time, however, there was also a concern about the attitude of Muslims and their organisations towards the principles and priorities of the integration program developed by the government. The new policies of integration took shape at a time when dramatic events, such as the revolution in Iran and the assassination of the Egyptian president Sadat, were taking place in the Islamic world. These events caused a tremendous increase in the number of publications about Islam and its adherents. Suddenly migrants from countries like Turkey and Morocco were "discovered" as Muslims. A new cultural category emerged: "Muslim migrants." For the sake of convenience, people with completely different backgrounds were lumped together under the heading: "Muslim culture." Since it was mostly Muslims facing problems of deprivation with respect to housing, labour and education, "Muslim culture" rendered specific meaning associated with backwardness and fatalism.

Islam increasingly became the explanatory factor, not only for specific (collective) behaviour of Muslims, but also for all kinds of societal problems they faced. This "Islamisation of the discourse" not only overemphasised Islam as an explanatory factor, but also produced a particular epistemology of Islam in which "Islam" was reduced or rather translated into certain features that were in line with specific policies (cf. Massad, 2015; see also Mahmood, 2015). There was a growing attention to Islam among the public.

The specific image of Islam that made its way into public and policy discourses was based on the idea that Muslims were the least integrated migrants. Just when the Netherlands did away with its religious past, a new religious group appeared and asked for provisions that had almost disappeared. A religious group that is known for its anti-modern character, it was assumed.

According to this view, Muslims were seen as passive, fatalist people who were turned inwardly and faced difficulties catching up with the pace of modern society, and easily fall back on their faith.

The origin of this image can be related to the so-called "rural bias." A majority of the first generation Muslim migrants had a rural background. They stood for the archetypical "Muslim." Rural habits and Islamic prescriptions were constructed into an amalgam that represented the religion as a whole. Despite the negative undertone in this type of discourse, there was a certain inclusiveness and compassionate undertone in this image. Muslims were not fundamentally excluded as a separate category; it is their faith that enforces rules upon them. But these problems can be overcome through systematic socialisation. The boundary may be temporary, provided certain conditions are fulfilled (Rath, Meyer & Sunier, 1997: 59).

As a result of the political and ideological developments that took place in the 1980s, a new type of Islamic leadership emerged among the migrant population. These leaders belonged to the earliest migrants and had lived in the Netherlands for a relatively long time; they knew society quite well and had acted as an intermediary between Muslim migrants and Dutch society. They were entrepreneurs rather than "ideologists" and were oriented towards mobilizing as many resources as possible. They successfully made use of their contact with Dutch policymakers and institutions. They emphasised that Islamic organisations must be considered as the main forms of "self-organisation" among migrants. These leaders increasingly took part in discussions on the position of migrants and as opinion leaders they gained influence. They represented the Muslim populations and articulated what needs existed among Muslims. They also articulated what it means to be a Muslim in a non-Islamic society. By stressing the "foreign" character of Islam, as something that is part of the cultural heritage of a specific group of migrants, they were able to convince policymakers that certain facilities were required (Sunier, 1996).

1990s

The late 1980s marked a turning point in the status of cultural diversity. The socio-economic integration of immigrants did not meet the expected results. To begin with, unemployment remained high. Several statistics revealed that the unemployment rate was higher among "ethnic minorities." Turks and Moroccans were in a relatively weaker position. School results and outputs remained relatively poor (WRR, 1989). But one of the most alarming developments in the eyes of many politicians was the increasing segregation in the neighbourhoods where most migrants resided (Koopmans, 2007). Most of these areas were of poor quality with cheap housing and little accommodation.

Tensions between several categories of residents often erupted. Although several community studies showed that the ethnic factor in these conflicts was rather complicated (see for example Niekerk, Sunier and Vermeulen, 1989), for many politicians cultural diversity was a source of problems rather than enrichment.

In 1989, the "Wetenschappelijke Raad voor het Regeringsbeleid" (Scientific Advisory Board for Government Policy), an influential advisory board of the government, issued a report in which they concluded that integration policies should be more oriented towards individual social mobility of migrants. They considered the government's policy too much based on migrants as ethnic communities. This would not only divert the attention from individual characteristics and individual trajectories of migrants, but it would also put the constitutional principle of equality in jeopardy. As we saw, the government had facilitated activities of migrant organisations that could contribute to the integration process. But the policies of the government had the opposite effect, the WRR concluded (WRR, 1989).

It was also in this period that migrants were increasingly referred to as "allochthonous." The WRR introduced the term as a central trope in the Dutch integration discourse, referred to ethnic origin and culture of migrants and their descendants, irrespective of their legal status, but without any substantial qualifications, and without any official policy status (ibid.). All inhabitants of non-Dutch descent are "allochthonous," even when they were born in the Netherlands to parents with a Dutch passport who were not born in the Netherlands and irrespectively of their social status.

In fact, the WRR proposed a gradual decoupling of culture from socio-economic status and a more neutral position of the state towards cultural diversity. To a large extent they proposed to follow the French assimilation trajectory. Where the relation between culture and social status had been formulated in terms of mutual reinforcement, they now should become separate independent fields. A neutral government should facilitate cultural expression without interfering materially and ideologically, a reformulation of the anti-discrimination article in the Constitution. Policies would only be directed towards social, political and economic assimilation. Inherent to the concept of "allochthonous" was the notion of "having a different cultural background" and a "different cultural make-up," a qualification that may or may not influence someone's attitude, *but not governmental policies.* Allochthonous has acquired a degrading and exclusionary meaning and it denotes an impermeable boundary between "Dutch culture" and "other cultures" (Vasta, 2007; Geschiere, 2009). Due to its vagueness and plasticity, the term is applied in a wide variety of situations. It gradually made its way into the dominant discourse and practical political matters in the early 1990s. Although the government had now abandoned its policy towards the cultural infrastructure of migrants, the idea that culture (that is, cultural attitudes) influences the migrants' relation vis-à-vis society remained intact, so did the relevance of a cultural hierarchy in the integration fabric. Just as in the 1980s, the Dutch government remained committed to the idea that integration could be influenced by explicit cultural politics. The following quote nicely captures the position of the state in those years: "The extent to which existing cultures develop in relation to each other is primarily dependent on the choices of the respective cultural actors" (Ministry of Interior, 1999: 7).

The beginning of the 1990s also marked a shift in integration policies from a pragmatic and pedagogical approach to one that was crucially connected to the emerging discussion about Islam and the character of the Dutch nation-state. Not only could we observe the gradual conflation of "culture" with "Islam" (Sunier, 1996), but we also saw the growing entanglement of integration trajectories with nation-building. As I have indicated, the Rushdie affair in 1989 was a catalyst for emphasizing this line of political thinking. The transnational networks that existed among Muslims were increasingly perceived as counterproductive to a "nationalisation" of Islam. Integration was not anymore just a matter of participation in society; it also touched on the very roots of the Dutch nation.

The first politician who explicitly referred to Islam in relation to immigration was liberal leader Frits Bolkestein in a speech in 1991 at the International Liberal Conference in Lausanne. In his speech he called on European societies to be aware of the presence of Muslims and to think about how "we" should relate to Islam and to "our" own liberal roots (Bolkestein, 1991). Bolkestein referred not so much to the assumed effects of Islam on the individual migrant's attitude, but more to the collective dimensions of the place of Islam in Western societies. In a later publication he predicted with typical liberal optimism that Muslims will eventually be absorbed by modern liberal society (Bolkestein, 1997: 175). He restated the dictum that there is an *inequality* of cultures and attached it to a discourse of civilisation. Islam, he argued, is a cultural complex that cannot be equally validated as "our" Western civilisation. In other words, it was not only a matter of cultural accommodation of a group of religious newcomers; the very character of the Dutch nation was at stake. The Western nation, according to Bolkestein, has accomplished a higher civilisational stage than Islamic societies. With reference to the claimed universality of these accomplishments, Bolkestein urged European liberal politicians not to give in to some sort of multicultural idea of cultural equality. By relating religion to citizenship, civilisation, integration and nation building, he opened up a new field in the debate soon to be taken up by others.

2000s

Towards the end of the 1990s, the relation between culture and social status became more complicated. Whereas the majority of Muslims still occupied the lowest social strata of society, there were an increasing number of young Muslims who performed relatively well. Their school results were close to the average. The assumption that "Muslim equals underclass" did not anymore correspond with the statistical realities (SCP, 1996, 2009). Young Muslims would demand their place in society more articulately. These young Muslims could not simply be discarded as "not-yet-integrated" individuals. Many of them were born in the Netherlands and considered it their society. Their ability to articulate their demands not *towards* but *within* society brought about new challenges to the existing cultural hierarchy paradigm. Muslims were increasingly visible in those sectors of society that were long exclusively "white." This threw into relief the fundamental question as to how society relates to these "new citizens." Some welcomed these developments as a sign of genuine integration; others feared a gradual "Islamisation" of Dutch society.

In the late 1990s, the debate took a more alarming undertone. The self-confidence that characterised the discourse in the 1980s and 1990s was gradually replaced by the awareness that the "cultural engineering" that dominated the "integration apparatus" until then did not work out. The increasing articulacy among young Muslims, their active engagement with transnational networks, the demands addressed by them towards Dutch society and not least their increasing visibility in the public sphere, prompted a reconsideration of the concept of "Dutchness." Many intellectuals argued for a deepening and dissemination of national awareness and protection of Dutch national identity, both in relation to the presence of ethnic minorities and European unification. Their plea for more attention to national roots fitted within a general change in the political climate that took place in the course of the 1990s. The main idea is that the Dutch seem to be at a loss when they have to define precisely what the Dutch nation is. What is Dutch about Dutch national culture? What does it consist of? Why is the nation (still) an important frame of reference (Van Ginkel, 1999)? The cultural feeling of national belonging has become so "natural" in the Netherlands that for a long time many thought it hardly needed contemplating. Some have mistaken this self-evidence for a lack of national consciousness, and even a denial of "Dutchness." This poses a dilemma for ethnic minorities: if they are willing to integrate into the nation, what is required of them? Exclusion may be a consequence of not knowing how to be included in a concept that is deeply hidden. How can they become full-fledged citizens when it is hard to know how to play by cultural rules that are unclear and changing all the time? How can one become a member of

Dutch society when it is unclear what this membership implies (Sunier & van Ginkel, 2006)?

So already prior to 9/11 a shift occurred in the thinking about the relation between culture and integration. The worries about the Dutch national character and the critique of the 1980s integration policies provided a fruitful basis for the anti-multicultural discourse that emerged at the start of the new millennium. Muslims were increasingly depicted as a border-defying category of the population, an image that went smoothly together with the quickly growing securitisation policies. But the focus on radicalisation among Muslims is part of a broader and more fundamental development in which the image of Islam shifted towards a continuous threat from outside. This shift coincided with the growing consensus that multiculturalism was dead.

In 1999 and 2000, two influential opinion leaders wrote an essay on multiculturalism in the Netherlands. Both authors strongly criticised "multiculturalism" and advocated assimilationist policies. Both commented on the developments and both concluded that multiculturalism was a dangerous myth that contributes to further cultural segregation in society. In *The Multicultural Drama*, the author Paul Scheffer (2000), in a worrying and alarmist tone, referred to the successful integration of poor Dutch people in the mid-20th century. This had been accomplished by a very active struggle against poverty, an effective schooling program, and all kinds of other measures meant to improve their position. Scheffer argued that this civilising mission had been successful. He wondered why a similar policy had not been implemented for present-day ethnic groups that live under similar conditions. According to Scheffer this was mainly for fear of interfering in their private sphere. Scheffer blamed the government for a slack attitude in these matters, arguing that the cultural diversity we can observe in the public sphere, such as Islamic schools, all kinds of language programs, the strong ethnic cohesion among many migrants and their children, and not least the increasing cultural assertion and visibility, are the direct result of this laissez-faire attitude. This, according to Scheffer, is multicultural policy in practice (see also Scheffer, 2007). We see a lot of ethnic tension in society just below the surface. But instead of trying to come to grips with those problems, we believed in the problem-solving capacity of multicultural equality. Scheffer then invites all those protagonists of multiculturalism to look at what happens in the poor neighbourhoods of the big cities. He also refers to the fundamental differences between Islam and Christianity and he chastises for their naivety all those who argue that one hundred years ago Catholics and Protestants were no less each other's adversaries than Muslims and Christians today (Scheffer, 2000, 2007).

Scheffer not only suggested a direct link between culture and backwardness, he also predicted that the problems will be even more difficult than those with "our own underclasses." He further argued that the cultural distance between "us" and "them" is much bigger than we seem to believe. Although Scheffer did not openly evaluate cultures, he implicitly assumed that it is in the best interest of migrants to assimilate into Dutch society. In other words, a lasting cultural diversity is the direct proof of a failed integration project and an open invitation for even bigger future problems. Such a "multicultural neglect" endangers the very fundament on which our society rests. Increasing cultural diversity implies diminishing national cohesion. Multiculturalism, a term which Scheffer nowhere explicated, is a typical example of an ideology born out of the lack of capacity to define what binds together a nation. "We boast of a national identity having no national identity," Scheffer argued; but this will certainly not invite immigrants to participate in that society. He then concluded, by stating that cultural reciprocity in an "open society" puts a limit to the extent of cultural diversity, that the only way to prevent a second Rushdie Affair is to make clear what Dutch national identity implies, and above all requires, a strictly neutral public sphere (Scheffer, 2000).

Paul Schnabel, former director of the influential Social Cultural Planning Institute (SCP), arrived at roughly the same conclusion as Scheffer, although emphasising slightly different issues (Schnabel, 1999). Like Scheffer, he started with a gloomy picture about the weak social position of many migrants. But unlike Scheffer, he then elaborated the concept of multiculturalism meticulously, by making a distinction between a "multi-ethnic" and a "multicultural" society. The Netherlands are multi-ethnic in the sense that there are people from many different backgrounds, but it is highly undesirable that they become a multicultural society. This, according to Schnabel would imply that cultures of whatever sort are principally equal to each other. This is an illusion, he argued. He then posed the rhetorical question what "other cultures" have actually contributed to Dutch culture besides some restaurants, some music, and some festivals. More than three decades of immigration did not produce any serious cultural hybridisation, according to Schnabel. The immigrant cultures are typical "lower class cultures" and they are no serious match for the Dutch general culture based on the principles of the Enlightenment. This is a well-known argument, but Schnabel proposed a distinction between what he calls "A, B, and C cultures." The first level – A – concerns the "general public culture which is normative to everybody in society," and which constitutes the constitutional and democratic foundation of society. B-culture refers to daily collective practices, ways of behaviour. People do have a certain freedom here to act as they wish, but there are limits to that freedom. C-culture refers to individual lifestyle, which is a personal pursuit. Evidently, according to Schnabel, A-culture is hegemonic and always overrules the other levels. Thus the wearing of the headscarf resorts to level B or C, as long as it does not interfere with the A-level.

It is clear that it is a matter of power what kinds of cultural traits belong to what kind of level. Schnabel admitted that, but he rejects the implicitness with which power inequality is often covered up. This, he argued, is the typical hypocrisy of multiculturalists. Under the banner of "anything goes" multiculturalists suggest a cultural equality while they know very well that multiculturalism as a political ideal only exists within the framework of an enlightened A-culture. This leaves, according to Schnabel, no option for immigrants but to assimilate completely into Dutch society. Even if they resist assimilation, they will in the end "lose the battle." Schnabel seemed to be confident that also his B and C cultural traits will eventually wane. He therefore proposes to put assimilationist pressure where it concerns the central values (A-culture) and be attentive though a bit lenient towards B and C cultural traits (Schnabel, 1999).

These foundational texts and subsequent reactions constituted a new turn in the political debate. It resulted in a breakthrough in the traditional dividing line between left and right on issues of integration and multiculturalism. These and other texts constituted the basis for a more elaborate anti-multiculturalist politics that, despite its political variants, took shape across the whole political spectrum. Although Islam was not explicitly referred to in these texts, it was clear that implicitly Muslims were seen as the proverbial examples in case.

Conclusion

In this article I have shown how Islam was "translated" into a policy category in the Netherlands over the past three decades. In the 1980s, Muslims were mainly depicted as inward-oriented rural people for whom religion was a last resort. Consequently, Islam was understood as a pre-modern phenomenon that may give Muslims emotional comfort, but to fully participate in society Islam is an obstacle. The international events around the beginning of the 1990s, notably the Rushdie Affair and the Gulf war, caused a shift in emphasis from Islam as a pro-modern religion to a border-defying force from outside. The "foreignness" of Islam rendered a new meaning from a religion of immigrants to a force that jeopardises national integration. From an initial general cultural characteristic among many, Islam became a category unto itself and "Islamic exceptionalism" made its way into policy agendas. As a consequence, a specific epistemology developed catered for policy interventions.

When we look at the research carried out among Muslims in Europe today, much of it resonates with this specific epistemology. This reductionism is understandable at a time when research budgets are shrinking and policymakers require ready-made answers to what they deem important and relevant in the study of Islam. However, the problem with this perspective is that one easily overlooks the broader historical, social and political mechanisms at work. This brings me back to the work of Jørgen S. Nielsen and the future research on Islam in Europe.

In my view, Nielsen has always emphasised the importance of this broader perspective and as such resisted the tempting "cheap solutions way." In assessing this future one finds oneself in a complex situation in which we need to strike a balance between sufficient "exceptionalism" and ontological substance on the one hand and the development of a comparative paradigm beyond the specificities of Islam on the other. To accomplish that in a fruitful and productive way we need to broaden up rather than narrow down the field of the study of Islam.

Religion as a field of study suffers from a gradual decline due to the decreasing numbers of students and the dominant assumption that religion has become an irrelevant issue. The study of Islam is trapped between a super visibility in public sphere resulting in an "over-Islamisation" of everything Muslims do and think, and increasing invisibility as a research field in its own right. Looking beyond the research field of Islam in Europe we can witness a sharp increase in studies dealing with radicalism, Salafi activism and the use of violence, security issues, and a negligence of the vastly increasing diversity in the ways the Islamic landscape in Europe is shifting. I consider the work of Jørgen S. Nielsen absolutely vital because it is precisely this broadness and thematic diversity that he addresses; not only in his own work but also in the way he motivates colleagues to study Islam. Without being insensitive to what goes on in Europe and to the contextuality of Islam, he continuously and critically takes issue with the reductionism that government programs entail.

References

Van Amersfoort, H. 1974. *Immigratie en minderheidsvorming: Een analyse van de Nederlandse situatie 1945–1973*. Alphen aan den Rijn: Samson.

Bolkenstein, F. 1991. *Address to the Liberal International Conference at Luzern*, Den Haag: VVD.

Bolkenstein, F. 1997. *Moslims in de Polder,* Amsterdam: Contact.

Engbersen, G. & R. Gabriëls (eds.). 1995. *Sferen van Integratie. Naar een gedifferentieerd allochtonenbeleid.* Amsterdam: Boom.

Geschiere, P. 2009. *Perils of Beloning. Authochtony, Citizenship and Exclusion in Africa and Europe.* Chicago: Chicago University Press.

Van Ginkel, R. 1999. *Op zoek naar eigenheid. Denkbeelden en discussies over cultuur en identiteit in Nederland.* Den Haag: Sdu.

ISEO. 2001. *Minderhedenmonitor 2001,* Den Haag: ISEO.

Koopmans, R. 2007. "Integratiebeleid is een mislukking," *Mens en Politiek,* 38 (2): 6–7.

Landman, N. 1992. *Van mat tot minaret. De institutionalisering van de islam in Nederland.* Amsterdam: VU-Uitgeverij.

Mahmood, S. 2015. *Religious Difference in a secular Age,* Princeton: Princeton University Press.

Massad, J.A. 2015. *Islam in Liberalism,* Chicago: University of Chicago Press.

Ministry of Interior. 1983. *Minderhedennota,* Den Haag: Ministerie van Binnenlandse Zaken.

Ministry of Interior. 1999. *Kansen Krijgen, Kansen Pakken,* Den Haag: Ministerie van Binnenlandse Zaken.

van Niekerk, M., T. Sunier & H. Vermeulen. 1989. *Bekende Vreemden. Surinamers, Turken en Nederlanders in een naoorlogse wijk,* Amsterdam: het Spinhuis.

Nielsen, J. 1992. *Muslims in Western Europe,* Edinburgh: Edinburgh University Press.

Rath, J & T. Sunier. 1994. "Angst voor de islam in Nederland ?" in: *Kritiek: Jaarboek voor socialistische dicussie en analyse 93–94,* Bot, W., M. van der Linden, en R. Went, Utrecht: Stichting Toestanden, 53–63.

Rath, J. et al. 1996. *Nederland en zijn islam. Een ontzuilende samenleving reageert op het ontstaan van een geloofsgemeenschap,* Reeks Migratie en Etnische Studies 5. Amsterdam: Het Spinhuis.

Rath, J., A. Meyer & T. Sunier 1997. "The Establishment of Islamic Institutions in a De-Pillarizing Society," *Journal of Economic and Social Geography,* 88/4, 389–396.

Rushdie, S. 1988. *The Satanic Verses,* London: Viking, Penguin.

Scheffer, P. 2000. "Het multiculturele drama" *NRC – Handelsblad,* 29/1/00.

Scheffer, P. 2007. *Het Land van Aankomst,* Amsterdam: De Bezige Bij.

Schnabel, P. 1999. *De multiculturele illusie- Een pleidooi voor aanpassing en assimilatie,* Utrecht: Forum.

SCP. 1996. *Sociaal Cultureel Rapport,* Den Haag: SCP.

SCP. 2009. *Jaarrapport Integratie 2009,* Den Haag: SCP.

Sunier, T. 1996. *Islam in beweging. Turkse jongeren en islamitische organisaties,* Amsterdam: Het Spinhuis.

Sunier, T. 2010. "Assimilation by conviction or by coercion? Integration policies in the Netherlands," in Silj, A. (ed.), *European Multiculturalism Revisited,* London: Zed Press, 214–235.

Sunier, T. 2011. "New Religious Leadership among Muslims in Europe," *Australian Religion Studies Review,* Vol. 24 (3): 275–296.

Sunier, T. 2012. "Beyond the Domestication of Islam in Europe: A reflection on past and future Research on Islam in European societies," *Journal of Muslims in Europe* Vol. 1(2): 1–20.

Sunier, T. 2014. "Domesticating Islam: Exploring Academic Knowledge Production on Islam and Muslims in European Societies," *Ethnic and Racial Studies* vol. 37 (6): 1138–1155.

Sunier, T. & R. Van Ginkel. 2006. "'At Your Service!' Reflections on the Rise of Neo-Nationalism in the Netherlands," in Gingrich, A. & M. Banks (eds.), *Neo-nationalism in Europe and beyond*, Oxford: Berghahn, 107–125.

Vasta, E. 2007. "From ethnic minorities to ethnic majority policy: Multiculturalism and the shift to assimilation in the Netherlands," *Ethnic and Racial Studies* vol. 30(5): 713–740.

Werkgroep-Waardenburg. 1983. *Religieuze voorzieningen voor etnische minderheden in Nederland: Rapport tevens beleidsadvies van de niet-ambtelijke werkgroep ad hoc,* Rijswijk: Ministerie van WVC.

WRR. 1989. *Allochtonenbeleid*, Den Haag: Staatsuitgeverij.

CHAPTER 2

European Muslims as Skilled Kite Flyers

Werner Menski

Introduction

The first major part of this article traces some early discussions about Muslims in Europe and shows how Professor Nielsen and a few others realised early on that Muslims, as part of the emerging scenario of deeper socio-cultural pluralism all over Europe, would not simply assimilate and blend into existing local populations and cultures. Rather, in a scenario of constant rapid flux, they would rebuild their own patterns and ways of life in efforts to maintain their identity, not without change, but certainly not by seeing their socio-cultural characteristics dissolve in the UK and elsewhere like salt in water. Early observers like Nielsen saw and treated Muslims as active agents, not as passive recipients or mere subjects of state-controlled power. They also argued that Muslims and other minorities should be allowed to play their part. Indeed, Nielsen (1993, 11), who clearly knows a lot about law and its operation, pointedly observed: "Our European nations now also include substantial Muslim communities who must be allowed to play their part in our continuing histories. In so doing they will both contribute and change."

Later sections outline how today we understand in more depth, also theoretically in terms of legal pluralism analysis, that such early perceptions and predictions about continuity and change were entirely appropriate and correct. Law never provides a static and complete regulatory framework of rules and processes. Both rules and processes are, visibly and often invisibly, shot through with exceptions and allow powers of discretion at all levels. And, as we understand today again much better than in purely modern times, law remains always connected to values, while value-neutrality is merely a nice ideal. Because this was not acknowledged for many decades, inevitably a lot of space has been left for Muslims (and other migrants) in Europe to cultivate and practise their own living laws. Indeed, I argue, many Muslims have meanwhile become skilled cultural and legal navigators. Focussing on how this works in terms of comparative legal theory, applying the highly dynamic model of the kite of law, I show specifically how this works in relation to marriage among Muslims.

Marriage as a central socio-cultural institution is paradigmatic for many other aspects of life in which private and public laws intersect and law and

---

© KONINKLIJKE BRILL NV, LEIDEN, 2018 | DOI 10.1163/9789004362529_003

religion meet. We see how skilful many Muslims have become in navigating and balancing competing expectations, risking all the time accusations of illegality, because they do not start their decision-making processes from a state-centric position of citizen, but think and act first as Muslim individuals and members of communities. The increasing strength of Muslim communities, not only demographically, but also in terms of what one could call "legal consciousness" and the vast capacity of private decision making and use of available choices is strongly evident today. Self-confident assertions of power and demands of respect for certain culture-specific ways of doing things are constantly raising new issues and concerns. Such matters arise in people's consciences, in families and communities locally as well as nationally and internationally. They seem to involve partial loss of control of mainstream European institutions, but also bring frequent infringements of supposedly strict Islamic prescriptions and idealised perceptions of what is to be done. Professor Nielsen observed early on that such processes existed and he predicted that they would be conducive to reconstruction of a new European Muslim presence. Such insightful early observations about European Muslims as skilled cultural navigators, also found in Ballard (1994), are actually replicated elsewhere in the world, since states everywhere, including Muslim states, are so blindly overconfident as centres of power that they fail to see multiple legal pluralisms in operation.

This scenario has huge implications for how we perceive and handle the theoretical and practical challenges of Muslim legal and cultural pluralisms in our own midst today. A complex problem, it is constantly affected by further events and changes anywhere in the world which may generate volatility, not only for state-centric regulatory efforts, but also for Muslims. As is only too human, they do not always make appropriate and correct decisions. This then justifies claims for state intervention, some justified, and some clearly not. A basic approach of mutual respect rather than efforts to ban or outlaw certain aspects might be advisable, but is manifestly not always maintained.[1] Lack of care and sensitivity on all sides make this field of study heavily contested, literally explosive and dangerous for health and well-being, both physically and mentally, resulting in well-known phobias of various descriptions. Yet in an assessment of plurilegal navigational skills, the largely silent but by no means inactive majority of European Muslims today comes out, in my view, as clear winners.

---

1   I endorse the warnings of conflict in Nielsen (1997, 142) and the observations in Nielsen and Christofferson (2010, xiii) that there has been too much polemical attention to such matters.

Plurality-Consciousness, Limits of Law and Resulting Tensions

Professor Nielsen's contributions have been so important, and remain so deeply relevant today, because he is one of the pioneers in this field who dared to tackle topics that many others were reluctant to raise, whether because of ideological constraints or lack of knowledge and insight. A perusal of his many early writings on this topic confirms the presence of an alert observer and an analyst with an open mind, willing to listen and engage. Fortunately, he was also equipped with the institutional means to bring many participants together for sustained debates. As evidenced in the bibliography of Pearl and Menski (1998, 521–522), by the late 1990s we were well aware of his numerous contributions to the field. What stands out for me in the celebrant's approach and methodology is the rich interdisciplinarity and deep respect shown for the views and claims of the Muslim "other," much in contrast to many observers who clearly had and have various issues with Muslim claims to a place at the global or local debating table. From a theoretical as well as practical perspective, denying anyone a voice in such global debates is, from the start, leading to a violation of that claimant's basic rights.

I therefore begin with some reflections on these early debates, which are surprisingly open-minded, and as I tend to call it now, "plurality-conscious," informed by history and memory (Menski, 2014b). I then move on to more contentious and acerbic discourses, marked by mutual distrust and frequent accusations that the "other," is engaged in intolerable forms of suppression and denial of certain basic rights. Such arguments reflect various efforts to silence minority voices and/or to assert majoritarian perspectives but also indicate Muslims" strenuous efforts at self-assertion. We thus observe basically two kinds of prominent conservative claims. Firstly, white backlash claims, as one might call them, including the "One Law for All" brigade, seek to ensure that everything stays the same even though many new migrants have moved into "our" spaces. However, some Muslim assertions are equally conservative, insisting that perceived patterns of "good" life from centuries ago and other parts of the world can simply be transposed into European spaces. Clearly, Muslim migrants bring their religion and cultural traditions with them, but to what extent are they going to adapt them to the new environment? Concretely, will Muslims go to pubs, but will they then drink alcohol? Or will they prevail on others to stop drinking? Indeed, we see all scenarios happening. Mutual willingness to balance competing views and expectations has, however, often been lacking and exaggerated claims may serve as a bargaining strategy. In our increasingly plural European spaces, what are and should be the guiding norms? Years ago, I caused aggressive opposition from sociologists in a conference by suggesting that the local normative systems of Bradford might now be different from those of rural environments. Arguing for custom as a source of law in the twentieth century was unacceptable for secular rational social scientists who had definite views about "the law." Asserting the presence of local Muslim customs of Bradford in the early 1990s was a red herring then; for many this is still so today.

Looking back in 2016 it sometimes seems as if the highly charged discourse about the role of Islam and Muslims in Britain and Europe has not actually moved. Entrenched positions persist both on the side of Christian – or more likely secular – Europeans who feel threatened by assertions of ethnic minority cultures and religiosity, as well as Muslims who insist on pursuing certain "traditional" ways of life and behaviour that clearly clash with European normative and legal orders. Symbolic gestures are visible everywhere, but interdisciplinary observers should perhaps wonder whether widespread veiling practices and use of new Muslim clothing fashions may not also have economic dimensions. If one can persuade hundreds of thousands of people to purchase certain items of clothing, one is clearly "in business." It is also evident that highly contested issues, like the Rushdie Affair of 1989, which Nielsen (1991: 467) identified as a symbolic moment,[2] as well as French concerns about the headscarf since around the same time, led to polarised views. Later of course, the Gulf Crisis of the early 1990s, and then more dramatically 9/11 and the current ISIS problems impinge on private and public perceptions and self-perceptions of Muslims worldwide. This torments Muslims, too, for not only are they major sufferers in these current upheavals, but it remains rather dangerous for the silent majority of Muslims to speak openly about their disgust of atrocities against fellow Muslims in the name of Islamic purity and wider geostrategic agenda.

A prominent German colleague (Rohe, 2015, x) now confirms my own experience that any effort to study Muslims and to write about them will upset the haters of Islam. What has significantly changed, however, is the capacity of Muslims, as individuals, families and communities, to make better sense for themselves of this confusing scenario and to quietly construct out of the various disparate elements some viable, albeit still contested strategies, not just for decent and ethical survival as Muslims, but also as increasingly successful members of British and contemporary European societies. They have often

---

2   On the negative fallout of this affair, see also Werbner (1991, 339), who identifies tensions over decision-making processes that only history will tell about (343) and emphasises awareness of multiple realities (345).

achieved this through pragmatism and application of common sense. This effort, which could also be called *ijtihad*, involves skilful balancing, avoiding to fall into either side of the extremist abyss by either abandoning or harming one's Islamic identity or completely subjugating oneself to fatalistic theocratic notions.

Today, many Muslims in Europe and elsewhere are working hard to find their own plural paths to success and happiness, aware that the divinely inspired system that they owe allegiance to, in whatever way, allows and in fact requires them to exert themselves to find an appropriate path. Hence I note with approval how Rohe (2015, 8), in his excellent book that is now finally available in English, "intends to take Islamic law into account as living law." Intriguingly, while Keshavjee (2013: 189) points to a "culture of reluctance to air problems," his study of alternative dispute resolution (ADR) argues convincingly that European/diasporic Muslims are probably freer than their co-religionists in Muslim countries to explore and navigate new options for developing this "living Islamic law." Keshavjee (2013: 181) observes:

> Diasporic Muslim communities today have a unique opportunity to do something creative that would be difficult to do in a Muslim country, and that is to improvise and think innovatively about their personal laws vis-à-vis the law of the land, provided they are prepared to organise themselves in a manner that respects the public laws of the countries in which they live. ADR provides them this opportunity.

Such arguments, significantly from a minority perspective within Islam, confirm appreciation that Islam as a comprehensive ethical value system is far from rigid and, with its many culture-specific manifestations, can be adapted to new socio-cultural and pluri-legal contexts. The question, from a legal perspective, then merely becomes to what extent the outcomes are perceived and treated as "legal." This is of course where "power" comes in, as formal legal systems (and religious and social systems, too) will seek to assert their respective authoritative positions, trying to maintain or even enforce uniformity and to draw boundaries between what is legal/good/acceptable and what is not. However, in lived reality, this is never going to match with the hybrid scenarios that arise if people adhere to different socio-cultural and religious patterns and values and seek to follow different legal orders. The vociferous proponents of "One Law for All" of course remain blind to such realities and merely press for majoritarian solutions that actually violate the very principles of human rights they pretentiously claim to protect. But political Islamists, on the other side of the spectrum, are no better.

As someone who has been studying such contested processes of social and legal change mainly among South Asian migrants of all backgrounds, I see, from a vantage point in 2016, much change and more confusions about how to interpret this. Today, subject-specific academics struggle to grasp the complete picture, let alone reconstruct what went on in earlier times, as much of what is going on is – partly deliberately – hidden from public view. Moreover, anything to do with Islam and its interpretation as a living system has quite evidently, since ancient times, been subject to never-ending disagreement, signified so well by the pluralistic concept of *ikhtilaf*, translatable as "tolerated diversity of opinion." This principle, based on recognition that no human interpretation of God's will could ever claim to be fully correct, means there will always be a residue of doubt. In this context, Rohe (2015, 28) goes back to the early stage of Islamic legal history, when after the death of the Prophet in 632 divine guidance in prophetic form ceased and "[g]aps would thus have to be filled after deliberations of common sense." This is a pertinent reference to the still today heavily contested notion of *ra'y*, personal opinion and interpretation, rather than literal interpretation or faithful, virtually blind acceptance of divine guidance among Muslims in its originally oral and later textual forms of Qur'an and Sunna/Hadith. The resulting never-ending debates and conflicts and tensions among Muslims arise from the complex nature of human society generally, but are also magnified by the specific constellation of Islam as a more or less strictly monotheistic faith system. In addition to all this internal struggling, we find continuing problems of distrust and accusations that these Muslim "others" in our midst are not fully playing by "our" rules, and thus are "dodgy Asians," or whatever else one might choose to call them (Menski, 2000). More recent quite nervous debates about the extent to which Britain now witnesses "parallel societies" or even "parallel legal orders" strongly reflect such kinds of apprehensions.

In the shadow of the formal law, as several recent doctoral studies at SOAS have emphasised, there is thus much more going on in the various minority communities than outsiders are allowed and able to see. A certain sense of partial loss of official control is therefore unsurprising. Muslims, Islam and the Law as a Legal Industry (MILLI, according to Grillo, 2015), focuses on the perceived need for legal control, a notion fed and strengthened by misguided presumptions that "the law" has comprehensive powers of control, when actually it faces huge limits, as we learnt earlier at SOAS.[3] Focused on Islamic

---

3 Allott (1980) is a highly sophisticated, now almost forgotten study, written by a law professor who was earlier a colonial officer in Africa and later observed, as a Magistrate, that the law he taught and applied was not followed by many people he encountered, even in Oxforshire.

jurisprudence and its highly contested internal methodologies of ascertaining authority is another seminal earlier study, highlighting the law's fluidity and constant potential for change and contestation among Muslims.[4] Such analyses cannot be dismissed today as outdated Orientalist scholarship. The latter study succinctly lays out the inevitable internal struggles for Muslims in a holistic ethical system in which divine authority is necessarily taken as supreme in religious terms, while individual discretion to find the right path (*shari'a* or *shari'at*) is in lived practice the most direct, arduous obligation of every individual. I have consequently written that "[a] good Muslim is therefore, of necessity, a pluralist" (Menski, 2006, 281) and see no reason to change that phrase, though it irks some of my colleagues. Indeed, Keshavjee (2013, 154) highlights that "legal pluralism among British Muslims is very much a fact" and proceeds to discuss Ballard (1994) and especially Yilmaz (2005).

While Nielsen and Christoffersen (2010) emphasise flexibility and fluid processes of decision-making among young Muslims, too, Nielsen suggests in that study that "substantial numbers simply want to be left alone in peace to get on with their lives!" (12). So there are numerous indications that many British/European Muslims have today become masters in what an expert on South Asians identified as "skilled cultural navigators" (Ballard, 1994, 31). That study shows, similar to Nielsen's work, but from a different interdisciplinary angle, how South Asian migrant communities are committed to cultural and religious reconstruction (Ballard, 1994, 2). In effect, so Ballard (1994, 5, italics in the original):

> ... both the older generation of settlers and their British-born offspring are continuing to find substantial inspiration in the resources of their own particular cultural, religious and linguistic inheritance, which they are actively and creatively reinterpreting in order to rebuild their lives *on their own terms.*

It is precisely this constantly changing and deeply confusing complexity we face today as academic observers and analysts. Such processes do not affect an easily researched small community, but are operated by millions of highly diverse people across Europe. No single academic subject or book on its own can handle this complexity.[5] Detailed fieldwork studies have become almost impossible, partly because of justified fears of intrusion, surveillance, breaches of

---

4 On this tension see excellently Coulson (1959), also relevant references in Menski (2006, Chapter 5) and now Rohe (2015, 28 et al.).

5 See to this effect already Nielsen (1992) and now also Rohe (2015).

confidentiality and targeted discriminatory practices. Multiple concerns about money laundering, terrorism and counter-terrorism mean that field researchers today may face walls of silence. Many early debates in which our celebrant was involved indicated that the complexities would grow, and such predictions were correct. Some prominent observers argued for assimilation strategies (Poulter, 1986), even stricter compliance with international human rights standards (Poulter, 1998), but today we know that these uniforming trends have not materialised. One can partly blame control-focused state centrism and its lack of sensitivity to minority concerns, as it generated symbolic and evasive protest actions, including changes of customary patterns, as the examples further below regarding registered buildings and recognition of Muslim marriages illustrate.

The Relevance of Pluralism Theory

As indicated, Nielsen has been aware of the important role of law in his interdisciplinary research. This section connects his work and legal pluralism theory, which has the potential to defy Eurocentric blinkers and strengthens the ability to deal with various culture-specific conflicts and tensions arising from competing claims by four major stakeholders in legal decision-making anywhere in the world, namely individuals, groups or societies, states, and today increasingly the international community. The still evolving kite model of law that I developed from an earlier triangular image (Menski, 2006, 612) has meanwhile become a more mature method to explore legal decision-making.[6] There is no space here to explain how the commonsensical, dynamic kite model of law with its four corners arose. Imagine at the top corner 1, the realm of ethics, religion, values, identity and psychology, which comprises the internal pluralities of people's individual and collective belief systems and values. This relates also to visions of secularism, has important connections to nationalism, and tends to be holistic and thus global as well. In fact, corner 1 includes some elements of all other corners within itself. Corner 2 on the right hand side concerns social normativities, including customs and various local traditions, the fields of sociology/anthropology as well as socio-economic concerns. Again, values, legal norms and global perceptions are part of this domain, too. Corner 3 on the left hand side concerns the state and its laws, and thus also politics. From a legal positivist perspective, this is the "proper" legal corner, but its management depends on power sharing and balancing of expectations

---

6   See Menski (2013, 2014a, 2014b).

from and with all the other corners. Finally, at the bottom, corner 4 represents the vast, internally plural realm of international law and human rights norms and processes, and thus also international relations.

The basic kite structure of four interconnected corners which each contains elements of all the other corners is clearly never static. A kite moves in the air, pushed and pulled by various forces; its movements need to be managed to avoid crashing. The highly dynamic nature of all aspects of the postmodern concept of law poses the key challenge, all the time, to find the right balance between the competing expectations emanating from the four corners. That is all I need to explain here to proceed to the next section, examining now to what extent European Muslim citizens as skilled kite flyers seem to win contests of pluri-legal navigation. As predicted many years ago by Nielsen, many Muslims in Europe are by now able to handle the challenges of balancing competing expectations by using plurality-conscious strategies. I observe that they do so much more skilfully than myopic, monist state functionaries.

Early Academic Discussions about Muslims in Europe and Muslim Citizens Today as Skilled Kite Flyers

After UMO, the Union of Muslim Organisations of the UK and Eire, had expressed their "demand for the 'domestication' of Islamic family law for Muslims in Britain" as a matter of priority in a conference in 1975 (Nielsen, 1993, 1), a somewhat sterile debate got underway whether Britain ought to introduce a virtually separate system of Muslim personal law. Another prominent contributor to those debates, David Pearl (1981, 10), then still a legal academic at Cambridge, concluded at that early point:

> The suggestion that a "personal regime of law" be adopted for the Muslim community as a whole, or for those sections of the Muslim community who opt for such a system, is not likely to find much support in the host community.

Indeed, such models prevail even today in Asia and Africa, but not in the state-centric global North. Significantly Pearl (1981, 6) identifies a "dual identity" which, he goes on to state, "allows the ethnic minorities in general, and in particular the Asia[n] and East African Muslim groups, to adopt their own cultural traditions away from areas of contact with the indigenous community." This, without saying so explicitly, identifies the balancing act between competing legal expectations, an attempted integration process of private and public elements of people's family life, inevitably semi-hidden, and not uncontested. In relation to marriage solemnisation, to take only the simplest first step of mature people's engagement with the official legal system, the emerging picture became evident by the early 1980s. Pearl (1981, 6) observes that from the perspective of English law, which we now see is clearly monist and recognises only corner 3 of the kite as law, only the registered ceremony of marriage counts as legally valid. However, for Muslims and other migrants, this is not seen as sufficient, so that hardly anyone would only have a registered ceremony. Muslims, this means, turn also to corners 1 and 2.

My own fieldwork from roughly the same time confirmed that Asian couples might get married even during a lunch break, as a matter of formality (Menski, 1987). We should not imagine that such arrangements are not made today as well. The parties might then return to their respective homes, waiting for the religious ceremony to be arranged. Pearl (1981, 8) writes that this happened usually a week later. However, my own research identified much longer periods between these two ceremonies, leading to many potential problems and often tragic confusions. Some young people, unsure whether they were really married or not, developed misunderstandings over the permissibility of closer contact, not to mention actual consummation of the relationship. Shame and deep concerns about honour (*izzat*) prevented that this became widely shared public knowledge.[7]

While the official law has not really changed, the various communities learnt fast to combine the two marriage ceremonies, keeping them as closely together as possible. This was not done by abandoning the ethnic minority component, however. Indeed, mostly the opposite trend is evident. As the risk factor remains the "first night" when there is only a religious ceremony first, Asians in Britain quickly understood the power of the formal law. As realisation dawned that the registered ceremony was the dominant legal element, this led to reported nullity cases that involved mainly Sikhs during the 1970s. Many years ago, I showed how a pattern began to emerge. In the first stage (Menski, 1988, 64–65) many Asians were simply unaware of English law rules, followed their customary or religious law and might not always register their marriage in Britain (Menski, 1988, 65). A Muslim couple might simply have an unregistered Muslim religious marriage (nikah) in the UK and believe themselves to be legally married.

---

7   Fieldwork during the early 1980s led me to several cases of Asian women who had simply been abandoned after "the first night," the "husband" taking advantage of the absence of a registered marriage. The woman, typically, was left to carry the blame and made to suffer.

When stage 2 involved learning about the existence of English law, normally there were now at least two marriage ceremonies. But in what sequence would they occur? One night in between might still be fatal for the woman's honour. Here kite analysis helps us today: A law-abiding couple would have the registered ceremony first. But a faithful Muslim couple could still start from corners 1 and 2, have the *nikah*, and might simply ignore state law. After all, God heard the agreement to marry, so there may not even be a need for human witnesses, though it is wiser/better to involve them.[8] Even today many Muslims ignore the state law's expectation, but many others register the marriage first so that their daughter/sister is legally safe. There is, so typically, no agreement among Muslims.

I observed in 1988 that the next stage of development would certainly not be, following assimilationist presumptions, that the customary/religious elements would be abandoned. Rather, the opposite happened, namely official registration ceremonies were skilfully built into the process of the respective Asian marriage ceremony. Observing this among Sikhs, Hindus and Jains, I realised that in the mind of the parties and their families, the Asian religious/ cultural ceremony had remained the dominant legal order (Menski, 1988, 65), even if there was now also a formal registration. From the monist perspective of English law, though, still only the formal registration counts, confirming the conflicting practical impact of perceptions in kite-based processes of decision-making.

As a lawyer, Pearl (1981, 6–7) typically discusses the registration of mosques for the purposes of becoming a "registered building" under the Marriage Act, 1949. He mentions enormous difficulties in this process, mainly because such buildings were supposed to be separate buildings. Hence only few mosques in the UK became registered buildings, a situation still prominent today. This meant that most Muslims who wanted to marry legally had to arrange a secular registration ceremony in a town hall. Researchers did not pick up, however, that Muslims changed their customs in response. They often neither register nor follow the officially presumed pattern of marrying in a mosque. Instead they would contract an Islamic marriage at home, in a community centre, or nowadays in elegant and often expensive special marriage halls, venues that can accommodate many people.[9] Kite analysis shows that this potentially completely bypasses the state law. Good Muslims would argue that the kite corner sequence is 1-2-4, protecting religious and social etiquette and the rights of the woman, while simply leaving out corner 3 and state law.

---

8   See on this also Rohe (2015, 29–30).

9   More recently the official law has caught up with this and now permits people, on payment of an extra fee, to call a marriage registrar to such venues.

Today many Muslim marriages in Britain remain officially unregistered, confirming that the *nikah* is still most important for many people. Legal problems may arise, and there is an ongoing campaign headed by Aina Khan to increase people's awareness about this. I am more interested in a different agenda than aiming to have all Muslim couples register their marriages, however. We need to ask more questions about how Muslim couples manage to live as married couples, despite absence of formal registration, and yet protect the rights of the women and children involved. Can we really trust them to manage this? The key issue is still, from a Muslim perspective, that a *nikah* is first of all contracted before God. But how will God protect the woman who has no legally valid marriage in the eyes of the state? Here again, kite analysis helps, as it emphasises the dominant perspective of the individual Muslim actor, who treats God's law as the law. Most likely now no longer an immigrant himself or herself, these are members of a subsequent generation, in all likelihood those skilled young cultural navigators that Ballard (1994, 30–34) so elaborately discussed. A good pluralist Muslim should not dishonour the pledge before God and could easily place this higher than a contract before the state. Some states, of course, treat this approach as a crime.

What human rights-focused scholarship in the various fields involved has simply not picked up is the quite obvious connection between lived legal practices relating to marriage solemnisation among Muslim immigrants and their descendants and global theorising about multicultural law and legal pluralism. The scenario of legal pluralism experienced by Muslims and others living and marrying in Britain is of course, first of all, not the same as that studied by experts of private international law. They examine and assess whether what was done in a foreign jurisdiction abroad should be legally recognised in the domestic forum. Here the issue is different. While a Muslim *nikah* of a couple marrying in Karachi, Delhi or Dhaka would be treated as legally valid under the respective South Asian national law, and should then also be recognised as legally valid in the UK, the same couple marrying in London or Manchester would not be legally married yet. However, English and other European state laws (Denmark being an aggressively negative example) may refuse legal validity to such overseas marriages and reject its consequences. Again, we see forceful assertion of the power of monist kite corner 3. It seems that the various legal problems thus caused by state systems have suggested to Muslims that they may be better off in self-regulating their marital relationships within *shari'a* norms. That this will not be easy, may be abused, and is likely to create other legal problems is evident by now. But it also explains, to some extent, why Muslims seem to need the assistance of Sharia Councils and other ADR-based bodies.

That these are not trusted to deliver justice is more than clear. Challenges of understanding this are clearly visible at all levels today. At the highest level of global legal theorising, Western hubris continues to claim that mostly anglo-centric and franco-focused concepts of law provide sustainable solutions for the whole world. Just transplant advanced versions of such laws, and the world will become a better place! At lower levels of theorising, customs and religious norms are defined away as "extra-legal" and only legal rules from corner 3, maybe strengthened by corner 4, have authority. Even academic commentators who should know better prefer to take such views and either deny that there is something to study about "ethnic minorities," as migrants should become part of "us" as soon as possible, or remain cagy about addressing important issues such as the construction and management of virtually "parallel legal lives" or unofficial laws in British cities. I faced such issues throughout as I insisted, in disagreement with Poulter and many colleagues at SOAS, that there was much to study about ethnic minorities and the law. Encouragingly, one former student, now a prominent barrister (Knights, 2007, xi), has written that this kind of course ought to be required study for all future lawyers.

But it matters how one studies such topics, which lenses one applies, and what one's agenda are. I was motivated to write about Muslim family law and how it was being handled at official and unofficial levels (Pearl and Menski, 1998), because the person who had been asked to produce this book was by then too pre-occupied with judicial duties. Today, there is continuing demand for an updated edition of this unique practice-focused study. Its key concept of "English Muslim law" (*angrezi shariat*), the skilful construction of British Muslim law, remains pertinent also for the present article. In many places in Europe today, Muslims have become the local majority, increasing "our" fears of being othered. I have lived in England long enough to see whole residential areas change character during the past few decades. More recently I met some German judges who are experts in dealing with various Muslim cases, while most lawyers struggle to understand such new pluri-legalities and their practical implications. While we avoid engagement with recent developments, demographic growth patterns and economic achievements of Muslims in the West provide the basis for a remarkable range of socio-cultural and also political and legal assertions of Muslim presence. That this further alienates those who still believe in neutrality and the possibility of being an enlightened, autonomous individual is another matter. Far too much of legal scholarship, even today, continues to treat Muslim, Hindu and other legal "others" as some kind of defective, orientalist phenomenon that is bad for human rights. For most observers, this is now simply the guiding yardstick, decision-making sequences follow a 3–4 or 4–3 pattern, and seek to disregard corners 1 and 2. Muslims, clearly, know more about skilful kiteflying and balancing acts.

When I first drafted my PhD proposal on European Islam to my home university in Rome in 2009, I had not read nor met the Danish scholar of Islam in Europe, Jørgen S. Nielsen. At the time, I first came across some of his ideas in his Foreword to Tariq Ramadan's *To Be a European Muslim* (1999). A particular idea remained in the background of my readings and reflections since then, and it would have developed into what I try to present here only with the passage of time:

> The irony of the situation has become that living on the margins of the Muslim world has taken European Muslims back into the theological centre. In doing so they are being watched also from the geographical center [i.e. the Muslim world].[1]

There are two major ideas expressed here: first, there is an acknowledgement, as early as 1999, that Muslims of Europe do think, and that a European Islam is taking ground; second, this European Islam can be inspiring to the Arab-Islamic heartlands. In this chapter I deal with the first point, and I develop it in the light of what has been produced in the field of "European Islamic Studies" for the last few decades. That is, I present two major divergent lines of thought that read European Islam differently, though this difference has hardly been problematised and remarked before, nor has it been put face to face in a scholarly debate. This chapter then presents the views of two major scholars of Islam and Muslims in Europe: those of the French scholar Olivier Roy, and those of the Danish scholar Jørgen S. Nielsen. My own reading of European Islam makes me stand with the latter on his position: European Muslims are making their own theology; it is a pluralist theology in progress.[2] It may even be inspiring to the Arab-Islamic world.

European Islam Does Not Think; It Only Acts: Olivier Roy

Olivier Roy argues that European Islam does not think theologically yet though there are European Muslim intellectuals and engaged imams involved

---

1 Jørgen S. Nielsen, Foreword, in Tariq Ramadan, *To Be a European Muslim* (Leicester: Islamic Foundation, 1999), xi–xiv.

2 I have made my first reference to this difference between the two scholars in my PhD Dissertation "On the Idea of European Islam: Voices of Perpetual Modernity," LUISS Guido Carli University of Rome, 2013, 584, and later in Mohammed Hashas "Tareq Oubrou's Geotheology: Shari'ah of the Minority and the Secularization of Islamic Theology in the European Context," Journal of Muslim Minority Affairs, 2014, 1–21, n.12.

CHAPTER 3

Does European Islam Think?

Mohammed Hashas

Introduction

"Does European Islam think?" is a question that puts many delicate themes together. It goes around another leading question, "Is European Islam possible?" If European Islam is possible, who says so? How does s/he argue about that? From which discipline he is doing that? Is he representative of a mainstream line of thought? If he Muslim or not? If non-Muslim, what is behind the question? Is it scientific-academic or policy-oriented? If Muslim, what is his intentions? Is he academic or a believer, or both? Is he representative of Muslim scholars, or Muslim believers, or all of these, or none of these? A longer list of questions can be further outlined here, but it may be enough to say the following for now – since this is part of a larger project that has been ongoing for the last eight-nine years. This question originates from an engagement with contemporary Islamic thought in general and Islam in Europe in particular from an academic perspective from someone from within the same studied tradition-religion (Europe and Islam), if that matters. What does Islam mean, and what does Europe mean are other iceberg-questions that eclipse a plural world beyond description here. The poetics of the question "Does European Islam think?" do not develop over a night by an indifferent mind; rather, it reflects an engaged and critical mind.

From the 1980s, a vast literature on Muslims and Islam in Europe has developed, mostly from political science, international relations, and socio-anthropological perspectives. Theological perspectives remain uncharted territories in what is now commonly referred to as "European Islamic thought" among some experts, maybe because theology requires a believing mind, or maybe because the secular university in Europe does not allow such an in-depth, or maybe there is no ideological interest in raising the question of theological insights about modern political issues, or simply maybe because Muslims in Europe have not produced enough texts to be studied from theological perspectives. It is for these various reasons that the thinking about the question "Does European Islam think?" becomes vital. Clarifying the debate on Islam and Muslims in Europe has to be made, and maybe here is the moment to reflect on that in utmost clarity.

© KONINKLIJKE BRILL NV, LEIDEN, 2018 | DOI 10.1163/9789004362529_004

Menski, W. 2000. "Chameleons and Dodgy Lawyers: Reflections on Asians in Britain and their Legal Reconstruction of the Universe," *Indo-British Review. A Journal of History*. [Millennium Issue on Britain, India and the diaspora. Changing Social and Historiographical Perceptions], XXIII(2), 89–103.

Menski, W. 2006. *Comparative Law in a Global Context. The Legal Systems of Asia and Africa*. Second Edn. Cambridge: Cambridge University Press.

Menski, W. 2013. "Law as a Kite: Managing Legal Pluralism in the Context of Islamic Finance," In Valentino Cattelan (ed.) *Islamic Finance in Europe. Towards a Plural Financial System*. Cheltenham: Edward Elgar, 15–31.

Menski, W. 2014a. "The Liquidity of Law as a Challenge to Global Theorising," *Jura Gentium*, Vol. XI: *Pluralismo Giuridico*. Annuale 2014, 19–42. [http://www.juragentium.org].

Menski, W. 2014b. "Remembering and Applying Legal Pluralism: Law as Kite Flying," In Séan Patrick Donlan and Lukas Heckendorn Urscheler (eds.) *Concepts of Law: Comparative, Jurisprudential, and Social Science Perspectives*. Farnham: Ashgate, 91–108.

Nielsen, Jørgen S. 1991. "A Muslim Agenda for Britain: Some Reflections," *New Community* 17(3), 467–475.

Nielsen, J.S. 1992. *Muslims in Western Europe*. Edinburgh: Edinburgh University Press.

Nielsen, J.S. 1993. *Emerging Claims of Muslim Populations in Matters of Family Law in Europe*. Birmingham. [CSIC Research Paper, No. 10].

Nielsen, J.S. 1997. "Muslims in Europe: History Revisited or a Way Forward?" *Islam and Christian-Muslim Relations* (82), 135–143.

Nielsen, J.S. and Lisbet Christofferson (eds.), 2010. *Shari'a as Discourse. Legal Traditions and the Encounter With Europe*. Farnham: Ashgate.

Pearl, David. 1981. "Islam in English Family Law," In Nielsen, J.S. (ed.) *Islam in English law and Administration. A Symposium*. Birmingham: Selly Oak Colleges, 6–10.

Pearl, David and Menski, Werner. 1998. *Muslim Family Law*. Third Edn. London: Sweet & Maxwell.

Poulter, Sebastian. 1986. *English Law and Ethnic Minority Customs*. London: Butterworths.

Poulter, S. 1998. *Ethnicity, Law and Human Rights. The English Experience*. Oxford: Clarendon Press.

Rohe, Mathias. 2015. *Islamic Law in Past and Present*. Leiden: Brill.

Werbner, Pnina. 1991. "Shattered Bridges: The Dialectics of Progress and Alienation Among British Muslims," *New Community*, 17(3), 331–346.

Yilmaz, Ihsan. 2005. *Muslim laws, Politics and Society in Modern NationStates. Dynamic Legal Pluralisms in England, Turkey and Pakistan*. Aldershot: Ashgate.

Conclusions

While I am certainly not claiming that all Muslims are skilled cultural/legal navigators, or that all arrangements within the community are acceptable,[10] it is clear by now that many European Muslims are more skilled and versatile than most legal professionals when it comes to handling Muslim living laws. They make decisions as Muslim individuals and members of communities, may or may not claim that Islamic law itself accounts for human rights, and they often have deep reservations about the *bona fides* of the approach that official laws take to matters of Islamic law and life or ethnic minority laws generally. I am not surprised that Muslims and others are reluctant to share their experiences of how they navigate competing pushes and pulls, but we have many indications that the lived reality is more plural than lawyers and bureaucrats realise and want to know. I rest my case here because of space constraints and would just like to add that our celebrant's work has significantly helped to inspire my research.

References

Allott, Antony N. 1980. *The Limits of Law*. London: Butterworths.

Ballard, Roger (ed.). 1994. *Desh Pardesh. The South Asian Presence in Britain*. London: Hurst & Co.

Coulson, Noel J. 1959. *Conflicts and Tensions in Islamic Jurisprudence*. Chicago and London: Chicago University Press.

Grillo, Ralph. 2015. *Muslim Families, Politics and the Law. A Legal Industry in Multicultural Britain*. Farnham: Ashgate.

Hasan, Khola. 2009. *The Medical and Social Costs of Consanguineous Marrriages Within the British Mirpuri Community*. London: Albatross Consultancy Ltd.

Keshavjee, Mohamed M. 2013. *Islam, Sharia & Alternative Dispute Resolution*. London: I.B. Tauris.

Knights, Samantha. 2007. *Freedom of Religion, Minorities, and the Law*. Oxford: Oxford University Press.

Menski, Werner. 1987 "Legal Pluralism in the Hindu Marriage," In Richard Burghart (ed.), *Hinduism in Great Britain. The Perpetuation of Religion in an Alien Cultural Milieu*. London: Tavistock, 180–200.

Menski, W. 1988. "English Family Law and Ethnic Laws in Britain," In 1988(1) *Kerala Law Times*, Journal Section, 56–66.

---

10   For example, Hasan (2009) researched a highly emotional subject of great relevance.

in debating how to interpret their Islamic sources. As will be shown below, his view that Islam is not being reformed theologically means that European Islam cannot think; it is only adaptive, and indirectly it is merely being forced into this adaptation without an accompanying intellectual exertion, and is thus theology-free. Otherwise said, European Muslims are passive (intellectual) agents, and passive religionists, though this passivity does not necessarily mean they are being passive citizens; they can and are active citizens since they abide by European laws and context requirements, but they do so only because secularism, laïcité and secularisation oblige them to.[3]

He writes in his *Vers un islam européen* [*Towards a European Islam,* 1999] that there is no theological new input to Islam among Muslims in Europe. All he sees is the age of "post-Islamism," characterised, among other aspects, by "individualization," "privatization," and "deterritorialization" without theological re-interpretations. I quote him in length:

> We see then that the minority fact does not necessarily bring about a theological or jurisprudential *aggiornamento* but rather a disconnection between the theological debate and the creativity of a religiosity which is centered on the individual. [...] It [i.e. individualized European Islam] is not a reformed Islam because not only the dogma but also the corpus of interpreters and jurists remain uncontested. [...] European Islam is deterritorialized, deprived of institutions that could impose norms. [...] *We are certainly wrong to wait for a theological reform, or a theological voice, for the liberalization of practices (like the veil, food, etc.) which would allow the Muslims to adapt to Occidental norms.*[4] [Emphasis added]

According to Roy, the resurgence of Islam among Muslims in Europe, and in the Islamic majority lands, is broadly anti-intellectual especially among fundamentalists and Salafis. This is the case for religion in general in the 21st century.[5] He calls this *"sainte ignorance"* (sacred or holy ignorance), because religionists are happy with the traditional way of practicing religion, with no

---

3   Roy differentiates between the three terms. Briefly, while laïcité is the French version of secularism, which in turn is the ideological separation of the Church and State, secularisation is a modern process, a way of conceiving the world that many factors contribute to (political, economic, social, intellectual, etc.); secularisation is "the persistence of the religious phenomenon without the sacred," Roy, *Secularism Confronts Islam,* trans. George Holoch (New York: Columbia UP, 2007), 59.

4   Olivier Roy, *Vers un islam européen* [*Towards a European Islam*] (Paris: Esprit, 1999), 89; 90; 91.

5   Roy, *Globalised Islam: The Search for a New Ummah* (New York: Columbia UP, 2004), 31; 35.

extra intellectual exertion.[6] In *Globalised Islam* (2004), Roy does not change his mind. He still views Islam in the West in general to be looking through the Western lenses, "The issue is not Western versus Muslim values. [...] The debate occurs within a single 'cultural' framework: that of the West."[7] Due to the fact that it works "within" the Western framework, Roy then sees no Islamic theology being revisited or developed, "Islam in the West is Western not to the extent it changes its theological framework, but because it expresses that framework more in terms of values than of legal norms, whatever the content of those values."[8] What Roy considers to be changing is not the dogma, but simply the practice of believers, "What is changing is not religion but religiosity," and he ascertains this since the "liberal [Muslim] thinkers do not meet the demands of the religious market."[9] That is, the thinkers are more reformist and progressive, while the religious market is dominated by conservatives. That is why "[L]iberal Muslims who accept the idea of a reformation of Islam" are "outside the purview of this [i.e. his] study."[10] There is a point that needs to be highlighted here, and it is recurrent in Roy's study of European Islam.

Roy argues that Muslims in the liberal societies of Europe are developing a new form of religiosity that underlines values instead of legal norms. They, he says, do not seek a "theological aggiornamento," or an Islamic reformation; they live it without questioning it; they do not think about it; their European Islam, then, does not think – to put it clearly. He says, "Islam has thus been *transformed*" by "*secularization*" [emphasis added], and by a "*negotiated* [emphasis added] political integration."[11] Then he adds, "[I]ntegrated Muslims have therefore *reformulated* their beliefs *according to the terms of the Western debate*" [emphasis added].[12] He recognises, however, that these "integrated or silent forms" are "simply forgotten in the debate, whereas they prove in actual fact the compatibility of Islam, laïcité, and secularism."[13] Still, this integration is not intellectual, not theological; it does not think. On the case of France, he says, "Muslims [...] have come to terms with laïcité through political steps, not through theological reformation."[14] On occasions he says that these new forms

---

6   Roy, *La sainte ignorance: le temps de la religion sans culture* [*The Sacred Ignorance: The Age of Religion without Culture*] (Paris: Seuil, 2008), 189.

7   Roy, *Globalised Islam*, 335–337.

8   Ibid., 31.

9   Ibid., 30–31.

10   Roy, *Secularism Confronts Islam*, trans. George Holoch (New York: Columbia UP, 2007), 82.

11   Ibid., 94.

12   Ibid., 83.

13   Ibid., 83–84.

14   Ibid., 91.

of religiosity will be legitimised theologically in the future, but until now there is none of such a process,[15] though he refers to engaged progressive imams like Ben Cheikh of Marseille, Hassan Chalghoumi of Seine-Saint-Denis, or the renowned public intellectual and theologian Tariq Ramadan. For comparative purposes he writes, "the secularization of religious behavior has occurred in the Western world without theologians necessarily drawing any conclusions from the process."[16]

While Roy's description of the new forms of religiosity may not be contested, the rest of his argument can be. At least three arguments may be deducted from his own contention that there is no theological thinking taking place among Muslims in Europe. First, one should be cautious of what the term "theology" includes and what it does not in modern times. If profound theological issues, especially on metaphysics and divine attributes are not so much on the scene, other aspects that concern especially rituals and law have become important in modern secular times to the extent that they have become to represent theological attitudes or meanings. A Muslim lady may wear the veil in France but without observing the daily prayers, which are the second pillar of Islam; her presence in the public sphere with the veil is a theological statement, because the context has made of it so. Similarly, a Muslim male may drink and not observe prayers (which may make him a visibly secular man), but observe Ramadan (which can hardly make him visible even when in the public sphere). Moreover, this transformation is not new; some Muslims in non-European societies also observe Islam this way; they are selective in so doing, though maybe less in the public sphere or in less intensity, depending on the country and its history with Islam (consider Muslims in Post-Communist countries, or Tatars, or post-revolution young Iranians). This is to say that the transformation of religious legal or ritualistic norms does not mean that they are theology-free.

Second, institutions like the European Council for Fatwa and Research, or "Embassy Islam"[17] and other various state sponsored councils established after 9/11, 2001, try to accommodate Muslims theologically in the new lands of Europe, either with reference to old legal schools these "embassy Islams" follow

---

15   He says: "Theological aggiornamento is not a prerequisite for the emergence of a liberal Islam in practice but will probably be able to give it theological legitimacy after the fact." *Secularism Confronts Islam*, 98–99. This is reiterated in a recent article, where Roy says that the Muslims' new forms of religiosity "will soon [sic] or later produce their own theological updating." In "Secularism and Islam: The Theological Predicament," The International Spectator: Italian Journal of International Affairs, 48: 1 (2013), 18.

16   Roy, *Secularism Confronts Islam*, 66.

17   Jonathan Laurence, The Emancipation of Europe's Muslims (Princeton, NJ: Princeton UP, 2012), 30–69.

back-home, or through new writings, like those of minority fiqh (Islamic juris-prudence). Some public imams have become iconic representatives of some parts of Muslim communities, and have written about the versions of Islam of/ in Europe they envision, like the imams quoted above, or others, like Mustapha Chendid in Denmark, or Yahya Pallavicini in Italy. These writings may not be theologically profound nor innovative nor liberal, but they still have an influ-ence on their followers, and a contribution to the debate with non-Muslims. Most importantly, the act of writing itself means that there is an intellectual engagement and theological accompaniment of the believers in liberal societ-ies. These writings may be mere adaptations to the new forms of religiosity, but still this means there is an intellectual-theological engagement of some kind. This questions Roy's comparative view that in the West, Church theolo-gians did not cope with secularisation, but were passively swallowed by secu-larisation process. I wonder where can he situate the work of Vatican Council II (1962–1965)? Was it not a theologically institutional response to secularism and secularisation and a contribution to it (even if considered by some a re-sponse from a weak position)?

Third, and maybe most importantly, Roy argues that Islamic history did not experience single religious authority as did the Catholic Church through the Pope since power was secular,[18] and religion held power at the societal level through *'asabiyya* [or *esprit de corps* in Montesquieu's terms] and sharia, which enjoyed flexibility.[19] Otherwise put, Islam was in most of its pre-modern his-tory a religion of civil society. If this is the case – which many scholars agree with – why is Roy not considering the emerging European Islamic theology within this framework? Roy does not suspect scholars like Tariq Ramadan of neo-fundamentalism, though he considers him within what he calls "orthodox liberals" school, i.e. a school that is theologically orthodox, but passively ac-commodative of modern changes and laws.[20] The point here is that despite the fact that he recognises Islamic classic sharia flexibility and its secular po-litical manifestations, and despite the fact that "orthodox liberals" adapt their discourse to the modern context and its exigencies, and despite the fact that he sees Muslims as components of civil society individualizing religiosity and internalizing modern values, he still does not recognise this as a theological work in progress, the way secularisation is in his framework, and only thinks that "Muslim liberal theology" may develop in the future, not now.

There is a clear contradiction here, and a clear inability to either recognise or see religiosity dynamics as part of intellectual dynamics of religion and its

---

18   Ibid., 62.

19   Ibid., 55.

20   Ibid., 43–44.

agents in society. It appears that Roy differentiates between reformists and the possible emergence of European Muslim [new] thought, and theology. It is as if there were religion without religionists/agents, or agents without religion. If there are reformists and engaged imams, even those involved only in adaptation and what he calls "orthodox liberals," let alone extremists, and he still sees no emergence of new Islamic thought in Europe, then something is missing: the lack of recognition of the emerging European Islamic thought/ theology. Roy's argument reads like Talal Asad's critical reading of Ernest Gellner's description of Muslim actors in *Muslim Society* (1981), they "do not speak, they do not think, they *behave*"[21] – Roy's actors do speak, but are unheard; they behave, but remain invisible.

At least two points can be advanced as informed but still assumed justifications of this lack of recognition or contradiction. First, Roy says it is out of the scope of his study to examine such discourses of Muslim reformists; yet, he does, and he gives his views that reformists and liberals exist, but not a new theology or a new comprehensive thought. Roy is well aware of the work of Muslim reformists also in the Arab-Islamic world, and not only in Europe. He mentions reformists-theologians like Mohammed Arkoun, Nasr Hamid Abu Zayd, and Abdolkarim Soroush. He, however, states: "We simply register the fact that there can be a Muslim liberal theology."[22] Are these theologians he quotes not advocates of liberal theology already?

Maybe the next point explains this contradiction and lack of recognition: Roy warns lest reformists are over-emphasised and mediatised especially in the West in these historical moments of turmoil in the Arab-Islamic world and the feeling of anti-imperialism that accompanies the turmoil. Such an over-emphasis of these reformists in order to make them prestigious "good Muslim" figures or to use them to show that they are good exceptions in the liberal West in front of the fanaticism of the region back there in the Middle East may just backfire and not allow them to do their intended service to their communities. If this is his point, then it is essentializing; it is depicting Islam as one-thing and any forms outside that are not Islamic – and certainly Roy is against such an essentialisation; it was noted that he speaks of past intellectual dynamics in Islam, which he now does not see evolving and being revisited in Europe. In both cases, Roy seems being against over-emphasizing reformists' work as theological to avoid making the Muslim community forced to choose one of the two (either liberal or fundamentalist thought), with no other alternative.[23]

---

21 Talal Asad, "The Idea of an Anthropology of Islam," Center for Contemporary Arab Studies at Georgetown University, Occasional Paper Series, March 1986, 8.

22 Ibid., 48.

23 Ibid., 49.

42 HASHAS

If he is against such a binary opposition, why does he remain blind to an alternative, or alternatives, he is aware of? This limited choice Roy portrays can be read as an irrecognition of not only an emerging theological debate in Europe, but an irrecognition of the profound theological debates among Muslims in the broad Islamic world as well – again, though he refers to renowned reformist theologians. To say that his study is not concerned with such a focus turns the argument against him, and here is why.

Roy's work studies Islam, especially political Islam in the age of secularisation, in secular and laïc contexts. Consider his major titles: *The Failure of Political Islam, Towards a European Islam, Globalised Islam, Secularism Confronts Islam*. Islam is at the centre of his political sociology, but it seems static, unable to think and interact with the politics and other factors it encounters in modern times; political Islam has failed, and the post-Islamic era is driven by the individualisation of Islamic values and internalisation of modern ones; as to the radical youth who resort to violence, they are a modern phenomenon and are mostly unfamiliar with the Islamic tradition and mainstream non-violent Islam; they are rebels against their parents, and society at large; Roy sees Al Qaeda and later ISIS foreign fighters in the West as a Youth Movement, and not a religious movement *per se*, a movement that reacts to socio-economic marginalisation, lack of integration, poverty, nihilism, corrupt and individualised interpretation of jihad, heroism, etc. Roy sees these radicalised Muslims – and new converts – are being active, also *just behaving* without *thinking*, in modern-secular contexts. The point is that even the radicals are passive in front of secularisation which Roy defines as a societal process to which various factors contribute, and is not a system of thought. Even the radicals then are passive reactors to secularisation, and to its forms of ideologies, be they [moderately] secular or laïc. But, are not these radicals creating a narrative, a new theology, however Islamic or un-Islamic it may be? By implication, this described passivity, or only behavioral activism, of a radical tiny fragment of Muslims, blocks the appearance to the surface of its counter-narrative, led by Muslim intellectuals and theologians. This is one of the other main points to be born in mind when trying to understand the implications of Roy's irrecognition of an emerging European Islamic thought.[24] Overall, it is not Roy's sociological details but

---

24   In his counter-narrative strategies, Roy proposes two approaches: 1) one vertical that examines the genealogy of violence in Islamic texts and history, and 2) the other horizontal, which examines violence as a modern phenomenon especially among the youth; "Al Qaeda in the West as a Youth Movement: The Power of a Narrative," CEPS Policy Brief, N. 168, August 2008, http://www.ceps.eu/system/files/book/1698.pdf; "The attractions of jihadism, and a generational nihilism stretching far beyond the Muslim sphere," 04 October

his misrecognition of the dynamics of European Islam, and contemporary Islamic thought in general, that does not correspond to my own findings, dynamics that Jørgen S. Nielsen saw developing more than a decade ago.

European Islam Thinks, Acts, and *Theologises*: Jørgen S. Nielsen

Jørgen S. Nielsen argues that European Islam does think, and it is forming a European Islamic theology that brings together the dynamic potentials of the Islamic tradition and European modern realities.[25] Nielsen brings his training as a historian to the socio-anthropological work and networks on Muslims in Europe he has prolifically contributed to since the 1970s. Nielsen's argument can be sketched out into four major "points of recognition": (1) recognition of perpetual renewal and dynamism in Islamic thought, which European Islamic emerging theology is part of, (2) recognition of the fact of pluralism within Muslims of Europe and their interpretations of Islam, (3) recognition of European Muslim's participation in major European debates, and the need of reciprocating this participation through engaging them institutionally, and (4) recognition of the potential of European Muslims and their version of European Islam can have on the Muslims and Islam "back home," i.e. in the heartlands of Islam. This means that European Islam thinks, speaks theology, and is not "subaltern"; it speaks and can be heard as a voice of alterity, and scholars should not be blind to it. These four points are explained below.[26]

2014, https://www.opendemocracy.net/can-europe-make-it/olivier-roy-nicholas-truong/attractions-of-jihadism-and-generational-nihilism-str.

Also here Roy is descriptive, though his intention is to propose a counter-narrative that is supposed to be active. More importantly, I wonder how could a vertical approach that studies Islamic texts, from the Qur'an to classical texts and their commentaries throughout the centuries, not be dynamic, and inclusive of contemporary anti-violence scholarship that Muslim scholars in Europe and elsewhere are contributing to. The point is that Roy insists on not underlying the internal dynamisms of a tradition in its encounter with the process of secularisation that modernity entails, in his view.

25   His argument saw materialisation also institutionally; he founded and directed the Centre for European Islamic Thought (October 2007–June 2013) at the Faculty of Theology, University of Copenhagen, a center I had the privilege of joining as a Vising PhD Fellow (September 2011–July 2012); I learnt a great deal from Nielsen, his research team, and the various activities the center organised.

26   A fifth point of recognition that deserves mention is that Nielsen, in his Inaugural Lecture cited below, recognises the role non-Muslim Western scholars of Islam play in the ongoing debates on Islam and modernity. Though he does not say much on this, but one could, for instance, say that Western scholars' choice of Islamic topics to research, Muslim

First, at the time when Roy published his book on European Islam in French, Jørgen S. Nielsen did the same, with a work bearing the same title in the same year in English, *Towards a European Islam* (1999). In the main, Nielsen imbues his sociological study of Muslims mostly in Britain with a historical note. He sees "grounds for optimism" in what concerns the integration of Muslims in Europe and Europe's ability to respond positively to that, if it brings up its past heritage of pluralism and tolerance, away from "restrictive and sometimes oppressive forms of nationalism."[27] More importantly, he argues that there is a lively intellectual debate going on within the Islamic community, and less attention is given to it. He compares it to the classical-formative Islamic intellectual era: "... less [attention] is being paid to the internal debates taking place. Here there is a range of philosophical and theological discussions, which in many ways remind one of the debates which ranged among Islamic theologians in the formative periods of the eighth–eleventh centuries."[28] This view on European Islam is based on Nielsen's belief that "regular renewal" has been an integral characteristic of Islamic thought over the centuries, and reflects the intellectual dynamism of the tradition according to various socio-cultural and political factors.[29]

For instance, Nielsen refers to the way part of the legacy of the renowned 13th–14th-century scholar Ibn Taymiyya (d. 1328) was appropriated by the 18th-century movement of Muhammad Ibn Abd al-Wahhab (d. 1792) in a different context and for different reasons. He also gives the example of how the 14th-century scholar al-Shatibi (d. 1388), who lived some four decades after Ibn Taymiyya, has become dominantly invoked by modern Muslim reformists, from Rashid Rida (d. 1935) to Mohamed Fadhel Ben Ashour (d. 1970) in the Arab world to Tariq Ramadan (b. 1962) in Europe; these and many others emphasise al-Shatibi's work on the objectives of sharia (*maqasid al-sharia*), and the prevalence of public good (*maslaha*) over rigid legalism. This example

---

theologians or reformists to study or invite for conferences or fellowships, and Muslim communities to stress or de-stress, all this plays a role in shaping the intellectual imaginary and direction(s) the overall debate take(s).

27   Jørgen S. Nielsen, *Towards a European Islam* (London and New York: Palgrave MacMillan, 1999), 10.

28   Nielsen, "The Question of Euro-Islam: Restriction or Opportunity?" in Aziz al-Azmeh and Effie Fokas, (eds.) *Islam in Europe: Diversity, Identity, and Influence* (Cambridge UP: 2007), 34.

29   Nielsen, "Islam in Europe: Retrenchment and Renewal," Inaugural Lecture, Faculty of Theology, University of Copenhagen, 8 February 2008, 1, at http://teol.ku.dk/ceit/doku menter/inaugural_lecture.pdf. I thank Niels Valdemar Vinding for having made access to this paper easy.

of medieval intellectual productivity, which happened in different times and contexts, is being borrowed by later generations of Muslims according to their realities. That is, Islamic scholarship approaches the text according to context, and, interestingly, brings about different approaches, which may later in history be re-interpreted even more differently. Consider the legacy of Ibn Taymiyya on logic and ethics, besides his fatwas, and how the Wahhabis-Salafis ignore a good part of this legacy and focus only on his fatwas that were issued in a particular context of political turmoil of the Islamic lands. As to the example of al-Shatibi and his emphasis on the objectives of sharia – an idea that was developed few decades before him by Izz al-Din ibn Abd al-Salam (d. 1262) – and how it is being re-appropriated by modern Muslim scholars, it is situated in Nielsen's contention about history of ideas and how they become either influential or neglected and only later on re-appropriated according to human needs. Otherwise said, lived Islam should not be neglected in the scholarly focus on ideas, because Islamic history has been "a history of interaction between realities and ideas," writes Nielsen.[30]

Second, Nielsen believes in the emergence of a theological debate among European Muslims because he recognises what he calls a "potential" the vast intellectual store of the tradition can offer them, and from which they are borrowing and to which they are adding. When he refers to theological differences among Muslim leaders in Europe in the debates he either got engaged in, witnessed or researched, he has in mind the diversity that early Islamic intellectual history experienced, and still does. By "potential" he means the following:

> [...] an understanding of the possibilities that the intellectual tradition has accumulated and an acknowledgement that the social, economic, cultural, and political changes of our times influence, and will continue to influence, the intellectual routes which Muslim thinkers globally, and particularly in Europe, are developing and will continue to develop.[31]

This potential that the context of Europe can bring allows seeing beyond the essentialisation of Islam as one theology, one movement, or one ideology. Nielsen recognises that this potential can be interpreted in ways that go against the mainstream of Islamic thought and European modern values, and thus against the mainstream in society. He refers here to the cases of violent Salafis and radical youth, but this should not hide the other majority voices that speak against violence. With Felice Dassetto, Nielsen speaks of three major models

---

30 Nielsen, "Islam in Europe: Retrenchment and Renewal," 2.
31 Ibid., 14.

within which the diversity of European Muslims can be categorised, and each of them is divided into further sub-models; suffice it to mention the general models: (1) the intra-European models, (2) the extra-European models, and (3) the in-between models. Overall, he believes that it is naïve to assume that the new generations of Muslims in Europe are assimilating without agency; on the contrary, they are assertive of both their religiosity and Europeanness, by various means, like the "spiritualization of Islam," "de-islamization," "inculturation," etc.[32] What is to be underlined here is that this pluralism within European Islam does not mean that there is no intellectual-theological debate going on, as Roy contends. On the contrary, according to Nielsen, it is a very clear example that Muslims think differently, give different theological interpretations to the same debated issue, despite their unifying creed and reference to the same major sources of Islam. This theological thinking is obviously first and foremost influenced by the countries of origin in the Muslim world, minority fiqh, the national established councils, Islamic confederations, the international networks operating in Europe, like the Muslim Brotherhood, Deobandi Movement, Jamaat e-Tablighi, the Muslim World League, the local leaders and imams, the young generation of Muslims, and the European Muslim scholars that advocate a European Islam. Put otherwise, European Muslims are making their theology; it is a pluralist theology in praxis, a theology in progress. That means that their epistemological compass is integrating Europe and its diversity.

Third, and as a continuity of the second point, in *Muslims in Western Europe* (3rd ed. 2004), Nielsen sees that young Muslims, born and educated in Europe, including and at times led by women, are being influential in leading their community of believers, and in giving shape to new forms of expressing and practicing Islam, forms and priorities "relevant to their European situation."[33] They are participating in public debates that concern their European societies and their international impacts as well. Nielsen gives the example of Muslims' engaging solidarity work with societies in the state of war, (like Bosnia-Herzegovina in the 1990s), and how their work led to the emergence of the international Islamic Relief. A related example concerns their demonstrations against the war in Iraq, and their overall organisation of demonstrations against Muhammad Cartoons in 2006, or veil-ban in France in 2004, or their work with various Islamic organisations and networks to issue denouncements of violence when committed in the name of Islam. Nielsen says that

---

32   Felice Dassetto and Jørgen S. Nielsen, "Conclusions," in Maréchal, Brigitte, et al., eds., *Muslims in the Enlarged Europe: Religion and Society* (Leiden and Boston: Brill, 2003), 531–542.

33   Nielsen, *Muslims in Western Europe*, 3rd ed. (Edinburgh: Edinburgh UP: 2004), 172.

DOES EUROPEAN ISLAM THINK? 47

this participation in the public debate over these issues and others should not be considered as opportunistic to avoid the accusation of being apologetic. He sees these important occasions that testify to both diversity in Islamic theology, and to new changes happening within it. It is here that his earlier idea of interaction between realities and ideas come back. At the same time, while these changes are taking place on the Muslims' side, he believes that such participation in the European public sphere plays an "integrative role" and finds listening ears in European institutions to accommodate such voices and their legitimate needs that the democratic constitutions of European countries guarantee. He speaks of renewing this basic value of an inclusive social contract, "a 'contract' where loyalty and consent are granted in exchange for participation and access to the social and political 'good.'"[34]

Fourth, and to reach the driving question of this paper, Nielsen believes that Muslims in Europe have the potential of influencing the centers of Islamic thought in the Arab-Islamic lands. In his words, European Muslims "are being watched" by their co-religionists in the Islamic majority countries, as if there was a shift in theological balance or a theological move in progress. This is expressed in his Foreward to Tariq Ramadan's *To Be a European Muslim* (1999), as quoted in the introduction above.[35] European Muslims, he adds, "are asking fundamental questions about Islam"; fiqh (which focuses on legal matters) is being questioned, and theology (which focuses on morality) is being given more weight.[36] This contention builds on the previous points, where Islamic intellectual dynamism and interaction between realities and ideas was stressed. The fact that Nielsen not only "forEwOrds" but also clearly states this "potential" influence of the debate Muslims of Europe experience on the debates in Muslim majority countries is a recognition that he very much believes that there is an interaction and dynamism in Islamic intellectual history, especially with the non-stop migration flows from the Arab world to Europe, the contact Muslims of Europe still have with the countries of origin, the globalising means of communication, and transnational movements and networking.[37] This may be further evidenced by the fact that Tariq Ramadan

---

34 Nielsen, "Islam in Europe: Retrenchment and Renewal," 542. For more on Muslim political participation, see Nielsen ed., *Muslim Political Participation in Europe* (Edinburgh: Edinburgh UP, 2013).

35 Nielsen, Foreword, in Ramadan, *To Be a European Muslim*, xi–xiv.

36 Ibid., *xi–xiv.*

37 Nielsen also notes in his inaugural lecture, op. cit., that there is another potential of interaction between the current developments of Islam in Western Europe with the Islamic old presence in south-east Europe. This is an intra-European interaction of Islams, so to say.

and Tareq Oubrou – figures Nielsen quotes, besides that of Abdennour Bidar – are invited to give lectures in the Arab world where they are allowed (i.e. Morocco), and some of their work is translated into Arabic. Ramadan is also the director of the Research Centre for Islamic Legislation and Ethics at Qatar University since September 2011, a fact which can testify further to his reputation and engagement with humanist-ethicist issues that bring European and Arab Islams into interaction.

What I have tried to show above is that there are at least two major views among non-Muslim scholars of European Islam – putting aside the Islamophobic camp. These two views, represented here by Olivier Roy and Jørgen S. Nielsen, do understand well the dynamics and history of ideas of the Islamic world and Islam in Europe in particular. They agree on various details, but their point of divergence is the one I have raised above, and tried to demonstrate. Roy sees Muslims but no emergence of a European Islamic theology, or European Islamic thought that can be read as theological projects. Nielsen, on the other hand, sees Muslims and a European Islamic theology emerging, and with this he not only recognises diversity within Islamic thought – which Roy also does – but underlines the fact that it is a category of thinking that is emerging, and it should be examined as such, instead of being ignored or considered non-authentic to the Islamic tradition, or to the European tradition as well. Nielsen recognises that there is an "emergent reason" that brings religiosity and modern values together beyond classical antagonisms of Islam vs. West, religion vs. politics, reason vs. revelation, etc. – to borrow a concept from the theologian-scholar Mohammed Arkoun (d. 2010).[38] European Islam in this sense tries to overcome classical exclusive epistemological paradigms and builds one that is plural and inclusive.[39] Socio-anthropological, theological, and literary works second such a perspective.[40]

---

38   Mohammed Arkoun, The *Unthought in Contemporary Islamic Thought* (London: Saqi Books and The Institute of Ismaili Studies, 2002), 23–24.

39   There is an epistemological revisionism taking place, at the background of which is a minor ontological revolution. This is further examined in my articles: "Is European Islam Experiencing an Ontological Revolution for an Epistemological Awakening?" American Journal of Social Sciences, Autumn 2014, pp. 14–49; "Pluralism within European Islam: Secularizing Theology, Sacralizing Modernity," in Carmela Decaro, ed., *The Legal Treatment of Religious Claims in Multicultural Societies* (Rome: LUISS UP, 2015) pp. 67–86.

40   For example, see the works of Felice Dassetto, Brigitte Maréchal, Stefano Allievi, Thijl Sunier, Jocelyne Cesari, John Bowen, Jonathan Laurence, Chi-Chung Yu, Dilyana Mincheva, etc. A clear statement from Jytte Klausen may illustrate this further. Jytte Klausen conducted 300 interviews with Muslim association leaders, politicians, businessmen and

Conclusion

The scholarly benefits of understanding whether a European Islam exists and thinks or not are numerous. First, it shows that the debate cannot be monopolised by politics or ideologues alone. Serious scholarly work that has been ongoing for years should be brought on the table for public discussions of the topic. Second, such an understanding can tell us how academics differ in their readings of the different productions of intellectual and activist Muslims in the European context; it helps in showing the dynamics of the community and its pluralism. Third, it importantly shows that Muslims in Europe, be they academics or community representatives or lay people, are aware of the challenges Europe and its modernity version pose to them; their engagement in its context is an engagement with the questions of modernity at large, which the Muslim world outside Europe has been engaged with for the last two centuries or so. This contextual engagement may be a minor reflection of a major engagement outside this context. Comparing how the context impacts such an engagement is scholarly speaking so enlightening from comparative perspectives. Fourth, and with this I close this reflective summary: Muslims of Europe and European Islam may be inspiring to the Arab-Islamic heartlands that have been discussing and interpreting modernity for good times now. Here comes again the importance of the work of Jørgen Nielsen; the quote I started with in the introduction is very relevant here. Nielsen thinks that European Muslims can influence the debate over Islam and modernity in the Islamic classical centres. This is a second major point in his work on European Islam, which deserves separate attention and space.[41]

---

intellectuals in seven European countries (Sweden, Denmark, Netherlands, Great Britain, France, and Germany) between 2003 and 2005, and arrived to the conclusion that there is an emerging European Islam. In her data analysis, and in a comment on Oliver Roy, she endorses the views of this paper. She says "I have more fundamental disagreements with Roy. He sees no evidence of any serious rethinking of religious dogma among European Muslims. I am convinced, on the contrary, that a 'European Islam' is emerging upon a new epistemology of faith and a new hermeneutics of textual interpretation." Jytte Klausen, *The Islamic Challenge: Politics and Religion in Western Europe* (Oxford: Oxford UP, 2005), 204–205.

41 The first version of this expanded article appeared as an opinion piece: "Can European Islam Be Inspiring to the Arab World?" Resetdoc Dialogues on Civilizations, 16 April 2014, http://www.resetdoc.org/story/00000022382.

CHAPTER 4

Churchification of Islam in Europe

Niels Valdemar Vinding

Introduction

Shortly after the Danish Cartoon Crisis in 2006, I had the first of many conversations with Jørgen S. Nielsen, as he had been appointed Danish National Research Foundation Professor of Islamic Studies and Director of the Centre for European Islamic Thought at the Faculty of Theology in Copenhagen. These conversations were about the struggle of Muslims in finding their place and position in Europe, and over the years continued into issues of social and legal integration, religious institutions and the struggles of identity formation of Muslims in Europe. A returning topic was the continuous challenge of accommodation for the rights of Muslims and the problems of the existing models of church and state in Europe and how Islam did not fit the dominant policies of religious governance. It seemed Muslim organisations needed to become more like the churches if they wanted their place in Europe. Jørgen S. Nielsen provokingly and charmingly has suggested thinking in terms of churchification – or ecclesiastification as he likes to say, teasing non-native English speakers – in order to better understand both the theoretical and practical complexities of fitting Islam and Muslims into the existing institutional framework of church and state. While such conversations sowed the seeds for the topic and themes of what would eventually be my thesis, *Muslim Positions in the Religio-Organisational Fields of Denmark, Germany and England*, and many of the ideas presented there resurface here, the idea of churchification needs a more thorough exploration, clarification and analytical unfolding. And what better way of doing so than by exploring Jørgen S. Nielsen's own understanding of the phenomenon with an outlook to other European scholars' observations and thoughts on the issue – in a book to his honour?

Thus, this chapter explores the concept of churchification in relation to Islam and Muslim organisations in Europe. The first part of the chapter surveys the word in variations, the phenomenon it describes and different observations of this phenomenon across a number of European contexts by a selection of European scholars on Islam in Europe. After the initial observations and conceptualisations of churchification and after discussing the promising institutionalist theories follows a process of analytical distinction into four

© KONINKLIJKE BRILL NV, LEIDEN, 2018 | DOI 10.1163/9789004362529_005

closely related but distinguishable logics of churchification. Firstly, churchification is understood as pedagogical, analogical or rhetorical usages comparing mosques to churches, or imams to priests, and so on. Secondly, churchification as normativisation is identified, which maintains that mosques *should* or *ought to* function like the churches, imams should act like priests, and that for a number of politically or ideologically motivated reasons. Thirdly, churchification can be identified in terms of structural and implicit hegemony emanating from the established paradigms of church and state relations, or from the churches themselves. Here, the sheer positional power and presence of the churches in Europe makes it almost impossible to avoid an influence on Islam and Muslim organisations. Fourthly and finally, churchification can be seen as a deliberate neo-institutionalist isomorphic strategy – or counter-strategy – where Muslim organisations and institutions deliberately model themselves on the churches either because they are structurally coerced to do so, because it raises standards or because doing so is smart and cost-efficient. Equally, there are Muslim organisations and communities who move in the opposite direction exactly because they want to distance and distinguish themselves from European churches, priesthood, Christian theology, and institutional expectations. This often proves to be a more difficult strategy and, although tempting, isomorphic institutionalisation might not yield the hoped outcome of resource mobilisation, acceptance or recognition for Muslims in the European context.

Of the many examples and observations given, most are drawn from Jørgen S. Nielsen and Olivier Roy. Thus a kind of discourse arises between the two, demonstrating significant convergence in their thinking, adding nuance and insights to the associated ideas of churchification. A convergence that does not extend to all aspects of their work, as Mohammed Hashas has argued in his chapter in this volume.

Finally, limited but important conclusions are drawn on the risks of thinking too modularly of churchification leading to an institutional misinterpretation of Muslim organisations with the resulting structural misrecognition of Islam and Muslim organisations.

Observations and Concepts of Churchification

The word churchification is not new in the English language, although the specification of the use for Islam is recent. In the Oxford English Dictionary, uses of the verb "to churchify" go as far back as to 1719 and means to "to imbue with the ideas, principles, or characteristics of the Christian Church; to make 'churchy,'" adding a specific use of "to churchify," meaning "to assimilate to

52 VINDING

the Anglican Church." By extension, churchification is the result of churchifying, meaning that some characteristic of the church has been imbued, or that something has become part of the church.

During the last 30 years or so – and very much in the light of recent history of Muslims in Europe – scholars from a number of countries have observed and described aspects of the phenomenon of churchification in a variety of contexts and with a variety of functions.[1] Amongst these scholars, I would argue, Jørgen S. Nielsen emerges with repeated documented observations of the phenomenon. Jørgen S. Nielsen gives some of the earliest accounts of the struggles of accommodation and recognition for the Muslim communities in Europe, and he recounts the assumptions and the myths that met the Muslim communities and institutions early on. Muslims had understood the elementary need for organisation and for resource mobilisation to build these organisations. "But the context in which they had to achieve this," writes Nielsen, "was one which had grown up around churches and which usually presumed that other religious denominations would seek to fit in as church-like organisation. The Jewish communities had over a long period of participation in European history adopted such a response. Their rabbis moved from being teachers, scholars and jurisconsults to being pastors and clergy, their synagogues become 'churches,' and their chief rabbis become 'archbishops.' The pressure was on for Muslims to move in the same direction" (Nielsen 1993, 98; also Nielsen 1999, 115–116). He goes on to summarise that such a pressure or effort to establish Muslim "fronts" or umbrella organisations, "often in response to government initiative, is evidence of an adaptation of structures in a pseudo-ecclesiastical direction" (ibid.).

As mentioned, others have observed the phenomenon. In French, churchification is akin to *eglisation*, defined as *action d'égliser*, where the verb *egliser* – to churchify – is understood as *attribuer á l'église, donner á l'église*, or *rendre dépendent de l'eglise*, meaning in turn, to attribute to the church, to give to the church or to make dependent on the church (Richard 1842). Out of a French context, but with a global outlook, Olivier Roy, too, has observed the phenomenon of churchification, and he is often cited with coining the phrase "the Churchification of Islam"[2] in his *Globalised Islam – The Search for the New Ummah*

---

1 Significantly, Ismail Serageldin, 1989: "Granted that the complexity of modern life has forced many communal public activities into specialized structures, the tendency towards limiting the mosque to its liturgical function, 'a churchification of the mosque' it to be deplored."

2 See Sara Silvestri, 2007, 180, "what scholars including Roy have called the 'churchification' of Islam." Also, Ayhan Kaya, 2009, 199: "This is what Olivier Roy (2004) calls 'Churchification of Islam.'" Later, Mårtensson & Eriksen, 2014, 162ff., "Roy's 'churchification of islam'" with

from 2004. However, in fact, the phrase never appears in *Globalised Islam*, and it seems his readers have coined the phrase in his name. It is not until some years later in *Holy Ignorance. When Religion and Culture Part Ways* from 2010 that he uses such a phrase, and there only twice. Nonetheless, he does discuss the phenomenon, but he uses the much wider concept of westernisation – most prominently in "Chapter 5, Islam in the West or the Westernisation of Islam" (Roy 2004). Significant to this wide idea of Westernisation he notes that as part of the identity constructions of Muslims, they follow a Western Christian model and produce purely religious "Muslim Churches" (Roy 2004, 201). In Roy's thinking, churchification specifically concerns a religious dimension of the much more general Westernisation which in turn is not clearly defined as opposed to globalisation and modernisation (Roy 2004, 14).

When Roy actually does use the phrase "churchification" in *Holy Ignorance* from 2010, he uses it to describe the process of how different religions conform to each other in contexts of interaction and mutual influence. He calls this standardisation or "formatting," and understands it as "a process of interaction, reciprocal adjustments and reformulation of norms from very different fields" (Roy 2010, 188). Regarding Islam and Muslims in the West, he asks: "when a Muslim couple living in the West marries in a mosque, bride and groom hand in hand, the bride dressed in white and carrying a bouquet as in a Christian church wedding, is this merely a superficial adaptation, a change in the conception of the couple or is it a redefinition of the religious value of Muslim marriage?" (Roy 2010, 188). As we shall see, Roy's use of standardisation resonate with the professionalization as employed by DiMaggio & Powell (1983).

In German, the word that comes closest to churchification is *verkirchlichung*. Here, too, the phenomenon has been observed and criticised. In Muslim contexts and at least twenty years ago, Ayyub Axel Köhler of the *Zentralrat der Muslime in Deutschland* observed in 1997 that many Muslim organisations are trying to gain public law recognition by "changing the Islamic religion with an essentially foreign Church structure" (Köhler 1997). Polemically, he labels this as an "official Islamic church" ("*islamische Amtskirche*") and observes how Muslim organisations are looking to the models of the reformed church and other successful church structures. The whole legal framework for recognition presupposes an implicit church structure, and therefore Islam must reform itself into what Köhler calls a secular deformity. In adjusting, Islam will sacrifice its religious particularity, and churchified Muslim organisations

---

reference to both *Globalised Islam* (2004) and *Holy Ignorance* (2010). None of these give a page reference in citing *Globalised Islam*.

will become instruments of state governance and policies towards Muslims (Köhler 1997). Köhler's observation and choice of words has influenced an on-going academic debate on the subject of the challenging struggle for recognition by German Muslims (Vinding 2013). At the 2011 session of the German Islam Conference, Heinrich de Wall, professor of ecclesiastical law, dismisses the idea that the legal framework for recognition would demand that Muslims submit to "verkirchlichung," but argues rather for a neutral, non-biased concept of religious community (Wall 2011, 92). He is echoed by minister of the interior, Thomas de Maizière, who maintains that Muslim organisations must adhere to the German constitutional law, and that such a demand has nothing to do with churchification of Islam (Maiziere 2011, 12). Years previously, Matthias Koenig, professor of sociology and sociology of religion at University of Göttingen, soberly states that whatever one might call it or however one is inclined to think about it, from a sociological point of view, "in the process of organisational incorporation, a formalisation and hierarchisation of Muslim community structures can be observed, which certainly leads to a churchification of Islam." (Koenig 2006, 2140). He, too, explicitly uses "Verkirchligung des Islam." There is a remarkable contrast between a politically informed official discourse on the framework of recognition as voiced by de Wall and Maiziere, on the one hand, and a sociologically attuned understanding of the impact of law on institutionalisation of Muslims as voiced by Köhler and Koenig, on the other.

In Denmark, the predominance of the Church of Denmark is significant and sets the frame for what could be seen as churchification in a Danish context. As such, the word churchification (*"kirkeliggørelse"*) is only used rarely, and only about internal shifts of balance within the church amongst those more secular and those more invested in the church as institution. However, while a word like churchification does not appear to be used about Islam or Muslims, there is a clear identification of what can be called "churchliness," (*folkekirkelighed*) informing the value or virtue of adhering to the church. Danish political scientist Hans B. Dabelsteen has written about such Danish churchliness between the established church and secularism (Dabelsteen 2011). He identifies in this concept both ideological, institutional and identity aspects in convergence with the secular value of having an established church. The model that the Church of Denmark provides is an ideological, institutional and identity-based way of understanding Danish secularism. This has been called "Lutheran secularism" or "Lutheran liberalism" (Dabelsteen 2011, 34), and "it pragmatically mixes liberal principles of state with the special status of the church and even ascribes Evangelical-Lutheran theology a constitutive role as a carrier of liberal principles" (ibid.). While it is historically questionable to make such a link, politically, nonetheless, it asserts that the church is not exempt from the liberal principles, but it confirms them and in effect aligns the Church with secular, liberal principles. As such, this value of churchliness becomes a way of making religion conform to an assertive secularism, and it goes beyond just the Church of Denmark, and very much also extends to Islam and Muslims, as well as to other religious minorities.

As we have seen, there are many who have taken notice of the phenomenon of churchification, using a handful of related terms and concepts. In one way or the other, churchification is discussed in a number of contexts across Europe and we have not at all considered the Eastern European context. However, so far we have moved little beyond description and raising important questions, and it seems that there are a number of different ideas and challenges at play. As such, very much inspired by Jørgen S. Nielsen and others, this chapter takes a step closer in order to systematise the understanding of churchification and to further unfold its distinct logic, nuances and implications.

Institutionalist Theory Relevant to Islam and Muslims Organisations in Europe

Larger organisations and institutions tend to follow similar paths, develop similar structures and appear homogenous across sectors, contexts or fields of similar interests or competition. Institutionalist theorists seek to explain this. Along with sociologists, cultural theorists and organisation scholars of the past few decades, such as Berger & Luckmann (1966), Giddens (1984), DiMaggio & Powell (1983, 1991), Jepperson (1991), Scott (2008) and many others, institutionalist theorists have posited that the behaviour, rationales and strategic choices by individual organisations are in a number specific ways informed by the context of the field or sector of similar organisations (DiMaggio & Powell 1983, 152). New organisations and actors, who have only recently entered into a field – or old organisations that are struggling to reinvent themselves – will naturally look to those who have done well, who have succeeded and have done so by being at the core of the changes that helped define the field and context as it is. In institutionalist theory, examples of this might be innovative or disruptive companies changing a given market, but in this specific context, the churches across Europe are the established and successful institutions, to whom the struggling new Muslim groups and organisations are obviously looking.

While doing as the great ones did does not necessarily guarantee success, it does remove a degree of trial and error, early mistakes, and unchartered territory in the complex dynamics of European state, church and religion relations. Such conformity or path dependence is a logical choice. As suggested by Paul J. DiMaggio & Walter W. Powell in their seminal article "The Iron Cage Revisited: Institutional Isomorphism and Collective Rationality in Organisational Fields" from 1983, this is what is implied in the idea of institutionalism, specifically the institutional isomorphism understood as a degree of strategic resemblance or homogeneity. This is important in the context of Muslim organisations in Europe, because doing as those who went before also lends a measure of credibility to those who follow, and from this kind of adaption new actors and organisations gain legitimacy. Institutional legitimacy is especially important in contested fields and contexts, and seems to be a potentially very powerful resource that aligns one's organisation with the rest of the field. DiMaggio & Powell identify in this a distinction between coercive, mimetic or normative strategies (ibid., 150–154). These are analytically distinct, but will most likely be intertwined in empirical realities. Normative isomorphism is understood as procedures, methods, definitions or professionalization to produce high standards and effective tools to deal with challenges and to define ways to solve problems (ibid., 152). Coercive isomorphism is seen as pressure, expectations, or intimidations to join into alignment by external force (ibid., 150). Mimetic isomorphism becomes a strategic choice to model or borrow from certain attractive properties (ibid., 151).

As opposed to such strategies of institutional isomorphism, a choice of counter-strategies can be devised in reaction to this normative expectation of institutional alignment. Being different may be the right choice in a number of contexts. Presenting your organisation as "not a church," when others do, opens a potential for authenticity and uniqueness in breaking with the structural forces of the field. However, it comes at a significant cost and resources for upkeep for there is no taken-for-grantedness and reduction of structural resistance. The rest of this chapter unfolds perspectives form this kind of thinking. When discussing aspects and implications of churchification, the institutionalist focus will be broken down in particular, but supplementary analytical observations.

Unfolding Churchification

Reading Jørgen S. Nielsen's early work on Muslim communities, organisations and institutions (1991, 1993, 1999, forthcoming) it is clear that the questions of establishment and recognition are predominant and important amongst Muslims. However, as he observes, a prerequisite for such establishment is the question of communicating what it means to be Muslim and navigating the elementary socio-religious field of existing church, state and religion relations. From these early observations, churchification is significant in a number of ways that develop as the Muslim community develops. Nielsen understood early on the government or policy driven pressure as a pressure for Muslims to adapt the structure of the church, in part because the Jewish communities had done so successfully before. He called this "pseudo-ecclesiastical." Recounting these observations at a conference on *Imams in Western Europe* in Rome in 2014, he argues for a continuously growing need among Muslim communities for communication with and mutual recognition of the governmental, administrative and social environment. This in turn "fosters a process of 'ecclesiastification;' of a professionalization modelled on Christian theological leadership" (Nielsen, forthcoming).

The analytical distinction in this article observes related but distinguishable logics of churchification that seem to evolve as the Muslim community evolves. Firstly, churchification is understood as a pedagogical or rhetorical device to comparing churches and mosques, or priests and imams, and so on. As such, it is a shorthand for communicating some very elementary similarities in the religio-organisational field. Secondly, churchification is observed as a normative position, mostly compulsory upon Muslim organisations and institutions. For a number of politically or ideologically motivated reasons, mosques, it is held, *should* or *ought to* become like the churches, who in turn are presented as models to be followed. Thirdly, a related structural level of churchification can be identified building on the established paradigms or models of church and state relations. Here, the hegemonic power of the churches in Europe makes it almost impossible to avoid an influence on Islam and Muslim organisations. Fourthly, churchification can be seen as a deliberate neo-institutionalist isomorphic strategy – or counter-strategy – where Muslim organisations and institutions deliberately model themselves on the church because doing so is smart and cost-efficient, or choose deliberately not to.

Churchification as a Pedagogical or Rhetorical Devise

In his study on *Can Islam be French?* John Bowen repeatedly uses the phrase "cathedral mosque" for the greater mosques that have been built in several large cities in France; in Paris, Lyon, Lille, Marseille, and so on (Bowen 22, 51–53). However, he does so without qualifying the use of Christian connotation with "cathedral" on the entirely Muslim institution of the mosque. As part of the interview material for the "Imams of the West" research project, I interviewed *Rectuer* Kemal Kebtane in the Grand Mosque of Lyon, who was familiar with the analogy between his mosque and the cathedrals. However, he did not consider it mere pedagogical shorthand, but noted that "this word has been invented by people opposing the construction of the great mosque of Lyon. It was a way of showing that the mosque would be in opposition with the cathedral church. Now that time has passed people see that the mosque is advantageous and that it reassembles Muslims and represents them. We never wanted to be equal or in competition with the church" (*Kebtane interview*, 19.04.2015). From how the *recteur* saw this, the shorthand was not just a pedagogical simplification, but rather a deliberate misrecognition of the mosque – an attempt to alienate the mosque from the Muslim community by tainting it as "Christian" in truth.

Roy, too, observes this simplification and speculates as to the motives in negotiating or soliciting the state, clearly equating Islam with Christianity, even if only rhetorically: "In every country most Muslim leaders ask for their communities to enjoy the same rights as other faiths. By doing so, they put Islam into the fold of the general Western perception of what a religion is. For example, Friday for Muslims (although it has never been declared by classical *ulama* to be a public holiday) is equated with Sunday for Christians, and *imams* are considered to be professional clerics, which historically they never were" (Roy 2004, 205).

Nielsen observes in the Belgian case for establishment of Muslim organisation the negative impact of an institutional oversimplification by the government: "When Belgium added Islam to its short list of recognised religious communities, it immediately had to adapt the administrative structure so that is was centered on the provinces rather than the smaller districts applied to the Catholic and Protestant churches, as well as to recognise the Brussels Islamic Cultural Centre as a kind of "cathedral." Now, almost twenty years later, the consequences of recognition have been virtually nil plus the creation of much ill feeling and mistrust across a spectrum of participants because of misunderstandings regarding intentions" (Nielsen 1993, 98–99). In turn, this kind of simplification of Islam and Muslim institutions goes beyond mere rhetoric and analogy, but when applied by politicians and practitioners (and scholars, too it) brings with it a crude fitting of Islamic institutions into the existing structures, without making any proper analysis of Islam or Muslims as such.

Churchification as a Normativisation

The step from assuming a similarity to insisting on it is short. Both Roy and Nielsen observe how the state and political institutions go beyond mere noting the similarity, to insisting on it. Roy notes what he calls "institutional convergence between religions," giving the example of how "the figure of the 'priest' or of the 'minister' tends to define all religious practitioners or professionals; *ulemas* (religious scholars) become theologians, imams and rabbis 'parish' leaders. In the name of equality between believers, the law, courts and also institutions tend to format all religions in the same way. For example, in extending the principle of chaplaincy to Islam, the army and the prison authorities reinforce the institutional alignment of Islam with Christianity. In this sense, we can speak of the 'churchification' of religions by courts and states" (Roy 2010, 190). Worth noting here, is that Roy considers this process not just applied to Islam, but to all religion – even to dissident or non-conformative Christianity that does not consider itself part of the paradoxical cooperation between the Catholic Church and the modern-day laic French State.

In his *Muslims in Western Europe* (4th edition with Jonas Otterbeck) Nielsen returns to the Belgian case of the establishment of the organisation of the Muslim community, the Islamic Cultural Centre, by royal decree in 1978. As part of the determining the official position and salaries of the imams a clear parallel was drawn to the Protestant Church with a three tier structure, thus creating ordinary imams, "first-rank imams" and at the top the "Imam Director of the Islamic Cultural Centre" with obvious structural references to a Bishop (Nielsen & Otterbeck 2015, 78). Forcing such alien structures onto the Muslim community speaks volumes of the generative structuration at play in the early decades.

There is a degree of political power associated with modelling of Islam on the Christian example or fitting it in the established framework for state and religion relations. When speaking of Islam, politicians hold that Islam *should* or *ought to* become like the churches, even if they don't want to. There is a normative assessment of the different religious traditions, were the Christian model produced as "objectively" better, or for historical reasons, the right way of organising religion.

A rather extreme case of this has been seen in recent Danish political discourse, where the assertive secularism of the Lutheranism liberalism became wrapped into a nationalist anti-Islam agenda following the recent terror attacks in both Denmark in 2015 and in Europe, generally. At the end of May 2017, Member of Parliament Marie Krarup of the right wing Danish People's Party argued that a NATO engagement against ISIS would not be enough to fight terror, but rather "… permanent border control, assimilation as the goal of integration and possibly also Christian missionary work amongst Danish Muslims, simply to reduce the massive presence of Islam in Denmark."[3] A few days later, she was ready to argue for funding on the national budget for this kind of

---

3   Danish TV2 News, "Danish People's Party Spokesperson: Need for Christian Mission among Danish Muslims," http://nyheder.tv2.dk/politik/2017-05-24-df-ordfoerer-behov-for-kristen-missionering-blandt-danske-muslimer, accessed 15 September 2017.

missionary work and to count conversion amongst the criteria for successful integration. She respects that politicians for a number of reasons cannot direct the work of the Church of Denmark, "but one could tell them nicely."[4]

Never mind the fact that Denmark does not have a massive presence of Muslims, with only a little under 5% nominally Muslim, but Mrs Krarup clearly argues for an instrumentalisation of the Church of Denmark as a state church to force Muslims against their owns ways and norms. In this case, obviously, churchification of Islam as a normative model has been wrapped into a call for Christianisation as such and become a political goal. Nonetheless, it illustrates well the point of normativisation of churchification. At this point, it seems that the implicit Christianity of the days of secularisation (Woodhead 2010) has identified itself once more as something far more normative beyond a pragmatic mix of liberal principles and the Church of Denmark.

Expressed in the institutionalist language of DiMaggio & Powell, this kind of expectation of normativisation can also be seen as a normative isomorphist strategy to produce high standards and professionalization in Muslim organisations. If imams and Muslim organisations on the one hand and religious leaders in the Church of Denmark, on the other, were equally professional and proficient, a much greater degree of interaction, alliance and common ground can be established – even across religious dividers.

Churchification as Institutionalisation

With the realisation of these normative expectations, it becomes apparent that the field and context around Muslims and Muslim organisations influence these significantly. In addition to the explicit normativisation of Christianity as a model for Islam, the sheer power of the churches in Europe makes it almost impossible to avoid an influence on Islam. The power of the paradigms of church and state relations (Ferrari 2002, 2008) is so significant that the structural power and hegemony it exercises is almost unseen and utterly taken for granted. Roy observes further on his term "Muslim churches" and notes how "Each Western country integrates Islam according to its own paradigms, and Muslim citizens tend to express their identity through these Western models, even if they oppose integration or if these paradigms theoretically contradict certain basic tenets of their beliefs (such as putting Islam on an equal footing with Christianity). Muslims in the West end up thinking in Western ways, even when they oppose Western values" (Roy 2004, 201).

---

4 Berlingske, "Marie Krarup: Drop the Dialogue Priests – Christian mission should be on the National Budget" https://www.b.dk/politiko/marie-krarup-drop-dialogpraesterne-kristen-missionering-skal-paa-finansloven, accessed 15 September 2017.

CHURCHIFICATION OF ISLAM IN EUROPE 61

This speaks to the power of institutionalisation as such, a significant influence of the churches on the public structures in general, and on the religio-organisational field, specifically. The example of Germany provides excellent illustration of this point, following on the discussion from above. Muslims in Germany are navigating a context of a strong leading culture, "leitkultur," that builds on the normative power of the existing church and state relations. Here Muslims are likely to become German Muslims rather than Muslims in Germany. Muslim organisations are treated, understood and they themselves start acting as if they were Christian churches, which becomes the *verkirchligung*.

However, the institutionalising of churchification goes beyond mere "being-as-church" with the fitting of the Muslim organisations into the model of the churches. In a Foucaultian reading of this process, it would be argued that state structure seeks to discipline a body of the population into the frames designed for them. Nonetheless, it seems Muslim organisations in Germany are failing and not becoming such Muslim churches, and it is not for lack of trying (Jonker 2002, 2003), because a number of Muslim organisations have met the criteria for public recognition (Vinding 2013, 187ff.). Rather, it seems the standards Muslims are expected to meet are impossible and the possibility of institutional recognition no more than a bar that keeps moving up, to the extent that it becomes impossible to be both "Muslim" and "German." In this context, Gerdien Jonker (2002) has presented a critical analysis, which demonstrates exactly that it is only those Muslim organisations willing to transform themselves and conform to Christian standards, into something non-Islamic that can be subject to the examination for the status of corporation under public law. Jonker's analysis furthermore demonstrates that this division is driving a wedge through the Muslim community:

> The wish to obtain the right to enter schools and provide religious instruction is a powerful motor indeed. It has set in motion forms of religious self-organisation that are foreign to the Islamic tradition. It also created a new divide among Muslims themselves. [...] Through the building of Christian-type community structures they hope to satisfy the majority society and gain acceptance. Even if they are treated with suspicion, in the eyes of German majority society these Muslims form the centre of Muslim religious life as they aim to meet the legal demands. [...]
>
> This is the trap that the German legislation has set up, and it is still likely to function. On the one hand, legislature has set up rules for the acceptance of new faith communities. In turn, these set into motion the building of a new centre and a new periphery, forcing activist believers

and secularised Muslims into two different camps. On the other hand, the legislation made the demand for loyalty – a rather vague notion that in public discourse seems to comprise both the legislation, the government, and German identity.

JONKER 2002, 44

Muslim organisations' attempts to gain the status as corporation under public law have so far furthered disunity in the Muslim community. It is clear that, if ever the Muslim organisations were to meet the structural standards set up for them they would be perfect Germans, which by default means being as Christian Germans. This again is, to many Muslims, utterly incompatible with being Muslim and clearly echoes Ayyub Axel Köhler's critique as mentioned above.

Churchification as a Strategy – and Counter-strategy

Following this identification of the power of institutionalisation, it becomes clear that churchification can be developed into a number of proper opportunities, as strategies or counter-strategies, for Muslim organisations – all unfolding under the framework of institutionalisation. For those Muslim organisations that effectively follow the path of the churches and manage to gain the kind of acceptance and recognition that the models of state and religion in Europe promise, there seems to be great rewards in terms of "taken-for-grantedness," automatic inclusion, the low maintenance and stability, which all follow from true institutionalisation, that is by conformity and synchronicity with the governing social order (Berger & Luckmann 1966, 65ff., Scott 2008, 51).

As we have seen, getting there is the difficult part, and in this one of the most efficient strategies has been mimetic isomorphism, as coined by DiMaggio and Powell (1991, 70). Here, challenged or struggling organisations look to those they perceive as successful in order to increase their legitimacy and to calibrate their choices after those that have proven successful to others.

Nielsen was very early on not just attuned to the process of churchification, which he called pseudo-ecclesiastical at the time, but he understands this in institutionalist terms and identifies the complex resource management and the institutional cost efficiency associated with establishment and recognition. In the early decades of Muslim communities in the West, observing the misunderstanding of who and what these Muslims were and the negative impact on integration this has, Nielsen notes that "the threshold of entry demanded by the host institutions is thus much higher than the newcomers can reasonably be expected to manage even while their expectations are being prematurely encouraged" (Nielsen 1999, 117).

CHURCHIFICATION OF ISLAM IN EUROPE

In his understanding of churchification, Roy stresses mutuality in this kind of institutional convergence, but he does not have a very deep understanding for the path dependency of institutional isomorphism at play (Roy 2004, 205). Christian institutions are already embedded and institutionalised, which makes it easier, more natural or even obvious for Muslim institutions to do as the Christians do. The religio-organisational field is a normative field, too. But here are cultural and deeply embedded norms, that may be difficult to see, define and navigate. Elsewhere in this volume, Werner Menski characterises European Muslims as skilled cultural and legal navigators, who understand and handle legal pluralism better than bureaucrats and politicians.

However, seen in the light of this often surprisingly difficult path-dependency that leads to churchification, there emerges an alternative to the strategy of conforming, and that is the deliberate counter-action (Vinding 2013, 42; Jepperson 1991, 148). We see repeated examples of Muslims taking counter-actions and being deliberately non-conformist, who actively assert their "otherness," and the distinct nature of an Islamic worldview. In institutional theory, this kind of action breaks or disrupts the institutional taken-for-grantedness. In his analysis, sociologist Ronald L. Jepperson maintains that institution is "non-action," just as the taken-for-grantedness can be characterised by the absence of active thought (Douglas 1986). In fact, Jepperson states that "... if one participates conventionally in a highly institutionalised social pattern, one does not take action, that is, intervene in a sequence, and make a statement. If shaking hands is an institutionalised form of greeting, one takes action only by refusing to offer one's hand. [...] The point is a general one: one enacts institutions; one takes action by departing from them, not by participating in them ..." (Jepperson 1991, 148–149). In such light, being Islamic becomes deliberate. Donning a headscarf, the refusal of shaking hands and the insistence on distinct dietary needs is making a statement. Churchification in turn becomes non-action, whereas by contrast islamisation becomes an empowering action. In his *Globalised Islam*, Roy presents a number of viable and authentic approaches and historic paradigms for Muslims to apply in negotiating what it means to be distinct and deliberate minority Muslims in the West, whether it be emigration, conversion, a millet model, a call for Islamising or a theological reduction to echo the "mere" religion of the Western context (Roy 2004, 111–116).

Conclusions

At every level of the churchification discussed in this article, there seems to be a significant risk, almost epistemic, of misunderstanding, misrecognising or misrepresenting Islam. There is risk in expecting too much of models when working with Islam and Muslim organisations, and understanding too little of the framework of the empirical world. After all, models are built on how things were and used to be, and are simplifications at that, but it seems clear that the changes we are seeing today are of a different kind that does not fit into the regular regimes of secularism and church and state relations. The risk, of course, is that we see only the models and adaptations that we want to see and that we are accustomed to seeing, and therefore overlook the actual phenomena or empirical realities of Islam and Muslims organisations in the West.

When adding up the different key elements presented in this chapter a governing logic of churchification begins to emerge, although with slight differences at each pace. When dealing with a new religious community and new religious organisations, like the Muslim, an institutionally embedded paradigm of churchification is applied. In treating Muslim organisations as if they were Christian churches, the expectations, the governing norms and the logic of perceiving that recognise religion are the same that have always been used. This is amounts to an institutional misinterpretation of Muslim organisations and the result is a structural misrecognition of Islam. Assuming that Muslims do as Christians do, will blind us – researchers, religious practitioners and politicians – to the fact that Muslims and Islamic institutions are different and distinct in a number of very significant ways. Assuming that imams in the mosques are like priests in the churches is misrecognition of the history, functions, training, ambitions, authority and leadership in Islam and Muslim organisations. Acting or even regulating on such misrecognition will at best yield no result, at worst do irreversible damage to state and religion relations and to the desired institutional integration of Islam and Muslim organisations.

Bibliography

Berger, P., & Luckmann, T., 1966. *The Social Construction of Reality, A Treatise in the Sociology of Knowledge*, New York: Anchor Books.

Bowen, J.R. 2011. *Can Islam be French? Pluralism and pragmatism in a secularist state*. Princeton: Princeton University Press.

Dabelsteen, H.B. 2011. *Folkekirkelighed: en undersøgelse af sekularismen i Danmark*. Copenhagen: Forlaget Politiske Studier.

DiMaggio, Paul J. and Walter W. Powell (1983). "The Iron Cage Revisited: Institutional Isomorphism and Collective Rationality in Organisational Fields," in *American Sociological Review*, Volume 48, No. 2, April, 1983.

Douglas, M. 1986. *How Institutions Think*. Syracuse, New York: Syracuse University Press.

DiMaggio, Paul J. and Walter W. Powell (eds.). 1991. *The new institutionalism in organizational analysis*. Vol. 17. Chicago, IL: University of Chicago Press.

Ferrari, S. 2002. "Islam and the Western European Model of Church and State Relations," in Shadid, W.A.R. and van Koningsveld P.S. (2002), (eds.): *Religious Freedom and the Neutrality of the State: the Position of Islam in the European Union*. Leuven: Peeters.

Ferrari, S. 2008. "State regulation of religion in the European democracies: the decline of the old pattern," in Motzkin, G., and Fischer Y. (2008), (eds.): *Religion and Democracy in Contemporary Europe*, London: Alliance Publishing Trust.

Giddens, A., (1984) *The Constitutions of Society. Outline of the Theory of Structuration*. Cambridge: Polity Press.

Jepperson, R.L. 1991. "Institutions, Institutional Effects and Institutionalism," in DiMaggio, P.J., & Powell, W.W. (1991) (eds.), *The new institutionalism in organizational analysis* Chicago: University of Chicago Press.

Jonker, G. 2002. "Muslims Emancipations? Germany's Struggle over Religious Pluralism," in Shadid, W.A.R., & van Koningsveld, P.S., (2002A) (eds), *Religious Freedom and the Neutrality of the State: the Position of Islam in the European Union*. Leuven: Peeters Publishers.

Jonker, G. 2003. "Forming Muslim Religion in Germany," in Daiber, K.-F., & Jonker, G., (2003) *Local Form of Religious Organisation as Structural Modernisation: Effects on Religious Community Building and Globalisation*," Philipps Universität Marburg 2003.

Kaya, A. 2009. *Islam, Migration and Integration: The Age of Securitization*, London: Palgrave.

Koehler, A.A. 1997. "Eine islamische Amtskirche–Anerkennung durch Körperschaftsrechte." *Islam hier & heute Jan*, 6.

Koenig, M. 2006. "Konstruktionen muslimischer Identität zwischen nationaler und europäischer Staatsbürgerschaft." In: Rehberg, Karl-Siegbert (Ed.); *Soziale Ungleichheit, kulturelle Unterschiede: Verhandlungen des 32. Kongresses der Deutschen Gesellschaft für Soziologie in München*. Teilbd. 1 und 2. Frankfurt am Main: Campus Verl., 2006.

Maiziere, T. 2011. "Islamischer Religionsunterricht in Deutschland: ein wertvoller Beitrag zur Integration." In: *Islamischer Religionsunterricht in Deutschland Perspektiven und Herausforderungen*. Dokumentation Tagung der Deutschen Islam Konferenz 13. bis 14. Februar 2011, Nürnberg.

Mårtensson, U. and E.A.V Eriksen. 2014. "Muslim Society Trondheim: A Local History." *Tidsskrift for islamforskning*, 8(1).

Nielsen, J.S. 1991. "Muslim Organisations in Europe: Integration or Isolation? In: Shadid, W.A.R., & P.S. Koningsveld." *The integration of Islam and Hinduism in Western Europe*, Kampen: Kok.

Nielsen, J.S. 1993. "State, religion and laicite: the western European experience," in: Speelman, Lin and Mulder, Muslims and Christians in Europe Breaking New Ground, Kampen: Kok.

Nielsen, J.S. 1999. *Towards a European Islam*, Palgrave Macmillan.

Nielsen, J.S. (forthcoming). "Preface." In: *Imams in Western Europe – Developments, Transformations, and Institutional Challenges*, Vols I+II, Mohammed Hashas, Jan Jaap de Ruiter, and Niels Valdemar Vinding (eds.), Amsterdam University Press.

Nielsen, J.S. and Jonas Otterbeck. 2015. *Muslims in western Europe*. Edinburgh University Press.

Richard, J.-B. 1842. *Dictionaire de Mots Nouveaux, Enrichissement de la Langue Française, Système d'éducation, Pensées politique, philosophiques, morales et sociales*. Paris: Pilout & Laloy.

Roy, O. 2004. *Globalised Islam: The search for a new ummah*. Columbia University Press, 2006.

Roy, O. 2007. *Secularism Confronts Islam*. Columbia University Press.

Roy, O. 2010. *Holy Ignorance: When Religion and Culture Part Ways*, London: Hurst.

Scott, W.R., 2008. *Institutions and Organizations*. 3rd Ed., Thousand Oaks, CA: Sage Publications.

Serageldin, I. 1989. "Faith and the Environment," in *Space for Freedom*. London: Butterworth Architecture.

Silvestri, S. 2007. "Muslim Institutions and Political Mobilization," in: Amghar, Boubekeur & Emerson, *European Islam. Challenges for Public Policy and Society*. Centre for European Policy Studies, Brussels.

Vinding, N.V. 2013. *Muslim Positions in the Religio-organisational fields of Denmark, Germany and England*. Copenhagen: Faculty of Theology.

Wall, H. 2011. "Mitwirkung von Muslimen in den Ländern: Religionsverfassungsrecht und muslimische Ansprechpartner" In: *Islamischer Religionsunterricht in Deutschland Perspektiven und Herausforderungen*. Dokumentation Tagung der Deutschen Islam Konferenz 13. bis 14. Februar 2011, Nürnberg.

Woodhead, L. 2011. "Five concepts of religion." *International review of Sociology, 21*(1), 121–143.

CHAPTER 5

"Perpetual First Generation": Religiosity and Territoriality in Belonging Strategies of Turks of France

Samim Akgönül

Introduction

Due to differences between the French and Turkish definitions of "nation" and "citizenship," it is not possible to determine the exact population of the "Turkish" community in France. The French census system has only two main categories: French citizens and resident aliens. However, a subcategory lists "naturalised French citizens" by their ethnicity. The Turkish system is a mix of the French (*jus soli*) and German (*jus sanguinis*) systems, and apart from the non-Muslim minorities identified *de facto*, it ignores the legal presence of minorities. The Turkish census is the continuation of the Ottoman *millet* system in that it identifies minorities by their religious affiliation. Although the proclamation of the Republic meant that the Turkish state was restructured with the individual at the forefront instead of groups, the Ottoman reflex of ethnic-religious classification had been internalised by the people and the government. Any citizen of Turkey may be a Turk according to the Constitution, but the criteria for possessing "Turkness" is very relative from a cultural perspective. A Turk must be a Muslim. A Muslim from another ethnic origin and/or using another language than Turkish can "acquire" Turkness, but a non-Muslim, speaking in Turkish cannot.

There are three distinct types of Turkish populations in France: "French of Turkish origin," "alien Turkish nationals" and "ethnic Turks." This is why a census of the "Turkish population" or "French population of Turkish origin" yields different results according to the procedure used. A census based on the legal definition of groups may be different from another based on ethnic, identical or cultural classifications. French and Turkish statistics differ widely, which sometimes sparks discussions far from objectivity (such as the xenophobic and/or nationalistic discourses of the extreme rightists in Turkey and Europe).

According to official Turkish data, there were 370,000 Turks or ethnic Turks residing in France as of 2014. If we add to this figure the French data and the non-official surveys, we may say that there are approximately 500,000

© KONINKLIJKE BRILL NV, LEIDEN, 2018 | DOI 10.1163/9789004362529_006

individuals living in France, originating from Turkey or with parents originating from Turkey.

The aim of this article is to discuss the qualification of "second and third generations" of people originating from Turkey living in France. This will be done by analysing religious belonging attitudes in the triangle of: France, as a belonging territory, insofar as these people are born and socialised in France; Turkey as a permanent reference, controlling solidly its diaspora and framing different groups abroad, especially by means of religion; and the Turkish community in France, which, pretending to self-protect from assimilation as a reaction to being aware of its minority status, shows enthusiasm towards everything coming from Turkey.

Perpetual First Generation Strategy

The transfer of the collective memory for the purposes of ensuring unity and integrity rests on three identity pillars:

- the longing for and loyalty to "the Motherland." It is Turkey in general and the hometown or village in particular;
- the transfer of the Turkish language to the younger generation despite French being the official language;
- and the continuation of customs and traditions believed to be rooted in religion.

The reason the community is so fervently attached to these three topics is its desire that the Turkish children born in France share the same sentiment of "Turkness" with them. Various methods are employed by the community to transfer these three elements to new generations. The leading method has to be the perpetual first generation strategy, i.e. the *positivation* of all features related to the Motherland and the *negativation* of the multi-belonging. Positivation involves three main pillars: popular culture related to Turkey (music, movies, television shows, newspapers), religious attitudes related to Turkey (imams, Turkish mosques, the Turkish way of celebrating religious festivities ...) and finally matrimonial habits related to Turkey ("imported" brides and grooms).[1] Young French people of Turkish origin rarely marry people who are of French or other nationalities, and seldom marry other members of the Franco-Turkish

---

1 Gökalp, Altan, S. De Tapia, and S. Akgönül, *Les conjoints des jeunes Français originaires de Turquie*, Paris, FASILD, 2005.

"PERPETUAL FIRST GENERATION." 69

community. From a statistical point of view, one of the parents (usually the mother) of all Turkish (and Kurdish) children born in France is a new arrival in France. The "fresh bloods" are received as the representatives of genuine "Turkness" (particularly in terms of language and religion) who will help to correct the degeneration in the "Turkness" of ethnic Turks who have lived in France for too long.

The loyalty of the ethnic Turks in France to Turkey becomes manifest even in how they call Turkey the "Motherland." The pillars of identity-building in the community are language (Turkish and/or Kurdish) and religion (Sunni Islam or Alevism). But the two pillars need a hinterland. The hinterland is primarily Turkey, but expands to concentric circles of the home villages, towns and provinces of the immigrants. The ties with their country are both physical and mental. Physical ties are the result of frequent travel to Turkey, whether for business, school or leisure, following the developments in Turkey via newspapers, television and other media, and contact with the country either by phone or over the internet. These three methods of contact have developed significantly in the last two decades: flights and voyages between the two countries are plentiful and the fares are low; the number of national and local television stations has seen a boom, and these stations are available abroad; the internet provides a means to communicate at minimal cost, while phone tariffs are also falling. All of these conduits enable the ethnic Turks in France to stay in contact with Turkey in an ubiquitous fashion.

More difficult to grasp are the emotional or mental ties with Turkey, which I believe correlate to two approaches:

(1) Firstly, the ethnic Turks in France are more interested in Turkish politics than French internal affairs. In fact, they pay close attention to the political atmosphere in Turkey and want the political context in Turkey either to change or remain as it is, much like their compatriots in Turkey. From this perspective, the change in the discourse of French Turks regarding the accession of Turkey to the EU is noteworthy. Although they desire Turkey and France to be members of the same union for emotional and practical reasons, they too have begun to voice the anti-French and anti-European discourse recently on the rise in Turkey. Meanwhile, none of the Turkish associations or organisations in France have attempted to block Turkey's accession to the EU. They desire the membership of Turkey for two somewhat irrational reasons: (a) the desire for the Turkish state to attain a better future and position, and (b) their hope that the accession of Turkey will legitimise their presence in France and improve their image in the eyes of the French public. This attitude emphasises that people

of Turkish origin have evolved into a "diaspora" as defined by Kim Butler (2001). According to Butler, members of the diaspora continue to be interested in the politics of the root nation. The interest is not necessarily in the way of support; on the contrary, a section of the diaspora may even side with the opposition. But it is interest that matters, not its direction.[2]

(2) Secondly, these irrational ties may be explained by Benedict Anderson's (1991) imagined communities theory.[3] In other words, the Turks in France associate themselves with other individuals comprising their community (even if they do not know all of them personally) and root for the success and victory of other Turks in a setting of competition with the majority, brought about by being in the minority.

The Motherland was in irrational ties with the Turks in Europe until recently. For years, every administration tried to prevent European Turks from acquiring citizenship of the countries they were living, and even born, in. They feared that by acquiring a different nationality, European Turks would detach from "Turkness" and Turkey. Legal attachment to the Motherland seemed more important than emotional and ethno-national loyalty. This was partly influenced by Germany's denial of dual-citizenship status. It should be remembered that the nationalist mindset considers national identity one and singular. As Max Weber suggests, nationalism is a system of belief over all, and just as a person may be loyal to only one religion, so must an individual choose to be loyal to only one nation. Multiple national loyalties are being condemned severely. Nevertheless, a recent radical change occurred in Turkey's approach to the issue: since the late 1990s, but particularly after 2002, European Turks are expected to acquire the citizenship of their country of residence. This will give them a voice in the national and local politics of their respective countries, and allow them to lobby in favour of Turkey.

President Tayyip Erdoğan's show of solidarity with the Turks in France with public lectures for huge gatherings in 2010, 2013 and 2015 may indicate that, contrary to belief, there is has been no significant change in the concept of "external Turks." This term is used for Turks – identified as such based on race and religion – who live outside the borders of the Republic of Turkey. The perception of the concept by political authorities and the society (consequently the media) is clearly evident in Article 66 of the Constitution of 1982 ("Any citizen

---

2 Butler Kim, "Defining diaspora, refining a discourse" in *Diaspora: A Journal of Transnational Studies 10*, no. 2, 2001, 189–219.

3 Anderson, Benedict . *Imagined communities: reflectons on the origin and spread of nationalism*, London: Verso, 1991 (Revised and extended edition), 6–7.

of the state of Turkey is a Turk. The child of a Turkish father or a Turkish mother is a Turk."). The first sentence forcibly includes those who live in Turkey but are not ethnically Turkish in the Turkish nation. The second sentence places the children of ethnically and religiously "Turkish" parents, even if they may live abroad, within the sphere of Turkness from an ethnic and especially religious perspective. In 2015, during an electoral meeting in Strasbourg, President Erdoğan emphasised the fact that Turks living in France were *Millî*, "Nationals," in the religious sense of the term.

In more open terms, the Greeks, Armenians, and for some the Kurds who live outside the borders of Turkey are not included in the concept of "external Turks" even if they are Turkish citizens and were even born and raised in Turkey.

Although seemingly narrow, the scope of this concept may expand depending on context and political view. Sometimes "external Turks" include the remnants of the Ottoman society in the Balkans, Middle East and the Caucasus. In other cases, groups like the Pomaks and Circassians, who are not ethnically Turkish but may be incorporated into Turkness via the *millet* system mind-set because of their religion, may be included. The racial approach may be expanded onto communities who lack even a relative relationship with Turkness or Turkish citizenship.

The confusion goes far enough for the establishment of a government authority under the name "Office of Expatriate Turks and Related Communities,"[4] or the legalisation of the concept of "aliens of Turkish descent" in Article 47 of the Turkish Citizenship Law dated 2009 (numbered 5901).

The emigration of Turks to Western Europe starting with the 1960s did help to expand the concept of external Turks. With the settlement of migrant workers from the mid-70s onwards, a group of immigrants scorned by the elite while being cherished for their accumulation and capital transfer emerged as the backbone of the so-called "external Turks." After 20 years of neglect, this group was framed within the "omnipresent fatherly State" in the wake of the 1980 junta. In other words, for almost two decades, the Turkish State left external Turks to fend for themselves in "civil society," especially with regard to far left movements and of course religious movements. To be exact, after the 1980s, one purpose of framing was to prevent external Turks from "taking the wrong path." The wrong path, of course, was paved with leftist movements and dissenting religious organisations.[5]

---

4   *Radikal*, 24.04.2010.

5   For more information cf. Akgönül, Samim. "L'État turc et les Turcs européens : une tentative permanente d'encadrement paternaliste," in Dumont Paul, Pérouse Jean-François, De

The real danger was assimilation, "forgetting" Turkness and losing loyalty to Turkey. So while this group was exposed to Turkish propaganda by print, media and imams and teachers commissioned from Turkey, they were prevented from entering into any kind of multiple loyalties. In the way of the knee-jerk reaction by nation-states whose strength is dubious, the perpetual first generation strategy was imposed upon generations born in Europe. The objective was to ensure that ethnic Turks born in Europe were at least as loyal to the country as those who came from Turkey, and the strategy was adopted and implemented by European Turks. The rejection of multiple loyalties applied to the change in legal affiliation – acquiring citizenship of the country of residence.

Administrations in Turkey considered change in citizenship or an additional citizenship dangerous for decades. Turks who acquired the citizenship of their country of residence would make compromises with their Turkness, and their loyalty would weaken. So they were expected to remain purely Turkish.

This policy has been amended since the 2000s. The relief brought by globalisation led Turkish officials to believe that European Turks were no longer under the threat of assimilation, decided that these communities would lobby for European relations, and encouraged them to acquire the citizenship of their countries of residence. Nevertheless, these groups are still viewed as instruments at the disposal of the Republic of Turkey.

From another angle, these people are being called upon as "soldiers," obliged to act like one single body, following the orders of Ankara: 10 years ago, their duty required them to be Turkish citizens; now, they are instructed to become French or German citizens. Wealth accumulation by migrant workers is still seen as a remedy to economic distress; the sentimental discourse around homesickness, loyalty and the Motherland is still maintained – to the extent of sheer emotional exploitation as seen in the 2012 Paris rally where 40 000 Turks marched in protest of the law criminalizing the denial of the Genocide of Armenians. All of the above makes it clear that the Motherland's view of the migrant communities has not changed radically.

The improvement and expansion of communication technologies removes the threat of assimilation that came with changing to French or German citizenship. Although having multiple legal affiliations has become acceptable, this is not the case with cultural loyalties. Multiple cultural loyalties are still viewed as dangerous and even treasonous.

We had mentioned that cultural loyalty was built on two pillars: language and religion. When in the minority, teaching the language to new generations

---

Tapia Stéphane, Akgönül Samim (eds.), *Migrations et mobilités internationales: la plate-forme turque*, Istanbul: Les Dossiers de l'IFEA, 13, décembre 2002, 79–99.

becomes particularly difficult. Naturally, the language of the majority immediately becomes the dominant language in a social environment. Furthermore, France insists on fluency in French as a prerequisite to integration into the country, and this has come to be accepted by the majority as well as the minority, who initially resisted the idea. Fluency in French is the most important measure of proper integration. As a result, lack of fluency in Turkish no longer poses a threat to loyalty to "Turkness."

Meanwhile, religious loyalty, being sacred and therefore immune to intervention, gained great importance and took priority. In a contradictory way, this type of loyalty became an indispensable and paramount element of "Turkness" for both Sunni and Alevi Turks in France. However, filling the gap left by language with religion gave rise to a number of issues in the French case: the French system is constructed on the principle of laicism and Turkish immigrants have diverse cultural and social backgrounds.

Religion as National Belonging

The solidarity among people of Turkish origin in France, or even across Europe, in the 1960s and 1970s expanded via two ideological movements. The community itself laid the foundation for solidarity when emigration to Europe began. At the time, neither the receiving countries (France, Germany ...) nor Turkey were interested in the matter. Both parties hoped for this migratory movement to be transient. According to both sides, Turkish migrant workers were in Europe for a limited period, after which they would return to Turkey. This did not require the countries to organise to meet the needs of this temporary community. Under these circumstances, Turkish immigrants were left to their own means and started to organise with what they had: either ideological or regional, familial and religious loyalty. The seeds of solidarity within the community of migrant Turkish workers, who were away from home, lonely, exploited and sometimes unemployed, were sown by leftist movements. Led by these movements and influenced by the unionist organisations gaining strength in Western Europe in the 1960s and the 1970s, European Turks began to organise and protest living and working conditions, if hesitantly. It is interesting to note that, as a consequence of the international aspect of Marxist ideology, these European Turkish leftist movements with time fused with French leftist movements.

The second ideology that creates solidarity among Turks is religion. It is not accurate to claim that the initial religious signs in the Turkish community in Europe were ideological: they emerged as a means of meeting the spiritual needs of the community. For example, rooms were set aside and furnished for prayer in worker housing facilities. These small prayer rooms came under the influence of the European factions of the *Millî Görüş* movement only after the 1970s. During the same period some other brotherhoods started to be locally organised like the *Süleymanci* in Cologne. As *Millî Görüş* expanded and gained popularity across Turkey in the 1970s, it became the prominent ideology within the diaspora of Turkish workers in Europe. The popularity of the movement in Europe was owed to its transition to a popular movement that appealed to worker and peasant classes. As most of the Turkish immigrants in Europe belonged in these classes and maintained their ties with their rural origins, the movement expanded and became deeply entrenched in Europe. Even today, *Millî Görüş* chapters are the leading representatives of Turkish Islam in France, Germany and Benelux.[6] However, one may notice that since 2011, when the AKP government succeeded in finally dominating the entirety of the Turkish State Apparatus, the role and the dynamism of the DİTİB[7] have increased substantially, especially in Western European countries but also in the Balkans.

During and after the junta established in the aftermath of the military coup in the early 1980s, the Turkish state realised the significance of Turkish people living in Western Europe, and subjected these communities to a rigid system of control and direction. This was done in order to prevent the spread of Marxist and religious fundamentalist ideas, which were considered dangerous. Another movement "dangerous" to the Turkish state emerged in the form of Kurdish nationalism in the 1990s.

The interest of the Turkish state in European Turks may be explained by two more developments – one domestic and the other foreign. An ideology of "Turkish-Islamic synthesis" was established within Turkey in the 1980s as a line of defence against communism. As the movement was conceptualised and shaped into a tangible entity, Sunni Islam regained its status as an indispensable part of the Turkish identity. The construction of mosques, prayer rooms and religious high schools was accelerated greatly, and political Islam became one of the leading movements of thought in Turkey. As a result, the State of Turkey had no option but to keep European Turks under religious control.[8]

---

6 Akgönül, Samim, "Millî Görüş: Institution religieuse minoritaire et mouvement politique transnational" in Amghar, Samir (ed.), *Islamismes d'Occident, les voies de la renaissance*, Paris: Lignes de repères, 2006.

7 The Diyanet İşleri Türk İslam Birliği (DİTİB) is a branch of the Turkish Administration of Religious Affairs for religious services abroad and the main control mechanism of the Turkish Diaspora.

8 For an in-depth analysis of the said control, cf. Akgönül, Samim, "L'Etat turc et les Turcs européens: une tentative permanente d'encadrement paternaliste," in Paul Dumont, Pérouse,

"PERPETUAL FIRST GENERATION."

The foreign development was that the migrant workers did not return to Turkey as expected. The families of the workers who were permanently residing in Europe began to settle in those countries in the 1980s. As the children of the emigrants also began to immigrate to Europe, the Turkish state undertook the duty to export "true Islam" to Europe. This attitude is legitimised in Article 62 of the Constitution of 1982:

> The State takes the measures necessary to preserve the family unity of Turkish citizens working abroad, to ensure that their children receive education, their cultural requirements are met and social security is provided, to maintain their ties with the motherland, and to assist them in their return to the country." Based on this article, a new division called "Turkish-Islamic Union for Religious Affairs (DITIB)" was established under the Administration of Religious Affairs in 1983 to serve the Turks living in other countries.

Starting in 1983 in Germany and 1985 in France, hundreds of associations gathered under the umbrella of DITIB. New associations were founded with the initiative of the Union. Nevertheless, joining DITIB did not necessarily mean adopting the ideology of the Union or accepting the official Islam that Turkey wanted to export to Europe. There are many significant advantages of membership, and these draw associations. Membership in DITIB means better relations with Turkish embassies and entitlement to request imams (and sometimes trainers) sponsored by the Turkish state. Considering the financial difficulties encountered by the associations of immigrant communities in France, this is an important source of financial support. Moreover, many associations assign their properties to the Administration of Religious Affairs, freeing themselves from repair and maintenance costs. In short, DITIB is not a predominantly ideological organisation like *Millî Görüş* or the "Süleymancı" movement.

An individual who believes to be a part of a minority chooses to join minority organisations for three reasons other than ideological motives:

- Increasing the number of minority members to ensure the group's survival;
- Joining the frontline against other groups and individuals who are perceived as a threat to the stability of the community;
- Sending out a message of strength and legitimacy to the majority.

Jean-François, De Tapia, Stéphane, and Akgönül, Samim, *Migrations et mobilités internationales: la plate-forme turque*, Istanbul: Les Dossiers de l'IFEA, 13 December 2002, 79–99.

The three points above should be kept in mind when looking into Turkish religious organisations in France. These organisations not only meet the spiritual needs of the community, but also cater to a series of diverse needs.[9] Analysis of the religious ideologies of people of Turkish origin in France shows that DİTİB does not represent a specific doctrine. The activities of DİTİB members and non-members alike are not restricted to religious events. The non-religious activities and officials of the associations are not affiliated with the Turkish state.

Religion as a Control Frame

As in the rest of Western Europe, people of Turkish origin in France are not limited to the *Millî Görüş* or DİTİB organisations. Ideological organisations that were unable to express themselves under the circumstances in Turkey enjoyed a legal and political environment that was conducive to growth and expansion in Europe. These organisations were born and nurtured in Europe, and then exported to Turkey. In the case of France, there are three main groups: the "Süleymancı" movement (congregational organisation), the "Idealists" (nationalist ideological organisation) and the Alevi (religious/cultural organisation). The Süleymancı community was established by Sheikh Süleyman Hilmi Tunahan, who died in 1959.[10] Members of the congregation began to play important roles in Turkish domestic policy starting in the 1950s but most notably during the 1980s. Many politicians today do not feel the need to hide their close relations to the Süleymancı community. Although very similar to the "Nurcu" community, the Süleymancı argue that the ancestry of their sheikh is rooted in the "Naqshbandi," meaning Central Asia. Although the Süleymancı do not have official houses of worship in Turkey, it is known that they are very active in many mosques that are under the supervision of the Administration Office of Religious Affairs, and provide informal religious education to large groups of students both in Turkey and abroad.[11] The Süleymancı in Europe have a large

---

9   Acquaviva, Sabino and Pace, Enzo, *La sociologie des religions*, Paris: Cerf, 1994, 123.

10 For one of many Süleyman Hilmi Tunahan biographies, cf. Akgündüz, Ahmet, *Silistreli Süleyman Hilmi Tunahan*, Istanbul: OSAV, 1997.

11 Yaşar Nuri Öztürk claims that the Süleymancı have 6 media channels, 2100 associations, 14 foundations, 1750 housing facilities and schools and 28 companies. The *Milli Görüş* organisation has 37 media channels, 330 associations, 33 foundations, 8 tutoring institutions and 48 companies. The same author claims that the followers of Fethullah Gülen operate 16 media channels, 23 associations, 220 foundations, 24 housing facilities, 570 schools and tutoring institutions and 96 companes (Öztürk, Yaşar Nuri, *Türkiye'yi Kemiren İhanet – Allah ile Aldatmak*, Istanbul: Yeniboyut, 2008).

number of mosques and religious complexes operating under their headquarters in Cologne. The congregation runs Qur'anic schools and summer schools in lavish houses of worship, providing religious education to children of Turkish origin to prevent them from taking the "wrong path." The Süleymancı actively organise Hajj and Umrah trips for immigrant Turks in Europe and protest against political acts thought to be targeting Muslims. An important example was how Süleymancı individuals rallied after the banning of headscarves in French schools in 2004. The fact that associations affiliated with the Süleymancı community appear as closed religious orders gave rise to rumours and worries about the community. The movement decided to open up to the society in recent years to become better known and understood in the public opinion. One of the results was increased communication and stronger ties with other Turkish associations and French authorities. For example, after a long period of refusing to take part in interfaith dialogue meetings held by Christian churches, they have begun to appoint representatives to these events since the 2000s, albeit still reluctantly. This quest for legitimisation in the eyes of the Turkish community of Europe, the European countries of residence, and Turkey made the activities and thoughts of the Süleymancı community open for everyone to see and follow, which played an important part in the opening up of the community.

Süleymancı associations usually carry names like "Turkish Civic Center" or "Turco-Islamic Culture Center" and aim to provide religious education to Turkish children via Qur'anic schools and summer schools. These activities are carried out in facilities owned by the community, sometimes complete with dormitories.[12] The Süleymancı community in France and Europe in general is more rigid in organisation and particularly with regard to the transfer of religious and moral values in comparison to other communities. This discipline is owed to the Süleymancı thought that all phases of socialisation, whether private or related to the community, must occur in accordance with the principles of the community. As is the case in other dogmatic communities, it is utterly meaningless to separate public and private life.[13] After being considered within the dissenting Islamic circles for a long time, the Süleymancı are

---

12   According to Ahmet Akgündüz, the Süleymancı community possesses approximately 2500 Qur'anic schools globally (Akgündüz, Ahmet, *op. cit.*, 114); Caymaz Birol believes this figure is exaggerated (Birol, Caymaz. *"Les mouvements Islamiques turcs à Paris*, Paris: L'Harmattan, 2002, 104).

13   Hervieu-Léger Danièle, "Peuple de Dieu, entre exclusivisme communautaire et universalisme" in Wieviorka Michel (ed.), *Racismes et modernité*, Paris: La Découverte, 1992, 98–105.

becoming closer to the ruling classes, integrating with the new conservative elite in Turkey and continuing expansion in Europe.[14] This domestic and international warming of relations has two aspects: the approach and discourse of community members towards the outside world is becoming moderate; however, this change is considered pretentious by the Kemalists.[15] On the other hand, the fact that some members of the new ruling elite were housed in facilities operated by the Süleymancı community during their university education helped them to establish closer ties with the community.

Associations of the nationalist "Idealist" movement should be considered in another context that is neither religious nor national. Gathering under the umbrella of the "Turkish Federation of France," these associations rarely take part in joint activities with Millî Görüş or DİTİB. Due to the negative image created by the French extreme rightist party, Idealist leaders keep repeating and underlining that they do not belong to any religious movement. Posters of the Idealist movement leaders (Alparslan Türkeş or Devlet Bahçeli) are on prominent display in their offices. In other words, the French context shapes the impression the Idealists want to make in France in an indirect way. Attitude-wise, they are very different from other Turkish organisations. For example, they stay out of debates on Islam in France or do not argue that French politics deserves more interest than Turkish politics. Almost all of the imams appointed to houses of worship maintained by Idealist organisations are affiliated with the Turkish chapter of the nationalist movement, and come from Turkey. Since the military coup of 1980, the Idealists have associated themselves with religion and began to view it as an aspect of "Turkness." The pan-Turkic ideology of "Turanism" was cast aside as it did not encompass the religious aspect, and was replaced by the Turco-Islamic synthesis ideology. Nevertheless and without exception, the Idealist imams in France are strangers to the country with no knowledge about it whatsoever. The number of Idealist organisations in France is very small compared to Millî Görüş or DİTİB associations.

In addition to these four prominent organisations in France (DİTİB, Milli Görüş, the Süleymancı and the Idealists), there are a variety of smaller organisations. For instance, the Naqshbandi order, which is highly influential in Turkey and Central Asia, maintains several lodges in France.

The "Kaplancı" congregation, founded by Cemalettin Kaplan but now almost facing extinction, has a few mosques in France. This is a Sunni extremist organisation that is inspired by Ayatollah Khomeini despite him being Shiite,

---

14   Çakır, Ruşen, "Le mouvement Islamique entre religion et Etat" in *Confluences Méditerranée*, no.23, 1997, 33–38.

15   For example, cf. Göçeri, Nebahat, *Dinî grupların eğitim anlayışı*, Adana: Karahan, 2004.

and wants the laic regime in Turkey to be overthrown and replaced by the caliphate.

In France, there are approximately 130 organisations under the umbrella of DİTİB, and approximately 70 under Milli Görüş. The number of Süleymancı and Idealist organisations is in the 10s and 20s.[16] The breakdown of organisations of Turkish origin in France as discovered by the author is shown below.

Disappearance of the Distinction between State Islam and Dissenting Political Islam

The aversion of Turkish associations to unite under one roof is the result of the presence of a dissenting Islamic movement that is in conflict with the official Islam in Turkey. An in-depth analysis of the division reveals that the rift is not as wide or severe as it seems or is commonly believed to be.

Dissident Islamic movements opposed to official Islam have existed throughout the Ottoman Empire and carried over to the Republic of Turkey. Both states, wanting to dictate and control religious thought and practice, considered those who reject whatever is imposed as subversive elements threatening unity and security, and branded them as heretics. Dissenting Islamic movements resisted annihilation when the Jacobin Kemalist regime saw them as a threat against the newly-founded laic regime, and their resistance brought them strength. People of the Anatolian Islamic culture, followers of heterodox faiths and practices in various congregations and even some Sufis were devastated when their religious orders, lodges or holy tombs where they congregated were banned and closed. However, contrary to the wishes of the state, the banning of religious orders did not diminish their importance, particularly in rural areas. They continued their existence in hiding. The state began to control and nationalise the religion within the Administration of Religious Affairs established in lieu of the abolished Caliphate. Religious orders that fell outside the planned official religious project were classified as dissident Islam, even though some were not even remotely tied to politics. These orders remained hidden until the 1950s, when the Democrat Party came to power with the votes of the rural population, and then began to take part in politics as the Democrat Party viewed conservative Islam favourably. The orders joined a variety of political movements until the mid-1960s, but "political Islam" was not yet developed. The foundation of political Islam took place in the relatively liberal environment created in the wake of the military coup of 1960. Millî Görüş completed its association in the 1970s and became one of the leading political parties in Turkey. To eliminate any previous misconceptions, it must

---

16   Akgönül, Samim, "Islam turc, Islams de Turquie" in *Politique étrangère*, 1/ 2005, 37–49.

be noted that the "dissidence" of this party is first and foremost political, and not tied to religion. To the contrary, Millî Görüş holds the belief that Islam already has a very special place in the private and social lives of the people in Turkey; it is only missing in the political arena. The purpose is not to discuss religion and draw a roadmap; it is to introduce religion in the world of politics. In this political environment, Millî Görüş managed to stay away from radical Islamic movements despite incorporating smaller fundamentalist groups. As explained above, despite the fact that the armed forces and other groups of the society did not acknowledge its legitimacy, the Millî Görüş movement became an indispensable part of politics, or the "system," starting with the 1970s. Kemalist circles were unable to prevent the political parties stemming from the Millî Görüş movement from entering coalitions and finally becoming the ruling party in 2002. Although the Justice and Development Party argues that it is separate from the movement, the leaders of the party are all from the Millî Görüş movement, and their constituency is composed of voters loyal to the same movement except the fact that the younger generation admire the new leader Recep Tayyip Erdoğan more than the founder Necettin Erbakan, mainly because Erdoğan brought the power and pride.

Due to these reasons, it is difficult to differentiate between official Islam and dissident Islam. In the European case, such a difference has lost its *raison d'etre*.

Considering Islam still as a system of belief that shapes all the aspects (personal and social) of an individual's life, dissident Islam may be said to be composed of individuals who desire a greater weight for religion in social life. Looking from this perspective, it becomes easier to understand why the people of Turkish origin in Europe place so much importance on religion. First and foremost, their inadequacy in the other loyalty measures of "Turkness" causes religion to gain more importance within these communities. The prioritisation of religion is a phenomenon that is observable in all minority groups, and even constitutes one of the minority theories in sociology today: minorities value religion more than their compatriots who are in the majority in another country; or, non-religious practices are accepted with more ease if the community in question is in the majority. European public opinion and state policies provoked also a self-identification as "Muslims." Minorities construct their identities in reaction to the majority's views. Therefore, as the perception of Arabs or Turks shifted from social class and/or ethnic affiliation in Europe to one of religious belonging – Muslims also present themselves as "Muslims."

In addition to the above, being a supporter of the widespread Millî Görüş movement in Europe has two advantages. Siding with this movement is not limited to supporting an ideology that plays a significant part in Turkish domestic politics. As the importance of Millî Görüş rises in Turkey, the proponents of the party in France become even more legitimate within the Muslim community and gain a surer foothold. In other words, members of Millî Görüş organisations in France are not there because they are interested in Turkish domestic politics; they are there to rise to a better social status in France.

Finally, while still valid to a degree in Turkey, the distinction between official Islam and dissident Islam is becoming irrelevant for the Turks in France. This is not in scorn of the thorough establishment of the Millî Görüş organisation in Germany and the importance of its activities there, or its legitimacy in Turkey: the movement represents a very important segment of the Turkish political system, and with the rise of a spinoff political party to power in 2002, this distinction needs to be curtailed, even in Turkey. Warming relations between the so-called official religion and its dissidents are apparent in many areas. From the close ties between the Turkish authorities and Millî Görüş organisations abroad to the communiqué of the Ministry of Foreign Affairs to its diplomats telling them to worry no longer about the Fethullah Gülen schools in their countries, examples are copious. But since the clash between AKP and Gulen's movements, the situation has reversed. After being the main ally of the government, this movement is now its main enemy and Gulen affiliated schools and associations are, since 2013, criminalised and marginalised.

The Alevi: Between Religion and a Philosophy of Life

Millî Görüş was an important wing of political opposition in Turkey in the 1970s and 80s. However, Turkey's most significant passive social opposition wing is the Alevi. As ideological loyalties lost their importance and were gradually replaced by religious and ethnic loyalties in the late 20th century, the religious element began to supersede other identity criteria in the Alevi. Consequently, the Alevi of France may be considered from two perspectives: first, there are Alevi organisations in France that have no connections to religion, whose activities are limited to social, cultural and sometimes political events. The members of these organisations believe that Islamists comprise the Turkish Sunni organisations and defend laicism as a reaction against these organisations, and are unhappy with the fact that "Turkness" is associated with Sunnism and is represented by Sunni organisations in France. Meanwhile, there are religious organisations that are tied directly to Alevism, therefore in opposition to the official Islam in Turkey. Of course, other organisations can be mentioned beside these two categories, including the ethnic Kurdish Alevi organisations and leftist political organisations whose members are Alevi.

In other words, it will be inaccurate to include all organisations whose members are Alevi in an umbrella category of "Alevi organisations." It must also be noted that the same applies to the Sunnis. Starting with the initial flow of migrant workers to France, but particularly during the 1980s when the migrants began to settle in France, Alevis established dozens of social solidarity associations or political organisations. The majority of these organisations are not religious in nature; they serve a purpose of social, cultural, political and/or ethnic solidarity. Nevertheless, as Sunnism began to dominate in Turkey in the 1990s, these organisations began to underline their Alevi identity. During the same period, a debate ensued in Turkey to shed light on the meaning and definition of Alevism, which was closely followed by the public in Turkey as well as the Turkish community in France. The society accepts the state's opinion of Alevism more than that of the Alevis' own. As an example, Turkish authorities reject the argument that the congregational houses of the Alevis (*cemevi*) are places of worship. At a time when all social and political problems were made ethnic or religious, the Alevis began to emphasise the religious aspect of their identity. This new quest for an identity caused political and social frictions with the established regime and Turkish Sunnism. In a display of power, more than 10,000 Alevis from all over Europe gathered at the Zenith concert hall in Strasbourg on 14 June 2008 for a celebratory event. The gathering was both religious and political at the same time. Until 2007 Alevis believed that political Islam as power in Turkey could improve their situation by recognizing their religious belonging. But the Sunni reflexes of the AKP prevent this recognition. As a result, the main organisation, which called to an anti-Erdoğan meeting in France in October 2015, was the Alevi Federation of France.

Nationalizing Religion: Rivalry between France and Turkey

Important changes have occurred in the attitude of the French state towards laicism and the perception of the French people of secularism in the late 20th and the early 21st centuries. Manifest both in discourse and in legislation, these changes are connected to the presence of Muslims in France and their quest for legitimacy in the simmelian sense of the term.[17] This situation has a direct and an indirect connection to the Muslims in France. The first is a structural connection. Four to five million Muslims may have acquired French citizenship but have yet to achieve legitimacy in the eyes of French society. These

---

17   Noreau, Pierre, "Le droit comme forme de socialisation: Georg Simmel et le problème de la légitimité," in *Revue française de Science Politique*, vol. 45, n° 2, 1995, 282–304.

"*nouveau*" French want their presence to be accepted, both individually and as a religious community with special rights. The quest for legitimacy causes tension in the French society from various perspectives. On the one hand, the French government has been trying to establish an authority that will represent the Muslims of France in an attempt to create a French Islam for more than 15 years; while the public is not in favour of such an authority, as they see it as a threat to divide communities further.

Speaking of the contextual reasons for the change in the French system of laicism, the dark image of Islam in Western societies after the 1990s, particularly in the aftermath of 9/11, must be investigated. Spreading fear as a symbol of threat, and even leading to Muslims being viewed as enemies, this new image had repercussions throughout French society. Although the French are not too keen on the "clash of civilisations," a large number of people want the Muslims in France to go through the laic system to adapt to society, effectively bringing the religiosity and its public visibility under state control. As part of the same approach, French society wants imams to be raised in the French culture and to address their congregations in French in order to keep abreast of the religious thoughts taking root in French soil. From this perspective, it can be argued that the French system of laicism, having clearly separated the state from the church in its time, is now evolving to overcome the issues brought by the Muslims – a new element in society. Similar to Turkey in the 1920s and 1930s, the idea that the state should keep religion under strict control is gaining popularity.

This is a process of localisation of Islam in France. After the oppression of the foreign and heretic French Protestantism, the nationalisation of French Catholicism with the law of 1905, and the digestion of Judaism which had been accused of dual loyalty for many years, the time has now come to nationalise and localise Islam. The objective is to replace Islam in France with a uniquely French Islam. The hottest debate surrounds the imams, and the leading issue on the agenda today is the education and training of imams who will work in France. There are three groups of imams working in French mosques. One group consists of the imams sent from Muslim countries. This is the group that is the least accepted by French society. Imams who will serve the people of Turkish origin in France are being appointed by DİTİB, or in other words the Administration of Religious Affairs, which has reported directly to the Prime Minister since 1984. These imams work within the Turkish organisations in France and their wages are paid by the government of Turkey through the "social affairs attachés" working in consulates. For *Milli Görüs* imams are "independent" but in 2010, most of them were former DİTİB imams. It is not difficult to understand why the organisations request imams from Turkey: on the one hand, due to their excellent grasp of the language and the religion, they are received as the representatives of the true "Turkness" that the ethnic Turks in France allegedly have lost over time due to their excellent grasp of the language and the religion, while their affiliation with the state of Turkey serves to confirm the allegiance of the organisation to the official religion of Turkey. Of course, all this and more is available and paid for by the Turkish government! These organisations are far from being rich, so not having to pay the wages of the imam comes as a great relief. In fact, the finances of some organisations are so precarious that they choose to assign their properties to the Office of Religious Affairs to ensure that imams are sent on a regular basis and building maintenance is paid for by the Office.

Despite the negative reaction from the public, French authorities do not object to the imams sent from Turkey because they are under the supervision of the Turkish state and present less of a threat than local imams who are not controlled by any country. For as long as there is no institution to provide education to local imams in France, it is important that foreign imams are under the supervision of the country they come from. If the country is laicist like Turkey was until the 1980s, this procedure becomes even more important. The foremost criticism of imams is that they do not speak French. Taking this criticism into consideration, the Office of Religious Affairs started a new procedure in 2005: about one hundred young individuals are chosen from the countries of immigration (France, Germany, Netherlands ...), they then travel to Ankara, Turkey to receive religious education, and then are sent back to their countries. In this connection, it must also be mentioned that the Office of Religious Affairs is not disturbed by imams being educated in Europe. The Office of Religious Affairs supports education abroad on one condition: contributing to the education so that the Office can continue to keep imams serving in Turkish mosques under its supervision. DITB is involved completely in education at three different levels. Firstly, all DITIB mosques have served as Qur'anic courses for years now, and many of them (approximately 50 out of 140 according to the Turkish embassy in Paris) welcome not only an imam from Turkey but also a "teacher" specifically dedicated to the Qur'anic courses. Secondly, since 2014, DITIB has run a imam Hatip High school in Strasbourg, within the DITIB complex of Cronenbourg, without a contract with the French ministry of national education. And finally, since 2015, again within the DITIB complex, a "free faculty of Islamic theology" has operated.

The second group of Turkish imams in France are those serving for non-DITIB organisations, such as Millî Görüş. Most of these clergymen come from Turkey. In their case, the wages are paid by the organisations themselves. Issues surrounding this group of imams are similar to those of the first group – mainly their lack of knowledge in the French language and culture. Some of the

"PERPETUAL FIRST GENERATION."

imams serving in Millî Görüş or Süleymancı mosques are former employees of DİTİB, although Süleymancı traditionally train their imams in France parallel to their school education there. They have either resigned and remained in Europe when their assignment was over, or chosen retirement.

The third group of imams have few members. They are from the North African community of France who have no affiliation with any national or international organisations and work on a voluntary basis in North African organisations. They are mostly elderly individuals who have been residing in France for a long time and have some command of the language. On the other hand, these imams usually lead the prayer only and do not deliver sermons. Unlike the imams in the other two groups, they are not responsible for giving religious education to children. The Turkish community in France does not have any unaffiliated associations that are not tied to an organisation, therefore there are no independent imams.

Attempts to nationalise Islam in France focus on the education and training of imams as a priority.[18] As explained before, French society harbours a distrust of imams sent from abroad. After a long and tense struggle to instate French as the language of Catholic worshipping – which succeeded in the end – France desires a similar outcome for Islam: the language of worshipping at last sermons should not be Arabic or Turkish, but French instead. It must be noted that Turkey went through a similar attempt at localizing religion in the 1920s and the 1930s. The attempt in Turkey has been met with a degree of success with the establishment of the Office of Religious Affairs, but there are hard limits, such as the rejection of the call to prayer to be pronounced and sung in Turkish.

To summarise the situation in France briefly: French laicism is undergoing change due to Islam, but French Islam is evolving alongside. This interaction has led to changes in the Turkish community in France too.[19] Differences from the old ways arise in subjects like covering the head[20] or sacrificial slaughter.[21]

---

18 Cf. Frégosi Franck, *La formation des cadres religieux musulmans en France*, Paris: Bayard Editions, 1999.

19 Changes in the Turkish community were small at first, but became more significant as Turks began to take part in national religious organisations and politics more recently. Nevertheless, the religious organisations of the Turkish community in France have not severed their strong ties with Turkey yet (Caymaz, Birol, *Les mouvements Islamiques turcs à Paris,* Paris: L'Harmattan, 2002).

20 For the new significance of covering the head for Muslims, see Weibel. Nadine, *Par-delà le Voile: femmes d'Islam en Europe*, Paris: Complexe, 2000.

21 For the significance and meaning of sacrifice in Europe, see Brisebarre, Anne-Marie and Gökalp, Altan, *Sacrifices en Islam: espace et temps d'un rituel*, Paris: CNRS Editions, 1999.

When in the minority, all religions take on two contradicting aspects. On the one hand, they resist changes that would have been readily adopted had they been in the majority, while trying to adapt to the country, if begrudgingly, on the other. This contradiction can be observed in the Turkish community of France. Meanwhile, because religious loyalty refers to national loyalty, individuals adopt a religious attitude in an attempt to prove their loyalty to the community and nation to which they belong.[22] This attempt at proving occurs through bringing rational explanations to religious behaviours (such as claiming that pork is bad for health), and arguing that religion has a very important place within the community because it constitutes a critical element of everyday life. By becoming an institution, the community manifests its existence in the eyes of the majority and reaffirms the fact that it will continue to exist regardless of time and place. As an example, while the Turkish community had kept its distance from the Muslims Council of France and the local councils in the beginning, they have since become a part of these organisations for strategic purposes.

Conclusion

Although more than 50 years have elapsed since the first emigration of Turks to France, terms like "French Turks" or "half French-half Turk" are still problematic today. The obstacles to overcome have structural and contextual elements. In Turkey as well as in France, "multiculturality" is asserted on the surface; however, the truth is different: both states are founded on national unity, above all. In other words, both states, drawing on their experience of nation building, prefer that their citizens belong to one and only one nation. National loyalty and the resulting notion of nationalism sharply reject the idea of multiple loyalties. Therefore, the French are unable to associate the immigrant communities with their idea of "nation," even when they have acquired French citizenship or even were born in France. There is a great difference between Turks and North Africans on this point: whereas the struggle of the North Africans is for being accepted as "French" and gaining legitimacy as French, people from Turkey fight to have their Turkish or Kurdish presence in France recognised and made legitimate. Between 2006 and 2008, I had the opportunity to ask a number of questions to 200 Turkish students taking their baccalaureate exams. A great majority of them were born in France (98%) and were French citizens (91%). Furthermore, 22% had a parent who was born in France. Despite this,

---

22   Deconchy, Jean-Pierre, *Orthodoxie religieuse et sciences sociales*, Paris: Mouton, 1980.

none of them answered the question "Where are you from?" with the name of the city they were born or living in. Without a single exception, all answered with the province in Turkey where their parents or at least the head of family (in most cases, the paternal grandfather) came from. This did not change even if those individuals had no familial or physical ties to these provinces, had never even been there and had poor command of Turkish. Based on these responses, we can confidently claim that neither the majority nor the Turkish minority have internalised the concept of multiple loyalties. This serves to prove that having dual citizenship is not an indication of feeling emotional ties to both nations.

This structural data should be accompanied by a contextual explanation: the "perpetual first generation" strategy. The intentional or unintentional practice of this strategy (marriage of people born and raised in France to spouses born and raised in Turkey) enables the Turks in France and across Europe to retain their close ties with Turkey, the Turkish language, and the Muslim religion, as worshipped in Turkey. Generations born in France do lose their command of Turkish, but this shortcoming is compensated for by religion, customs, loyalty to the "motherland" and the cultural accumulation of the parents who had recently emigrated from Turkey. In other words, multiple loyalties are experienced but not expressed, and are even rejected.

Minority theory may explain the situation: all minorities create rules for socializing that will prevent their members from becoming individual. Even if a member of the minority gains the freedom to define himself as an individual, he will continue to be perceived and treated as a member of a minority by the majority and the minority alike. Weber's theory of methodological individualism cannot be used for minorities where the unity and integrity of the identity is paramount. But the antithesis, Durkheim's holism, is inadequate as far as the socializing system is considered. Among the theories that will answer this paradigm is the methodological complex individualism conceptualised by Jean Pierre Dupuy.[23] This appears to be the best way to break down the rigid barriers of the individual/minority/majority triangle. I believe that focusing solely on multiple loyalties[24] in a situation where the minority is still not legitimate in the eyes of the majority is inadequate. To religious minorities that are yet to become legitimate in the society, the demand of the majority from them to adapt their religious customs and practices to the new context in which they settle

---

23 Dupuy, Jean Pierre, "Vers l'unité des sciences sociales autour de l'individualisme méthodologique complexe" in *Revue du MAUSS*, n° 24, 2004, 310–328.

24 Sutter, Jacques, "Overture" in Bauberot Jean (ed.), *Pluralisme et minorités religieuses*, Louvain, Paris: Peeters, 1991, 2.

can be viewed as oppression: by submitting to the demand, they will lose touch with their culture. Although not accepted by the members of the minority for the purpose of preserving their uniqueness, religion – or religious practices – like all other aspects of a cultural whole, is expected to adapt to new circumstances and surroundings. It cannot be denied that the religious attitudes and overall approach of the people of Turkey in France changed as a result of this interaction. On the other hand, because the same group is also in danger of being alienated from their cultures and compelled to assimilate, these developments win the favour of neither the Turkish society nor the minority itself. Returning to Turkey, the people in France are confronted with changes in their behaviour as if they were a crime. The worst insult to Turks coming from France is to tell them they have become French. Owing to the phenomenon of interaction, a member of this community very naturally brings together and uses religious symbols that belong to the Turks in Turkey with those belonging to the majority in France. Collective behaviour is shaping the behaviour of the individual, and individual discourses are creating the collective behaviour.[25]

---

25   Mead, George, *Herbert Mind, Self and Society: From the Standpoint of a Social Behaviorist*, Chicago: University of Chicago Press, 1934.

PART 2

Producing Islam and Muslims in Europe

∵

CHAPTER 6

Alternative Dispute Resolution among Muslims in Germany and the Debate on "Parallel Justice"

Mathias Rohe

I dare to choose this topic for my contribution to this *liber amicorum*, since Jørgen S. Nielsen and I have been partners in the EU-funded RELIGARE consortium, which worked on selected issues regarding religion and secularism in Europe, including ADR under religious and cultural auspices.[1] In addition, Jørgen was among the first scholars, if not the very first, to publish on Muslim family disputes and the application of Islamic law in Britain in the early 1990s.[2] I have always admired Jørgen's capabilities and interest in linking the research on minority issues with society as a whole. By this Thereby, he avoids the perspective on minorities as being restricted to reaction to the majorities' demands, and instead demonstrates the necessities and perspectives of mutual influence and understanding, without neglecting the problems arising from these constant developments.[3] I beg his pardon for the level of English language used here – in this exceptional case it was impossible to ask him for language editing, which I was always grateful for in other contexts.

This article aims at linking new factual knowledge on ADR among Muslims in Germany with the existing legal framework and the public debate on these phenomena. It might also contribute to the ongoing debate on normative pluralism.[4] While considerable scientific work on ADR among Muslims has been

---

1   Cf. Mathias Rohe, Alternative Dispute Resolution in Europe under the Auspices of Religious Norms, RELIGARE Working Paper No. 6, January 2011, available at http://www.religareproject .eu/system/files/Alternative%20Dispute%20Resolution%20by%20Rohe%20e-version.pdf (accessed 26.4.16). http://www.religareproject.eu/system/files/Alternative%20Dispute%20 Resolution%20by%20Rohe%20e-version.pdf (accessed 27.06.2017).

2   Cf. Jørgen S. Nielsen, Emerging Claims of Muslim Populations in Matters of Family Law in Europe, CSIC-MR Birmingham, CSIC Paper no. 10, November 1993; cf. also Jørgen S. Nielsen, United Kingdom: An Early Discussion on Islamic Family Law in the English Jurisdiction, in: Maurits Berger (ed.), *Applying Shari'a in the West*, Leiden 2013, 79–96 (LUP).

3   Cf. Nadia Jeldtoft and Jørgen S. Nielsen (eds.), *Methods and Contexts in the Study of Muslim Minorities*, Abingdon and New York 2012 (Routledge).

4   Cf. e.g. Andrea Büchler, *Islamic Law in Europe? Legal Pluralism and its Limits in European Family Laws*. Farnham and Burlington 2011 (Ashgate); Marie-Claire Foblets, Accommodating

---

© KONINKLIJKE BRILL NV, LEIDEN, 2018 | DOI 10.1163/9789004362529_007

done in several European states (in the UK in particular,[5] but also e.g. in the Nordic countries[6] and in the Netherlands[7]), Germany with its Muslim population of certainly more than four million people[8] has been close to a blind spot so far. Therefore it might be appropriate to concentrate on our recent findings regarding Germany.

ADR and the Role of State Law

No legal order whatsoever would claim an exclusive role in resolving human conflicts, including legal ones. Having served as a judge at the Court of Appeals of Nuremberg for a number of years, I am well aware of the fact that state courts are often unable to implement sustainable conflict resolution by simply issuing judgments. Therefore codes of civil procedure demand to figure out possible ways to settlements between the parties in every stage of court

---

Islamic Family Law(s), in: Maurits Berger (ed.) (n. 2), 207–226; Mathias Rohe, Family and the Law in Europe: Bringing Together Secular Legal Orders and Religious Norms and Needs, in Prakash Shah et al. (eds.), *Family, Religion and Law – Cultural Encounters in Europe*, Farnham 2014 (Ashgate), 49–78; Russell Sandberg, Religious Law as a Social System, in: Russell Sandberg (ed.), *Religion and Legal Pluralism*, Farnham 2015 (Ashgate), 249–278.

5 Cf. S.N. Shah-Kazemi, *Untying the Knot: Muslim Women, Divorce and the Shariah*, London 2001 (Nuffield Foundation); Samia Bano (2007) "Islamic Family Arbitration, Justice and Human Rights in Britain," *Law, Social Justice & Global Development Journal* 1: 2–26. <http://www2.warwick.ac.uk/fac/soc/law/elj/lgd/2007_1/bano/bano.pdf> (accessed 27.06.2017); Samia Bano, *Muslim Women and Shari'ah Councils: Transcending the Boundaries of Community and Law*. Basingstoke 2012b (Palgrave Macmillan); Maleiha Malik, *Minority Legal Orders in the UK*. London: British Academy Policy Centre. Available for download at http://www.britac .ac.uk/policy/Minority-legal-orders.cfm: (accessed 27.06.2017); John Bowen, *On British Islam. Religion, Law, and Everyday Practice in Shari'a Councils*, Princeton and Oxford 2016 (PUP).

6 Cf. e.g. Maarit Jänterä-Jareborg, On the Cooperation between Religious and State Institutions in Family Matters: Nordic Experiences, in: Prakash Shah et al. (eds.) (n. 4), 93 ff. with further references.

7 Cf. Susan Rutten, The Netherlands, in: Maurits Berger (ed.) (n. 2), 97–109; ongoing field research is done by Arshad Muradin in a doctoral project (information is available at http://law .leiden.edu/organisation/metajuridica/vvi/staff/muradin-arshad.html).

8 According to the most reliable figures dating from 2008, a number of 3.8 to 4.3 million Muslims lived in the country at that time (information is available on the website of the German Islam Conference at http://www.deutsche-islam-konferenz.de/DIK/EN/Magazin/Lebenswelten/ZahlenDatenFakten/ZahlMLD/zahl-mld-inhalt.html (accessed 27.06.2017). Since then, the number has certainly increased due to an estimated immigration of around 800.000 Muslim refugees in 2015 alone.

proceedings.[9] New mediation laws[10] further encourage extra-judicial conflict resolution in matters beyond the limits of mandatory law.

Nevertheless, the scope and intensity of state intervention into the legal relation between private persons largely differed, and still differ, in the different parts of the world. The less centralised and institutionalised states are, the more tribal, ethnic, religious or local stakeholders are capable to exercise power in setting and enforcing legally or socially binding norms. In our days there is a huge gap between most of the European states governed by more or less developed structures of public welfare under the ultimate responsibility of the state on the one hand, and dictatorial, but socially weak states e.g. in the Middle East, South Asia and Northern Africa on the other. The latter by and large are used to accept the distribution of normative power in favour of extended families, clans, tribes etc.

In consequence, family related conflicts are perceived to be first and foremost a private matter, in which the state would only interfere in cases of gross violence of rights. Customary law and customary practices are broadly accepted based on parallel normative orders, including non-state-run mechanisms for the enforcement of decisions.[11] In contrast, strong European states are used to organise unity in diversity by one legal order granting far-reaching "internal" dispositions (dispositive law) instead of establishing parallel legal systems,[12] and to enforce law first and foremost by state institutions.[13] Within this frame, ADR is generally encouraged. These different models co-exist territorially, but increasingly meet because of migration processes whereby immigrants and their descendants are confronted with social exigencies as well as claims of regulation by the law of their new home country. This can lead to normative conflicts, but also creates opportunities for innovative solutions reconciling

---

9 Cf. sect. 278 subsect. 1 German Code of Civil Procedure: "In all circumstances of the proceedings, the court is to act in the interests of arriving at an amicable resolution of the legal dispute or of the individual points at issue."

10 Cf. e.g. The German Mediation Act (2012).

11 Cf. Mathias Rohe, *Islamic Law in Past and Present*, Leiden and Boston 2015 (Brill), 87 ff., 391 ff. with further references.

12 Cf. Mathias Rohe, in Prakash Shah et al. (eds.) (n. 4), 51 ff.

13 For an overview on the factual and legal situation in different parts of the present world cf. only Matthias Kötter, Non-State Justice Institutions: A Matter of Fact and a matter of legislation, in: Matthias Kötter/ Tilman J.Röder/ Gunnar Folke Schuppert/ Rüdiger Wolfrum (eds.), *Non-State Justice Institutions and the Law. Decision-making at the Interface of Tradition, Religion and the State*, Houndmills, Basingstoke 2015 (Palgrave Macmillan), 155–187; Gunnar Folke Schuppert, From Normative Pluralism to a Pluralism of Norm Enforcement Regimes: A Governance Research Perspective, ibid., 188–215.

the indispensable claims of the law and the social, cultural and religious needs of the persons involved. Nevertheless, the mostly simplistic public debate on the issue does not facilitate a fact-based approach.

The European and German Debate

In 2008, the speech of the then Archbishop of Canterbury Rowan Williams on the application of Sharia legal norms in the UK[14] triggered a heated debate on legal pluralism – and on real, as well as perceived, conflicts between Sharia and European legal orders. It has not yet come to an end, since a bill on virtually banning Muslim ADR in Britain (Arbitration and Mediation Services (Equality) Bill 2001 proposed by Baroness Cox is still pending in parliament.[15] In late 2015, a superficial PhD thesis[16] based on only 15 hours of poorly documented fieldwork and selective studies of literature was given extraordinary public repercussion. It was sold as "one of the most detailed academic studies of Sharia courts ever printed."[17] Thorough previous studies e.g. by Samia Bano, Maleiha Malik and others[18] seem to be ignored by sensationalist journalists. In Germany, the public climate has become unfavourable even to academic debate on these issues. I myself was repeatedly accused by the prominent feminist journalist Alice Schwarzer[19] and one of her epigones, the sociologist and

---

14   Cf. Rowan Williams, "Civil and Religious Law in England: A Religious Perspective," available at http://www.archbishopofcanterbury.org/articles.php/1137/archbishops-lecture-civil-and-religious-law-in-england-a-religious-perspective (accessed 27.06.2017); John Milbank, The Archbishop of Canterbury: The Man and the Theology Behind the Shari'a lecture, in Rex Ahdar/ Nicholas Aroney (eds.), *Sharia in the West*, Oxford 2010 (OUP), 43–57; Jean-François Gaudreault-Desbiens, Religious Courts' Recognition Claims: Two Qualitatively Distinct Narratives, ibid., 59–69.

15   Cf. John Bowen, *On British Islam*, Princeton and Oxford 2016 (PUP), 205 ff. The last hearing took place in January 2017. The text is available at https://www.publications.parliament.uk/pa/bills/lbill/2016-2017/0018/17018.pdf (accessed 27.06.2017).

16   Machteld Zee, *Choosing Sharia? Multiculturalism, Islamic Fundamentalism & Sharia Councils*, 2016.

17   Cf. "Inside Britain's Sharia Courts," Mail online 13.12.2015, available at http://www.dailymail.co.uk/news/article-3358625/Inside-Britain-s-Sharia-courts-EIGHTY-FIVE-Islamic-courts-dispensing-justice-UK-special-investigation-really-goes-doors-shock-core.html (accessed 27.06.2017).

18   Cf. the references n. 4.

19   Cf. Patrick Bahners, *Die Panikmacher. Die deutsche Angst vor dem Islam*, München 2011 (C. H. Beck), 233–251.

ALTERNATIVE DISPUTE RESOLUTION AMONG MUSLIMS IN GERMANY   95

activist Necla Kelek,[20] of promoting the replacement of German legal order by Sharia, simply because I *inform* the public about the *existing* German legal order with respect to the treatment of Islamic norms. Such debates demonstrate first and foremost a widespread lack of knowledge regarding the complexity of Sharia as well as with respect to the basics of the rule of law in European countries.

My topic does not cover the scope and limits of the application of Sharia norms in Germany as a whole.[21] Instead, I will concentrate on the legally most complicated field of ADR under religious (and cultural) auspices in the country. This is not only aimed at legal reasoning, but will also demonstrate the impact of public debates on governmental action and its results. It relies on first-hand information, since I was involved in all these governmental initiatives.

Research on Muslim ADR in Germany

Regarding ADR among Muslims in Germany, only one monograph has been published on the issue by the lawyer and journalist Joachim Wagner in 2011 under the title of "Judges without Law – Islamic Parallel Justice Endangers Our Rule of Law."[22] The book describes 16 cases of ADR predominantly among members of Kurdish-Lebanese family clans who immigrated to Germany in the 1980s and 1990s as refugees. The cases dealt with crimes (severe bodily harm, attempt of homicide) and attempts to settle conflicts between the families of the offender and the victim, partly to avoid subsequent blood revenge. Victims and witnesses were put under pressure to stay silent vis-à-vis state institutions, evidence was distorted, only in rare cases a fruitful cooperation between mediators and state officials was reported. The book stressed the role of the so-called justices of peace (Friedensrichter) who mediated the conflicts

---

20   Cf. "Das ist Kulturrelativismus," *FAZ*, February 15, 2011 (available at http://www.faz
      .net/aktuell/feuilleton/islam-debatte-das-ist-kulturrelativismus-1592162.html (accessed
      27.06.2017)) and my reaction in "Das ist Rechtskulturrelativismus," *FAZ*, February 22,
      2011 (available at http://www.faz.net/aktuell/feuilleton/debatten/islam-debatte-das-ist
      -rechtskulturrelativismus-1595144.html (accessed 27.06.2017)).

21   Cf. Mathias Rohe, Shariah in Europe, in: Jocelyne Cesari (ed.), *The Oxford Handbook of
      European Islam*, Oxford 2015 (OUP), 656–700; id., Islamic Norms in Germany and Europe,
      in: Ala al-Hamarneh/Jörn Thielmann (eds.), *Islam and Muslims in Germany*, Leiden 2008
      (Brill), 49–81.

22   Joachim Wagner, *Richter ohne Gesetz. Islamische Paralleljustiz gefährdet unseren
      Rechtsstaat*, Berlin 2011 (Econ).

under the principles of the Islamic Sharia. In a later edition,[23] cases of family conflicts (mainly marriage and divorce-related ones) were added.

Wagner's book gained intense interest in German politics and administration. The Bavarian Ministry of Justice established a working group lead by me and consisting of attorneys general, judges, police officers, lawyers, members of migrants NGOs, institutions working in the social sector and Joachim Wagner (the author of the book). Its aim was to evaluate whether similar phenomena were to be found in Bavaria, and to consider preventive measures to protect victims and witnesses against undue pressure.

First of all, it was necessary to formulate criteria for distinguishing ADR as an appreciated means of conflict resolution in general[24] and "parallel justice" as a challenge for the law of the country. The starting point has to be the protective function of the law and the institutions implementing it. Far-reaching normative pluralism is granted by the German and other European legal orders within the limits of mandatory rules. The latter aim at protecting the interests of the weaker parties, including vulnerable minorities (within minorities),[25] and maintaining the minimum standard of common rules of conduct laid down and defined in parliamentarian legislation. Granting easy access to state institutions is an integral part for the efficient implementation of legal protection.

Thus, ADR under the auspices of any cultural or religious norms is acceptable or even desirable as long as it meets the following prerequisites:

- The parties must freely agree on the ADR mechanism, and opting out at any time has to be granted;
- undue pressure or the exercise of violence against the parties, witnesses or other persons involved must be avoided;
- the ADR process must be performed neutrally and professionally;
- the limits of mandatory law of the country must be respected.

---

23   Berlin 2012 (Ullstein). The subtitle "How imams in Germany apply the Sharia" (Wie Imame in Deutschland die Scharia anwenden).

24   For the scope and limits of ADR under religious auspices cf. Franziska Hötte, *Religiöse Schiedsgerichtsbarkeit*, Tübingen 2013 (Mohr Siebeck), 195 ff. with further references; Kathrin Bauwens, *Religiöse Paralleljustiz. Zulässigkeit und Grenzen informeller Streitschlichtung und Streitentscheidung unter Muslimen in Deutschland*, Berlin 2016 (Duncker & Humblot); for international experiences cf. Michael A. Helfand, Religious Arbitration and the New Multiculturalism: Negotiating Conflicting Legal Orders, New York University Law Review 86 (November 2011), 1231–1305.

25   Cf. Ayalet Shachar, *Multicultural Jurisdictions. Cultural Differences and Women's Rights*, Cambridge 2001 (CUP), 45 ff.

"Parallel justice" would thus describe cases in which at least one of these criteria is violated. With respect to the fields of law covered by "parallel justice," there has been evidence from previous research that criminal cases, family disputes and civil cases regarding contracts (black labour in particular) or property disputes were typical for this phenomenon for various reasons.[26] On the other hand, it should be clear that the definition of "parallel justice" in accordance with institutional criteria is misleading. The debate in Britain on "Islamic Sharia Councils" clearly demonstrates the shortcomings of such an institutional approach. ADR-institutions working in religious or cultural contexts cannot be judged in an abstract way, since European laws open broad space for non-state bodies to engage in conflict resolution. The only relevant question is whether these institutions operate within the framework of the law defined above, or beyond it.

Empirical Evidence Regarding Muslim ADR in Germany

We know that the Ahmadiyya Muslim Jamaat[27] has set up an internal board to decide on religious disputes in Frankfurt. This board has the legitimacy to excommunicate members of the community in cases of gross violation of core convictions of the Ahmadi confession, e.g. if a member has committed a capital crime.[28] Such sanctions would fall under the (collective) freedom of religion according to German constitutional law. No scientific research has been done on the work of this body so far. The same has been true for ADR-related issues among the Muslim population as a whole, forming the second largest religious group in the country.

The more anecdotal information available on "parallel justice" suggests that there are massive problems of violence in structures of organised crime, particularly regarding Eastern European mafia-like organisations. Singular cases similar to those reported by Wagner could be found among several population groups (Yezidis, Roma, Albanians and Africans of different religious

---

26   Cf. Mathias Rohe (n. 1) with further references.

27   The German organisation forms the oldest Muslim community in the country. In 2013, it has been recognised as a corporation under public law in the states of Hesse and Hamburg as the first Muslim organization. This status grants far-reaching rights in public space; for details cf. Mathias Rohe, On the Recognition and Institutionalisation of Islam in Germany, in: Marie-Claire Foblets et al. (eds.), *Cultural Diversity and the Law*, Brussels 2010 (Bruylant), 145–194.

28   Information given to the author by Mr. Wajih bin Sajjid in Berlin in January 2015.

affiliations, East Asians, not least native Germans), but they were not typical for any of these groups. In addition, imams and other members of the Muslim communities reported cases of domestic violence and forced marriage[29] in Bavaria. At first glance it appeared that, given the religious diversity of the persons involved, the main motivation for ADR was rooted in socio-economic and cultural specificities, and in a lack of information about the structures and contents of the German legal system and its institutions. In family matters, Sharia norms played a role. Therefore a publication was prepared in several languages for being distributed among migrant communities. It is re-printed now in large numbers for distribution among refugees arriving in Bavaria, in addition to introductory courses by legal officials organised by the Ministry of Justice.

A working group consisting of representatives of several states and experts elaborated papers for courts and judicial administrations which were approved in November 2015 by the Conference of the Ministers of Justice (of the 16 German states).[30] As a result of the findings of the working group, the Conference agreed on developing measures to ban parallel justice in the country.[31] In late 2014, the Parliament of the State of Berlin had decided to finance a broader study on the particular situation in the State, since Berlin was described as the major hotspot in Wagner's book, and criminal structures of Kurdish-Lebanese

---

29   It should be noted that traditional Islamic law, while demanding the consent of the spouses in principle, has established forced marriage (zawaj al-jabr) as an exceptionally accepted institute; cf. Mathias Rohe (n. 11), 108. Besides that, customary law prevailing within some Muslim communities is even more apprehensive to this institute. Thus, it is untenable to claim that forced marriage was simply an imagined construct of colonial consciousness (this is the opinion of Prakash Shah, Shari'a in the West: colonial consciousness, in: Elisa Giunchi (ed.), *Muslim Family Law in Western Courts*, Abingdon 2014 (Routledge), 14, 23–31). For Germany, cf. Bundesministerium für Familie, Senioren, Frauen und Jugend (BFSFJ), Zwangsverheiratung in Deutschland, 2008; Filiz Sütcu, *Zwangsheirat und Zwangsehe: Fallagen, rechtliche Beurteilung und Prävention*, Frankfurt a.M. et al. 2009 (Peter Lang).

30   Cf. the proceedings of the Parliamentary Law Commitee of the Parliament of North Rhine-Westphalia, 53rd session 9 December 2015, available at https://www.landtag.nrw .de/portal/WWW/dokumentenarchiv/Dokument?Id=MMV16/3523 (accessed 27.06.2017).

31   Conference of the Ministers of Justice, 83rd Session, unanimous decision of 13/14 June 2012:

1. Parallel justice directed against the value system of the Constitution shall not be tolerated.

2. Preventive measures are needed by intense information about the ruling legal system in connection with trust-building measures.

3. Sensitivity regarding parallel justice shall be fostered within the legal administration.

ALTERNATIVE DISPUTE RESOLUTION AMONG MUSLIMS IN GERMANY 99

clans who had taken over the public space in parts of the city were well-known already. The legal fields to be covered were limited to criminal cases and family disputes; the majority of the latter consisted of marriage and divorce cases, including custody issues and matters related to property. The Erlangen Centre for Islam and Law in Europe (EZIRE) was chosen to conduct this study.[32] At the EZIRE, we decided to concentrate on the situation within the Muslim communities, due to their large number and the fact that cases of "parallel justice" were already known to have occurred there. We also briefly looked into the Roma communities, since cases of "parallel justice" within these communities were also reported during our previous work in Bavaria, and because of the religious heterogeneity of these communities.

During the year 2015, we[33] evaluated existing reports[34] and scientific literature. The core part of our work consisted of interviews with representatives of religious Muslim organisations and Muslims working within secular organisations from different ethnic, social and cultural backgrounds,[35] Muslim clan elders and drug dealers, judges, attorneys general, police officers and other members of the administration. In sum, 93 interviews were conducted, some of them repeatedly, lasting between one and four hours. In addition, we attended several meetings of Muslim groups, where in up to 50 persons took part (women's meetings). We used our previous knowledge of the scene for starting the interviews and then relied on a snowball system. Even though our findings cannot claim to be representative, they nevertheless are based on a sample which is the broadest by far until now in Germany, and embedded into

---

32   The German text of 197 pages is available on the website of the Berlin Senate for Justice and Consumer Protection, EZIRE (Erlanger Zentrum für Islam und Recht in Europa/FAU Erlangen-Nürnberg) und Senat von Berlin/Senatsverwaltung für Justiz und Verbraucherschutz, Paralleljustiz, Dezember 2015, available at https://www.berlin.de/sen/justv/service/broschueren-und-info-materialien/ (accessed 27.06.2017).

33   The largest part of the fieldwork was done by Dr. Mahmoud Jaraba, who succeeded in gaining access to interviewees from different migrant groups, including clan elders involved in criminal activities, drug dealers, etc. The author conducted several dozen interviews as well, partly among members of the Muslim and Roma communities, mostly among state officials from all levels.

34   Cf. e.g. Federal Ministry of Justice and Consumer Protection, Gibt es eine Paralleljustiz in Deutschland? Streitbeilegung im Rechtsstaat und muslimische Traditionen, available at https://www.bmjv.de/SharedDocs/Archiv/Downloads/Studie-Paralleljustiz.pdf?__blob =publicationFile&v=4 (accessed 27.06.2017).

35   The interviewees had an ethnic background from Germany, Bosnia-Herzegovina, Albania, Macedonia, Turkey, Morocco, Tunisia, Egypt, Palestine, Jordan, Syria, Lebanon, Pakistan and Bangladesh.

ongoing research in other parts of Germany. Most of our interviewees were only ready to talk frankly under the condition of full anonymity. Having granted this, many interviewees were unexpectedly open and ready to give information about very sensitive issues. Some of them (clan elders) seemingly enjoyed their social power due to "armies"[36] of family supporters behind them.

All our findings are based on cross-check interviews with interviewees from different positions presumably having conflicting interests. If such persons agree on certain observations, it is likely that these observations meet the reality. It might be disappointing that no figures or percentages can be presented. In fact, the Parliament of Berlin initially wanted to know e.g. how many Muslims living in the State resort to ADR mechanisms, as compared to filing claims in state courts. Since secular German courts would not even be allowed to ask the parties about their religious affiliation, no such statistical data can be provided. In addition, experience shows that if figures of percentages are presented in qualitative (non-representative) studies on topics of public relevance, there is no hope that even clear remarks on the very limited value of such figures will be listened to.

Major Findings

Other than in the UK, there is no evidence in Germany for any kind of institutions (MAT, Sharia councils, etc.) providing Muslim ADR in Berlin or in Germany as a whole. Instead, ADR is mostly performed within informal extended family/ clan structures, and by some religious actors in family disputes. The role of so-called Muslim justices of peace is heavily overestimated in public, due to media publications during the debate about Wagner's book. Some of them now make use of the PR granted by media reports.[37] Only within the extremist Salafi spectrum is there first evidence for the establishment of a counter-structure, which explicitly ignores German law and legal institutions for being irrelevant instruments of the "kuffar" (infidels), and provides all sorts of "legal" services for those asking for them. Many imams complained that they would e.g. assist in religious marriages without any regard to the existing laws or the Islamic normative tradition, which leads to legally invalid and Islamically disputed

---

36 In cases of conflict, they are able to gather dozens or even hundreds of persons within a few minutes, who are ready to use violence in promoting the clan's interests.

37 I was contacted by a larger number of journalists who wanted to get in contact with such persons. I refused to provide any information not only because we granted anonymity, but also because I did not wish to support probably misleading reports.

marriages and family bonds. We even heard of cases of polyandric marriages, where the Muslim wife did not disclose an already existing marriage.

Regarding the actors and the norms applied, we have to distinguish criminal cases from family disputes, while there is a certain overlap between the two, e.g. in cases of divorce requests as a consequence of domestic violence.

Criminal Cases

In criminal cases, religious aspects rarely play any role. Typical cases of "parallel justice" arose in the consequence of criminal offenses between members of Kurdish-Lebanese or Arab family clans, who immigrated in huge numbers (up to 8,000) in the 1980s and 1990s mostly as asylum seekers. Many of them[38] are now involved in intense criminal activities, ranging from human and drug trafficking, prostitution, dealing with weapons and blackmailing to capital crimes. A typical case would be a knife attack against another person of a similar ethnic and social background, which might cause blood revenge or at least unrest within the communities. Sometimes clan elders would try to reconcile the parties (more the families than the victims themselves) by offering to pay a certain amount as a compensation and by formal gestures of appreciation, e.g. by visiting the victim in the hospital.[39]

German law does not object to such efforts at all; to the contrary, under the Criminal Code (Sections 46, 46a), efforts of compensation by the offender may reduce or even waive the punishment in case of penal court proceedings; procedures of offender-victim mediation are encouraged by the law. As opposed to some simplifying juxtapositions of informal and formal state systems of conflict resolution regarding offences, the victim is not at all side-lined in these cases of state-controlled reconciliation.[40] Nevertheless, massive problems arise if the victim is pressed to accept unfavourable solutions and severely threatened in case of cooperating with the police and the courts,

---

38   According to interviewees belonging to such clans; cf. Mathias Rohe/ Mahmoud Jaraba (n. 35).

39   Cf. Joachim Wagner (n. 22), 33 ff.

40   Cf. the model developed by Gunnar Folke Schuppert, (n. 13), 191 s.: He considers the victim to be central in informal systems of community-based conflict resolution and "side-lined" in formal state systems. This juxtaposition ignores the possible implementation of the victim's interests in penal proceedings as well as the fact that the victim is free to file a civil claim against the offender, in which he/she is the central actor (claimant).

or if witnesses are threatened the same way. Furthermore, the application of Section 46a of the Criminal Code[41] requires an active role of the offender himself, who is expected to acknowledge his offense and to express his repentance in a credible manner.[42]

This requirement based on a "culture of guilt" might conflict with a "culture of shame," the latter considering such acknowledgment as a "loss of honour" and replacing it by family-based procedures of demonstrating respect instead of re-entering into a debate on the offense and the responsibility for it. Stable conflict resolutions dependent on extended family and clan structures are taken to be more important than state interests regarding the punishment of offenders or preventive goals. Loyalty towards the extended family/clan based on strong patriarchal structures is expected and mostly given. Some clan elders, in full pride of their social power,[43] expressly stated that they would not accept the state's authority over them.

In fact, there were a considerable number of enquiries by attorneys general and court proceedings which came to an end after the victims had withdrawn their formal notification of the crime or their testimonies for unclear reasons.[44] In addition, I was informed about a case of a surprising involvement of a lawyer in assisting the accused, who was sued for having forced a girl into prostitution. The lawyer advised her to withdraw her testimony and to rely on

---

41   The text reads as follows: "If the offender,

    1. in an effort to achieve reconciliation with the victim (offender-victim mediation), has made full restitution or the major part thereof for his offence, or has earnestly tried to make restitution; or

    2. in a case in which making restitution for the harm caused required substantial personal services or personal sacrifice on his part, has made full compensation or the major part thereof to the victim,

    the court may mitigate the sentence (...) or, unless the sentence to be imposed on the offender is imprisonment not exceeding one year or a fine not exceeding three hundred and sixty daily units, may order a discharge." The full text of the German Criminal Code is available at https://www.gesetze-im-internet.de/englisch_stgb/englisch_stgb.html#p0242.

42   Cf. e.g. the decision of the Regional Court of Berlin of 14 November 2014 (unpublished), quoted in Mathias Rohe/ Mahmoud Jaraba (n. 35), 82 ff. with further references.

43   One of the interviewees, a man in his 70s, was asked how he would enforce his decisions in cases of conflicts. His answer was "there is an army behind me." In fact, there were repeated cases of mobilisation of dozens of young men ready for any kind of violence within a few minutes.

44   Besides the information from our interviews cf. the report "Es war nichts, es ist nichts" – Tumulte in Kreuzberg um eine junge Mutter", Der Tagesspiegel 14.01.15, 10 regarding an Arab family well known for criminal activities.

ALTERNATIVE DISPUTE RESOLUTION AMONG MUSLIMS IN GERMANY 103

the right to refuse giving a witness statement according to Section 55 of the Code of Criminal Procedure. The reasoning was that she had professionally earned money, which her "lover" had immediately taken – but not paid business tax for this income. Obviously, this milieu is capable of financing well versed lawyers who are not reluctant to accept mandates whatsoever.

While challenges of the rule of law become evident in such cases, the suspicion of introducing "Sharia mechanisms" into the German legal system by accepting compensatory payments ignores the very same opportunities under German law (damages for pain and suffering). In addition, it is highly unlikely that the actors referr to the Islamic legal concept of "qisas"[45] in this regard: while they might be Muslims indeed, the field of their activities does not form part of the core areas of activities for devout Muslims. Furthermore, very rarely are imams or other religious persons involved in the procedures of reconciliation. It is mostly clan elders who negotiate and decide in accordance with culturally based customary practices. Regularly, imams and other members of mosque associations are more than reluctant to engage in such cases, partly due to fears of exceeding the limits of German law, partly because of the intricate personalities involved. It should be also mentioned that occasionally police officers cooperate with renowned (non-criminal) members of these families/clans for preventing major crimes, e.g. if dozens of persons of inimical families are gathering at the brink of an outburst of heavy fights.

In sum, the criminal cases demonstrate existing problems of parallel justice, but on the basis of customary, culture-based practices rather than religious ones. This conclusion is reaffirmed by a small number of interviews with experts from the Roma communities, who reported similar phenomena irrespective of the religious affiliation (Christians, Muslims, others) of the persons involved, and by other reports from courts and attorneys general regarding members of African communities.

Family Disputes (Marriage, Maintenance and Divorce Cases)

The borders between family disputes and the aforementioned criminal clans' activities, which partly even demonstrate a fundamental conflict between the religious affiliation and the socio-cultural background of the persons involved, are fluid. In some cases of domestic violence committed by clan members, imams and other religious representatives tried to assist the wives and were severely attacked in consequence. In many other cases, there is a mix of religious

---

45   Cf. Mathias Rohe (n. 11), 179 ff.

reasons and aspects of migration driving Muslim family members to resort to ADR mechanisms based on Islamic and/or customary rules.

One of the major reasons for the reluctance to use state institutions for resolving legal conflicts is a widespread lack of information about the contents of German law and the ways how legal institutions operate in daily practice. Many people are not aware of the easily accessible forms of legal aid for those in need, which only require a form available for 10 euro to obtain a lawyer's first advice. Particularly in family conflicts including domestic violence, parties are often advised not to make these conflicts public, in fear of losing their children to state-run shelters. While in fact the Child Protection Services apply this means of last resort only in rare cases of massive damages,[46] the fear is still present in wide circles. One interviewee who had lived in Germany for years opposed marriages of Muslims concluded at the civil registry office, which is the only authority under German marriage law to validly register marriages. The reason given was that this (secular!) office was "the church," which would not be appropriate for Muslim spouses. Others are not informed about the prerequisites for valid marriages concluded in Germany, or are lacking the necessary documents for that, and then resort to merely religious marriages. Until 2009, it was prohibited under German marriage law to have a religious marriage registered before being married under civil law. Since then, solely religious marriages are simply ignored by German law. While there are no representative statistics available for Muslim "religious"[47] marriages in Germany, experts estimate that between 20 and 50% of Muslims would either additionally, or even solely, conclude a religious marriage. Many Muslim organisations refuse to solemnise religious marriages before a civil marriage has taken place, while Salafists do not hesitate at all to participate.

Some imams and organisations declare the German civil marriage (which enables e.g. the presence of two witnesses chosen by the parties if they wish so pursuant to Section 1312 of the Civil Code) to fulfil the prerequisites of an Islamic marriage, while others disagree. In many mosques, marriage contracts are formulated, some of them in a legally professional manner e.g. regarding financial aspects, others lacking any sound legal basis.[48] It has to be mentioned

---

46   Cf. Mathias Rohe/ Mahmoud Jaraba (n. 35), 98 f. with further references.

47   Marriage is a civil contract under Islamic law. Nevertheless, it has a "religious flavor," and thus Islamic family law regulations are taken to be part of the religion of Islam by considerable numbers of Muslims, particularly those from Arab countries and from South Asia, much less among Muslims originating from the Balkans and from Turkey.

48   In our research projects, we have collected around 2,000 mostly hand-written marriage and divorce documents which will be evaluated in the future.

here that under German family law, Islamic marriage contracts are accepted in principle with respect to their non-status-related aspects).[49] Nevertheless, some Muslims are at unease with contemporary German family law, based on gender equality and individual choices, equal treatment of children born out of wedlock and the protection of same-sex relations, and prefer to stick to traditional Islamic rules. Others would purposely avoid the legal consequences of a civil marriage and potential costs of a divorce, but enter into an Islamic religious marriage to make their relation socially acceptable within their families and communities. An increasing number of polygynic relations on such informal basis were reported by many interviewees, partly leading to undue payments of social security funds. In one case, a Muslim wife was religiously married in polyandric marriages, because she had hidden her previous and still existing marriage. While Islamic law is famous for creative practical solutions, this case remains a particular challenge. A feasible solution was indeed found in another case of a marriage which had already existed for 20 years, with three children arising from it. Then the couple found out that they were linked by common breast-feeding, which could render a marriage invalid under traditional Islamic law.[50] A solution was then found on the basis of takhayyur (combining rules of different schools for feasible regulations),[51] given the fact that no witnesses were available for that fact, and that according to some opinions this would be a prerequisite for barring a marriage between those linked by breast-feeding.

In both cases of an additional or a solely religious marriage, there is a religious and even more a social need for many to obtain a religious divorce in cases of fundamental conflicts between the spouses. Otherwise, even in the event of a civil divorce, the parties are still taken to be married within their social environment. While husbands can make use of the easily obtainable institution of talaq[52] and might take more than one wife, wives are in need of mechanisms dealing with their rights to tafriq or khul' under Islamic law. Here, imams and other representatives of religious associations are frequently consulted for assistance.[53]

---

49   Cf. BGH NJW 1999, 574; Nadjma Yassari, *Die Brautgabe im Familienvermögensrecht*, Tübingen 2014 (Mohr Siebeck).

50   Cf. Rohe (n. 11), 104 with further references.

51   Cf. Rohe (n. 11), 240 ff. with further references.

52   Cf. Rohe (n. 11), 116 ff., 275 ff. with further references.

53   For details cf. Mahmoud Jaraba, *Khulʿ in Germany: Mutual Consent as Opposed to Litigation*, to be published in ILAS 2017.

According to many interviewees, domestic violence, criminal activities, drug addiction, gambling and the neglect of the family by the husbands are the main reasons for divorce pleas of the wives. Regarding the benefits of the comparatively generous German social welfare system, the family gains economic independence from the husband, who is solely responsible for family maintenance under traditional Islamic law. In one case, a wife told her children when passing a bank ATM counter: "This is your father." In other cases, wives earn their own living and do not accept the gender-biased family regulations of traditional Islamic law linking male rule with the male role of providing for maintenance. More generally spoken, there is a potential for conflicts between wives who have grown up in Germany, and immigrant husbands who maintain their patriarchal convictions and attitudes to compensate the factual loss of their traditional role by using violence.

Representatives of religious organisations often lack information about the scope limits of German law regarding ADR as well as sound knowledge of Islamic law. According to Jamal Malik's and Misbahur Rehman's observations, "most of the leaders of diasporic religious communities are self-made scholars who have been nominated by their communities due to their socio-economic, in seldom cases also religio-cultural capital."[54] In addition, a lack of cultural sensitivity among members of state administrations and courts, and real or perceived discrimination are important factors for distrust, or at least reluctance, to cooperate. Some interviewees said that they felt embarrassed by the procedures dealing with highly sensitive personal issues. The "culture of shame" might collide with the typical German way of a very direct and outright mode of conversation, which is unfamiliar to many other peoples in and beyond Europe. In recent years, courses for state officers on religio-cultural factors and needs in communication are increasingly offered and sought in the academies for vocational training.

In sum, regarding family disputes among Muslims regulated by ADR mechanisms, we have to distinguish between cases of professional aid willingly asked for by all the parties involved within the limits of German mandatory law, and other cases. The latter cases, which form part of the "parallel justice," occur relatively rarely due to a deliberate rejection of German law; the Salafist spectrum and criminals stand for that. Much more frequently, decisions are made under ignorance of the existing law and the lack of legal enforceability of the decisions. Furthermore, many imams complain about excessive demand by members of the community, for which they are not prepared, neither regarding

---

54   Jamal Malik/ Musbahur Rehman, Islamic Law and Mediation, in: Werner Gephart et al. (eds.), *Legal Cultures in Transition*, Frankfurt a.M. 2015, (Vittorio Klostermann), 202–230.

their professional skills, nor with respect to resources. An attempt to form a common board of Muslim representatives to set up standards for dealing with the aspects of marriage and divorce apt for ADR has recently failed due to deep internal controversies.

We are continuing research on ADR among Muslims in Bavaria as a part of a study on Muslims in Bavaria for the Bavarian Academy of Sciences and the Bavarian Government, and in other parts of Germany (greater Frankfurt, several cities in North Rhine-Westphalia, Hannover) to get a broader picture on the situation in Germany as a whole, which will hopefully be published in book form in the foreseeable future.

Conclusion

In sum, a number of conflicting areas can be identified regarding religio-cultural ADR and the law.

(1) Fact and fiction – the public debate often lacks sound information and the necessary distinction between acting under the freedom of religion and violations of the law. In addition, socio-cultural motives driving the actors are frequently attributed to their religion without proper evidence.

(2) Crime and the rule of law – Some of the ADR mechanisms qualify as "parallel justice" in the sense of rooting (mostly) in criminal activities and using criminal methods for "resolving" conflicts.

(3) A clash of legal cultures/cultures of resolving conflicts – The German legal order and its institutions, like others within the EU, are reliable and protect the rights of the individuals on a high level of the rule of law, despite all shortcomings in daily practice. In contrast, many immigrants had good reasons to fundamentally distrust the regimes and institutions of their native countries. This lack of trust might be "imported" and maintained under certain living conditions. In addition, the self-understanding of European legal orders does not allow to treat law-related conflicts as being merely private issues, thus protecting the interests of the weaker parties even in case of formal reconciliation by mandatory rules and state activity.

(4) Applying the law equally. Theory and practice – German law grants a fair and equal application of the law. Nevertheless, in practice there are experiences of lacking cultural sensitivity in administrative and court procedures, and of real or perceived discrimination, all of which may prevent people from resorting to state institutions. Measures to further improve

the relatively high standard of efficient legal protection are increasingly developed and applied, but still need to be extended. On the other hand, there is an urgent need formulated by Muslim representatives themselves for professionalising persons involved in ADR. Professionalisation is equally needed regarding the mechanisms of ADR and the contents, opportunities and limits of German law as well as of Islamic normativity, and the possibilities of cooperation with state institutions and professional secular NGOs.

(5) Religion and religious extremism – While the overwhelming majority of Muslims in Germany subscribe to the principles of the existing legal order,[55] some extremist groups like political or jihadist Salafis openly reject it, and seemingly start to establish a counter-system without building up fixed institutions so far. Thus, it is the common interest of German society as a whole, including its Muslims, to broaden the basis for making the law an accepted, living experience for the overwhelming majority who wish to live a self-determined life with the efficient protection of the state for those in need for it.

---

55 Cf. Mathias Rohe, *Der Islam in Deutschland: Eine Bestandsaufnahme*, Munich 2016 (C.H. Beck), 235–242, for further references.

CHAPTER 7

Islamic Law in Lithuania? Its Institutionalisation, Limits and Prospects for Application

Egdūnas Račius

With the numbers of people of Muslim cultural background steadily increasing in most European countries in the past quarter of a century, recently discussions have emerged on the feasibility, scope, place and role of Islamic law in Europe. By now, several dozen studies (McGoldrick 2009, Christoffersen & Nielsen 2010, Büchler 2011, Mehdi & Nielsen 2011, Cumper 2014, Karčić 2015, Kruininger 2015 etc.) dealing with one or more aspects of the issue have been published in English. Since 2014, Brill Academic Publishers has been publishing Annotated Legal Documents on Islam in Europe under the editorial team headed by Prof. Jørgen S. Nielsen, who has personally been particularly interested in the feasibility and application of Islamic law in Europe, and to whom this article, as indeed the entire volume, is dedicated.

Speaking generally, in regards to the inclusion of Islamic law into their legal systems, European countries fall into two broad, and heterogeneous, categories: those that prefer to keep it out and those that have allowed it in. Among the first is Slovakia, where Islam is not yet even officially institutionalised, or Moldova, where much of the political elite is vehemently opposed to it having been institutionalised, exemplifying the extreme end of the former category. Of the latter category are the UK, Bosnia, Ukraine, and ... Lithuania.

This chapter is devoted to an analysis of the potential for the application of Islamic law in Lithuania, directly enshrined and indirectly implied in the current Lithuanian legal system. It investigates the state of the art and future prospects, in view of the ongoing changes in the composition of the Muslim community, in terms of cultural background, religiosity, and the understanding of the contents of Islam and the place of Islamic law in the personal and communal life among the country's Muslim population. This chapter also takes into account the credit of tolerance in both the politico-legal system and society at large for the prospective increase in demands from the Lithuania's Muslims to apply Islamic law in the country. The analysis of the situation up to date leads the author to make the conclusion that although there is nominally comparatively much space for the application of the Islamic law in Lithuania, because of low demand from the Muslim side, it has not been realised. On the

© KONINKLIJKE BRILL NV, LEIDEN, 2018 | DOI 10.1163/9789004362529_008

other hand, if and when the demand for the application of the Islamic law among the country's Muslims grows, there is a high likelihood that the legal regulations and the social attitudes will become less accepting of it.

Islam and the State in Lithuania

The Constitution of Lithuania (Article 43) explicitly makes a distinction between what it refers to as "traditional" and merely "registered" churches and religious organisations, however, without indicating which ones fall under which category. Nevertheless, Islam, albeit only in its Sunni version, was included among the nine traditional faiths in a *lex specialis*, as Article 5. Traditional Religious Communities and Associations of Lithuania of the Law on Religious Communities and Associations (adopted in 1995) states: "The State shall recognise nine traditional religious communities and associations existing in Lithuania, which comprise a part of Lithuania's historical, spiritual and social heritage: Roman Catholic, Greek Catholic, Evangelical Lutheran, Evangelical Reformed, Russian Orthodox, Old Believer, Judaist, Sunni Muslim and Karaite." This makes Lithuania rather unique in the European Union context, though, admittedly, several other Eastern European non-EU countries, particularly those with significant numbers or share of Muslims in their populations, have also recognised Islam as a traditional religion on the territory of the respective country.

The uniqueness of the Lithuanian case, from the legal point of view, first of all stems from the fact that there is no state religion (as stated in Article 43 of the Constitution) in Lithuania and formally all traditional religious communities are equal, both vis-à-vis the state and among themselves. This way, the Sunni Muslim community, whose share in the country's population, which according to the most recent census figures (2011) was less than 0.1 per cent, has the same rights as the Catholic community, which stood at over 77 per cent!

Secondly, the Law distinguishes between traditional and non-traditional religious communities (Articles 5, 6), and, despite Article 3. Equality of People Regardless of their Religion of the Law, which states that "All individuals, regardless of religion they profess, their religious convictions or their relationship with religion, shall be equal before the law. It shall be prohibited to, directly or indirectly, restrict their rights and freedoms, or to apply privileges.", Articles 10. Formalisation of Legal Personality of Traditional Religious Communities and Associations, and 11. Granting of Legal Personality to Other Religious Communities and Associations establish a clear distinction between the two categories of religious communities and associations, not least in respect of the status and rights of their legal persons. For instance, Article 14. Educational, Charity and Benevolent Activities of Religious Communities, Associations and Centres, *inter alia*, stipulates that "Educational and training establishments of traditional religious communities and associations providing general education of the national standard shall be funded and maintained in accordance with the procedure established by the Government or an institution authorised by it, allocating the same amount of the budget funds as allocated to state or municipal educational establishments of the corresponding type (level)"; and in this way clearly prioritizing traditional religious communities over non-traditional ones.

Following the Constitution and specifically the Law on Religious Communities and Associations, and particularly its Article 5., which explicitly includes Sunni Muslims among traditional religious communities of Lithuania, non-Sunni Muslims by default fall into the category of non-traditional religious communities. In consequence, Shi'i, Ibadi, Ahmadi and any non-denominational Muslims are formally separated by law from Sunni Muslims. From the point of view of history, this is justifiable – on the territory of Lithuania, there have historically been only Sunni Muslims of the Hanafi legal tradition, in the person of an ethno-confessional group regionally known as Lithuanian Tatars.[1] And though the Law on Religious Communities and Associations does not mention them by name, it is them and only them who are implied under the designation "Sunni Muslims" in the Law. However, as the Law is more inclusive, non-Tatar non-Hanafi Sunnis by default are also included into the category of this traditional religious community. Ultimately, from the legal point of view, Muslims in Lithuania fall into two distinct categories: the traditional religious community, comprising besides the historical Sunni Hanafi Tatars all other (non-Tatar and / or non-Hanafi) Sunnis irrespective of their cultural background or place of origin, on the one hand, and non-traditional religious community(ies) comprised of non-Sunnis of whatever origin and cultural background.

The Law on Religious Communities and Associations foresees that religious communities may operate without formal registration. However, if they want to become "state recognised" religious communities, i.e. to be recognised as "being a part of Lithuania's historical, spiritual and social heritage," they first need to formally register with the Ministry of Justice, i.e. become legal persons

---

1 On the history of Islam in Lithuania, see Račius, E. (2009) "Islam in Lithuania' in Larsson, G. (ed.) *Islam in the Nordic and Baltic Countries* (London and New York: Routledge), 116–32; Račius, E. (2011) "Muslims in Lithuania. Revival at the expense of survival?' in Górak-Sosnowska, K. (ed.) *Muslims in Poland and Eastern Europe. Widening the European Discourse on Islam* (Warsaw: University of Warsaw Press), 207–21.

("state registered") and after the period of 25 years after their first registration they may apply for the status of "state recognised religious community." But the Law also stipulates (Article 6) that such applicant community needs to have a "back[ing] by society" and the "instruction and rites thereof are not contrary to laws and morality." In the case of rejection, they may reapply after a period of another ten years.

So, any non-Sunni Muslim community might expect to become a "state recognised religious community" only after 25 years after its initial registration and only if it has widespread support in the society, something that is rather difficult to imagine in the overall atmosphere of latent and at times manifest Muslimophobia[2] in Lithuania – in public opinion polls Muslims constantly rank among the three least liked social groups by the Lithuanian population. Therefore, non-Sunni Muslims, who may never expect to be recognised as a traditional religious community, might have a hard time attaining even a status of "state recognised" religious community and might have to choose between mere registration with the state, which gives few benefits, and remaining unregistered. There, of course, is yet another option – register as a public enterprise rather than as a religious community / organisation.

The legal distinction between the several categories ("traditional," "state recognised," "registered," and unregistered) of religious communities in the country implies their unequal status (actually, endorsed by the Constitutional Court in several of its decisions, particularly the one of 2007 in reply to a request by the Ministry of Justice (Vitkauskaitė-Meurice 2017), which becomes particularly evident in practical application of the law in various fields to be discussed below. In this regard, one is to always keep in mind that Sunni Muslims in Lithuania have a distinctly different status, with all the ensuing consequences, from any non-Sunni Muslims.

It may be noted that traditional religious communities in Lithuania for the past 20 years have been receiving, through their legal persons, annual pay-outs from the state, the amounts of which are divided proportionally, based on the number of believers recorded by the Department of Statistics (the question on religious identity is included in the population census). This way, the Catholic

---

2 Though the more common term is Islamophobia, I find Muslimophobia to be a more adequate term as it refers to contempt for a category of people, who are seen as a collective body with a set of common features of habitual behavior, which, though erroneously may be attributed to the religion of Islam, is often of non-religious and sometimes even anti-Islamic nature. So, while Islamophobia is confined to strictly religious matters, Muslimophobia goes beyond religion to encompass lay culture also.

Church gets the bulk, with the Orthodox Church being a distant second and the remaining seven traditional religious communities receiving peanuts. But it is not the size of the amount that matters here but the fact that the state, in the person of successive governments has been since 1997 distributing such pay-outs exclusively to traditional religious communities based on the annually adopted Law on the Budget, which routinely grants a right to the government to allocate such funding. The traditional religious communities may use the received funds at their own discretion and not even need to report back to the state on how they were spent. Sunni Muslim community, on its part, spends the money (ranging between three and four thousand euros) mainly on the maintenance of the mosques and other communal premises as well as cemeteries.

Muslim Communities and Demography

As of 2017, of the nine officially registered Muslim religious communities in Lithuania under the category of "traditional religious community," only five had the word "Sunni" in the title. Six were established and are run exclusively by Lithuanian Tatars, while three (all in the seaport city Klaipėda in the west of the country, where historically there was no Lithuanian Tatar presence) have mixed memberships, comprised of Muslims of immigrant background, converts and Lithuanian Tatars.

Irrespective of whether the word "Sunni" is or is not present in their title, all nine registered Muslim communities are, at least nominally, Sunni, as either their representatives were the founding fathers of or the founding of these communities themselves was endorsed by the pan-Lithuanian umbrella Muslim organisation – the Spiritual Center of Lithuanian Sunni Muslims – the Muftiate, itself founded in 1998 in direct reaction to the Law on Religious Communities and Associations and particularly its Article 10 Formalisation of Legal Personality of Traditional Religious Communities and Associations, on whose board representatives of these communities sit. The founding fathers of the Muftiate were Lithuanian Tatars who made sure the title of the organisation includes the word Sunni, as only then, it was argued (Sitdykovas, 1999, 1), the Muftiate may have hoped to be put on the books as a legal entity representing a traditional religious community in the country, namely Sunni Muslims. Article 1.1. of the Muftiate's Statute states that the Muftiate is "the supreme governing body of Lithuanian Sunni Muslims" (Muftiate, 1998), implying that all current and future Sunni communities (presumed by default to fall under the category of "traditional religious community") are to be subordinated to the Muftiate and that there may be no rival or alternative "supreme governing body" or Muftiate.

In 2013, the Muftiate jointly with the Turkish Presidency of Religious Affairs, Diyanet, founded a public enterprise "Center of Islamic Culture and Education." This organisation, which in its nature is Sunni – its board is comprised of Turkish and Tatar Sunni Muslims, owns premises in central Vilnius bought on Turkish money and houses the Muftiate and the Vilnius Muslim community. The Center's headquarters serve as the sole public Friday prayer space in the town and also provide classrooms for the makeshift Islamic weekend school. One may say that, in the absence of a purpose-built mosque, the Center's premises are the sole public space for communal activities of the city's Muslim population.

Another Muslim public enterprise "Education and Heritage" was founded in 2014 by Lithuanian converts to Islam and is housed in Kaunas mosque. However, unlike the Vilnius-based "Center of Islamic Culture and Education," which is by all means Sunni, "Education and Heritage" may not as easily be assigned a denominational label. In fact, as a large number of Lithuanian converts to Islam, who are both rank and file of "Education and Heritage," are of non-denominational and / or revivalist leanings, with some of them identifying with Salafi creed, it is best to be described as a denominationally nondescript organisation. Nonetheless, the "Education and Heritage" for the past several years has been the most (if not the single) active Muslim organisation in Lithuania with its educational and missionary activities aimed at primarily converts and the wider public. It has been cooperating with the "Center of Islamic Culture and Education" through using its premises in Vilnius for the Islamic weekend school.

One needs to point out that for a quarter of a century of Lithuania's independence (1990) there has been only one attempt to register a non-Sunni Muslim organisation in the country – an Ahmadi, back in the early 1990s, before the Law On Religious Communities and Associations of 1995 was drafted. But even in that case, it was done through the Tatars who soon realised that they had been used by Ahmadi missionaries to their own advantage. And though the Ahmadi community was formally registered with the state, it never actually existed and no activities were carried out in its name. Ahmadis retreated not to return to Lithuania until the 2010s. However, to this day, there hardly is an Ahmadi presence in the country and no second attempt has been made by them to register their community anew.

A New Age type Hazrat Inayat Khan Sufism Study Circle was officially registered with the Ministry of Justice in 2002 as a non-traditional religious community – a "community of non-Islamic Sufism," which itself was put under the category of "stocks of Islamic nature." However, as its members do not identify themselves as Muslims, and, moreover, the community's activities appear to have dwindled by the mid-2010s, it is of no relevance for the present discussion.

There has not yet been any attempt by any of the Shiʻi denominations to formalise their presence in Lithuania in the form of a religious community, though there are well over 500 Lithuanian citizens of Azerbaijani origin, some, if not most, of whom may be of Shiʻi Ithna ʻashari (Imami) cultural background, as well as several dozen of other individuals of Shiʻi, mainly also Ithna ʻashari (Imami), cultural background. However, there is a little known public enterprise "Center of Shiʻi Muslims in the Baltic States" with formal headquarters in the Lithuanian capital Vilnius.

Though Lithuanian Tatars are the historical backbone of the country's more than six-hundred-year-old Muslim community, today they make just slightly over half of Lithuania's Sunni Muslims – 1,441 (or 52.8 per cent) of 2,727, according to the 2011 census results. By comparison, in the 2001 census, of 2,860 Sunni Muslims, 1,679 (or 58.7 per cent) were ethnic Tatars. Moreover, the 2011 census showed that the number of ethnic Tatars in the country decreased by 13.7 per cent in a decade: from 3,235 in 2001 to 2,793 in 2011 (Statistics Lithuania, 2012, p. 20) and only 51.6 per cent of them identified with Islam in 2011. The second biggest ethnic group in the Lithuanian Sunni Muslim community in 2011 was Lithuanians with 374 (in 2001 – 185) Sunni Muslims (Department of Statistics 2013: 14), presumably of convert background. There also were 73 ethnic Russian and 15 Polish Sunni Muslims (many if not most of whom were also of convert background), with 794 (from among 157 Uzbeks, 144 Kazakhs, 93 Arabs, 88 Turks, 84 Bashkirs, 76 Chechens, 43 Tajiks, 30 Turkmens, 29 Egyptians, 19 Pakistanis) assigned to a general category "others." There were also 648 Azerbaijanis in the country at the time of the census but it is not known how many of them, if at all any, identified as Sunni Muslims.

In view of the demographic composition of the Sunni Muslim community in Lithuania, one may draw a conclusion that though Islam in Lithuania is still first and foremost represented by the more than half a millennium old Lithuanian Tatar segment, with their numbers dwindling and the steady increase in the ethnic Lithuanian and other convert component, the face of Islam in Lithuania is slowly but surely changing. If, or when, Lithuania becomes a more attractive destination for migrants from the Muslim majority lands, the demographic balance may take yet another turn. But for now, in the realm of Islamic beliefs and practices in the country, it is the Lithuanian Tatars (through their controlled state-recognised traditional religious communities and other

Muslim organisations, like the Muftiate and the "Center of Islamic Culture and Education") on ethnic Lithuanians and other Muslims of convert background (individually and in the person of their founded public enterprise "Education and Heritage"). As is shown further below, such division of the Lithuania's Sunni Muslim community into two groups of actors and their juxtaposition is imperative for the discussion on the practical application of the Islamic law in the country.

Islamic Law in Lithuania – The Potential, the Reality, and the Prospects

A   *The Potential*

The official recognition of Sunni Muslims as a traditional religious community appears to directly and even more so indirectly confer the right to them to practice certain aspects of Islamic law as part of the overall legal system in Lithuania. However, Sunni Muslims should not be seen as having been separately granted exceptional rights vis-à-vis other, particularly, traditional religious communities. Rather, the overt (stated in the Law on Religious Communities and Associations and other legal acts) and implied rights for the country's Muslims come as a corollary to the rights conferred to and further claimed by the mammoth traditional religious community, the Catholics, for, as indicated above, all traditional religious communities are equal, both before the state and among themselves. Consequently, whatever right the Catholics are provided with by the state, it by extension applies to other traditional religious communities. The Catholic Church in Lithuania has claimed a wide spectrum of rights directly ensuing from or indirectly implied in the aforementioned Law and a range of other legal acts, including but not limited to establishing religious organisations, construction of churches and other buildings for religious uses (such as monasteries), religious instruction in public schools, confessional educational establishments (kindergartens, primary, secondary and high schools), religious marriage and funeral rites, chaplaincy in public institutions (armed forces, prisons, hospitals), state-provided health insurance for clergy and those studying at clergy-training seminaries, diplomatic immunity to ecclesiastical leadership, and celebration of and days off during religious holidays. These and many other rights have by extension been granted to the country's Sunni Muslim community. Most of these rights are enshrined in separate relevant laws, where traditional religious communities are specifically mentioned, albeit as a group, with no individual ones mentioned by name.

ISLAMIC LAW IN LITHUANIA?

Admittedly, not all formally and informally granted rights for Muslims to practice Islam in Lithuania need to be viewed as manifestations of the Islamic law. However, if the Islamic law is taken holistically (as expression of Sharia, an arguably wider concept), as it indeed is in this chapter, in order to lead as Islamic way of life as possible, Muslims need to have these and many more rights. In other words, the right to live their religion as comprehensively as possible means that the Islamic law is implicitly included in that right, which itself generally stems from the legal system and, in particular, from concrete laws.

In practical terms, such aspects of the Islamic practice (and by extension, the wider understood Islamic law) as *nikah* marriage, donning of *hijab*, *halal* slaughter and *halal* meals at state institutions, *janaza* funeral, *qitan* circumcision, and many others, following the Law on Religious Communities and Associations, have been legalised by the state.[3] In this regard, comparatively viewed, Lithuania is among the few European countries with such a vast array of Islamic practices (aka aspects of Islamic law) that have been included into the legal system of the country.

Islamic Marriage

Traditional religious communities in Lithuania are granted by Civil Code the right of religious marriage, which is recognised by the state as legally valid with all the ensuing consequences. So, Sunni Muslims, instead of using municipal registry office for the occasion, may resort to the way envisioned by the Islamic law and perform *nikah* marriage in front of an imam (of a Sunni Muslim religious community), who is recognised by the state as a surrogate public registrar and charged with doing the needed paperwork and submitting the relevant documents to the municipal registry office for formal registration of the marriage. Meanwhile, the newlyweds are not required to show up in person at the registry office. The marriage contract signed at the *nikah* ceremony is also recognised by the state, unless it contains something illegal under the Lithuanian laws, as the civil law in Lithuania recognises the institute of marriage contracts.

Islamic Funeral

The Law on Burial of Human Remains establishes that traditional religious communities may have denominational cemeteries, therefore Sunni Muslims in Lithuania are entitled to exclusive Muslim cemeteries. Though the Law

---

3   For a comprehensive overview of the Lithuanian legal documents covering Islamic practice / Islamic law, see Vitkauskaitė-Meurice, Dalia. *Annotated Legal Documents on Islam in Europe: Lithuania*, Brill, 2017.

generally requires a period of 24 hours since the moment of death to have passed before the corpse may be buried, its Article 25 notes that religious convictions of the deceased and his / her relatives may determine the actual timing of burying. This clause allows Muslims to perform burial sooner than the lapse of the required 24 hours. Furthermore, Article 20 of the Law stipulates that the process of burying needs to respect the religious convictions of the burying people. This may be read as implying that, *inter alia*, Muslims may bury their dead according to the Islamic regulations.

Islamic Religious Instruction and Education

As indicated above, Article 14 of the Law on Religious Communities and Associations explicitly states that "Educational and training establishments of traditional religious communities and associations providing general education of the national standard shall be funded and maintained in accordance with the procedure established by the Government or an institution authorised by it, allocating the same amount of the budget funds as allocated to state or municipal educational establishments of the corresponding type (level)." Sunni Muslims, therefore, may not only establish denominational educational institutions of all levels (including imam-training seminaries) but such institutions would be financed from the state coffers. Additionally, the laws regulating the Lithuanian educational system envision religious instruction in Sunni Islam to Sunni Muslim pupils in public schools with catechists paid by the state. Though in itself the right to Islamic religious instruction in public schools and denominational education is not directly related to the Islamic law *per se*, educational institutions of Sunni Muslims and Islamic instruction in public schools would be the environment in which the Islamic law (in the form of Islamic morals and ethics) would be taught.

Islamic Chaplaincy in State Institutions

Though Lithuania constitutionally is a secular state, traditional religious communities are granted by the Law on Religious Communities and Associations the right to engage in religious worship and have their chaplains in state institutions including the armed forces, hospitals, and penitentiary institutions if there is demand from the side of believers. The right also covers premises – chapels – devoted to religious services.

Islamic Slaughter and Halal Meals at State Institutions

Through an exception in the Animal Welfare Law, Sunni Muslims, together with two other traditional religious communities, Judaists and Karaites, are

ISLAMIC LAW IN LITHUANIA? 119

granted the right to religious ritual slaughter, in this case Islamic. Consequently, trading in halal meat and meat products is also legal. By extension, offer of religiously sanctioned meals, in the case of Muslims, halal, in state institutions is implied.

Islamic Dress

There are no rules limiting religious dress in public or for pupils in schools in Lithuania, and members of traditional religious communities are even allowed to submit personal photos with headgear and other religious attire for official documents. It is only required that such a person produces a document issued by the authorities of his / her religious community stating that wearing of a particular attire is required in his / her religion. Ultimately, donning of hijab or other Muslim women's dressing which does not cover the face is perfectly legal. Niqab and burqa, though, are proscribed through the ban, on security grounds, on face covering of any nature, secular or religious.

The provided list of Islamic practices is not exhaustive and is only meant as an indication of to what extent Sharia has been allowed into the country's legal system in Lithuania, either as exceptional rights relevant to Sunni Muslims or as rights granted more generally to traditional religious communities. And although (Sunni) Muslims certainly do not have a privileged position vis-à-vis other traditional religious communities, and one even might reasonably argue that it is the Catholics who do, the spectrum of Islamic rights granted to them is arguably impressive. On the other hand, having a right is not the same as using it – the supply needs to be actualised by demand to practice those rights granted by the state to traditional religious communities.

B   *The Reality*

The supply (in the sense of the facilitation of the conditions conducive to practicing of the Islamic law) on the state's side may be met only if there is a corresponding demand sustained by the Muslim community and particularly its leadership in the person of imams led by the mufti. On this count, one may observe that the Muslim religious establishment has been conspicuously quiet in the public domain on the issue of the applicability and scope of the Islamic law in the country. Consequently, whatever public demand there is for the application of Islamic norms in the country, it comes from the grassroots of the community, however, not from the majority segment, the Tatars, but mainly from the Muslims of convert and immigrant background. In the end, the implementation of religious rights of the country's Muslims mainly involves non-Tatar Muslims.

Islamic Marriage

Annually, up to a dozen of *nikah* ceremonies, with the signing of a marriage contract, are presided over by the mufti and other imams. In most cases, it is a foreign groom and a local bride, as a rule of convert background. In some cases, the brides are non-Muslim Lithuanian nationals. In this regard, one may conclude that this aspect of Islamic law is not only available to but rather actively implemented by Muslims in Lithuania.

Islamic Funeral

Historically, Muslims in Lithuania, in the person of Lithuanian Tatars, have had their separate cemeteries since their settling in Lithuania. Most Muslim cemeteries were located next to mosques. A dozen cemeteries (in Nemėžis, Raižiai, on the outskirts of Vilnius, and elsewhere) have survived to the present day, and some still serve as burial sites for the community. A separate section was allocated for the Muslim community in one of the cemeteries of the western seaport city Klaipėda in 2011. Though many of Tatars today are buried in a regular Lithuanian fashion – in a coffin, some are still buried in an Islamic way – without a coffin, with the body having been wrapped in shroud. So far, as most expatriates and converts are of young age, there have been very few funerals of them in Lithuanian cemeteries and it is not known to what extent Islamic requirements are followed.

Religious Instruction and Education

Though the law grants the right to denominational educational institutions to Sunni Muslims, there have yet been no attempts to set up any such institution, apparently because of the absence of demand, which in itself is directly related to low numbers of school-age Muslim children. The lack of demand for Islamic instruction in public schools also meant that after several aborted attempts by the local imams to provide it to Tatar Muslim pupils in the 2000s, for the past ten years, providing of Islamic religious instruction in public schools has not been offered in any Lithuanian public school. By the way, Sunni Muslims are the sole remaining traditional religious community in Lithuania, which has no Ministry of Education approved curriculum of Islamic religious instruction in schools.[4] On the other hand, informal Islamic education is provided in improvised weekend schools with volunteer "teachers" of convert and

---

4 For a comprehensive analysis of Islamic religious instruction in Lithuania, see Račius, E. "(Re)discovering One's Religion – Private Islamic Education in Lithuanian Muslim Communities" in Jenny Berglund (ed.), *European Perspectives on Islamic Education and Public Schooling*, Equinox, 2018 (forthcoming).

immigrant background. The "students" are mainly converts and their children or children of mixed parentage.

Islamic Chaplaincy in State Institutions

There are no permanent Islamic chaplains at any Lithuanian state institutions such as armed forces, prisons, or hospitals, as there is virtually no need for their services, though imams, at the request of individual Muslims, do occasionally visit hospitals and prisons. A notable case in this regard was a formal complaint submitted to the Ombudsman of Equal Opportunities by a Muslim inmate (apparently of a convert background) at a Vilnius prison who argued that he, being of a traditional religious community, like his Christian fellow inmates, who are regularly served by a Catholic priest, has the right to such services by an imam. The mufti was asked to pay a visit to the inmate.

Islamic Slaughter and Halal Meals at State Institutions

There are several meat-processing plants in Lithuania with halal certification provided by either the mufti or foreign imams. The slaughter is performed by local and expatriate Muslims and the bulk of produce is exported abroad, as there is very little demand for halal meat and its products locally. There are a few food stores that cater for Muslims' needs with locally produced and imported halal food and there are just a handful of restaurants in the major cities serving dishes made from halal meat. None of the state institutions have halal option and Muslims are instead offered vegetarian option. There have been several formal complaints submitted to the Ombudsman of Equal Opportunities by illegal migrants of Muslim background at the Foreigner Registration Center, who complained of having been deprived of their dietary rights to have pork-free meals and also utensils that had not been use for pork storage or cooking. The Foreigner Registration Center was obliged to split food preparing process to facilitate Muslims' dietary requirements.

Islamic Dress

Only a handful of Muslim women (mostly of convert background) wear hijab publicly in Lithuania, mainly on Fridays while attending communal prayer. No niqab-wearing Muslim females have been observed in Lithuania. Although some of the female Lithuanian converts to Islam have informally complained of being insulted for wearing hijab, no formal complaints have been filed and no cases of discrimination on the basis of Islamic attire have been reported.

When checked against each other, the potential and the reality reveal a picture in which it is evident that while the Lithuanian legal system is nominally exceptionally open to and inclusive of the Islamic law, the country's Sunni Muslims, due to a variety of reasons, first of all because of their miniscule numbers, but more importantly, because of the lack of demand for the practicing of the Islam law, have used the system to their benefit to a very limited extent. Furthermore, among those who make use of the Islamic law, it has been mainly Muslims of convert and immigrant background, while the Tatars have remained on the margins. To tell the truth, Tatars are least inclined to apply Islamic norms in their lives, something for which they have been constantly reprimanded by convert and expatriate Muslims.

C   *The Prospect*

So long as the Muslim community remains both numerically insignificant and, more importantly, reluctant to push for the implementation of more religious rights implied (or presumed to be included) in the recognition of Islam by the state as a traditional religion in the country, the comfortable *status quo*, with Islam being recognised as a traditional religion in the country, will not be upset. However, when more observant (and thus demanding) Muslims (prospectively, of convert or immigrant background) either ascend to the power positions within the existing community structures or create their own alternative power bases and proceed to claim the presumed rights, the status of Islam in the country might start changing significantly, both on the official and public levels, as this would cause friction and tension not only between the officially secular state and the generally post-religious majority, on the one side, and the increasingly visible observant part of the Muslim minority, on the other side, but within the Muslim community itself.

The system with "traditional" religious communities, especially in the Lithuanian case, is itself very problematic in at least two respects. The first problem is the registration of new "traditional" religious communities of the same faith. As the official of the Lithuanian Ministry of Justice who has been personally supervising registration of religious organisations laments, "there have been a number of problems related to registration of traditional religious communities. The Law on Religious Communities and Associations does not name particular organisations that the state recognises as traditional, it only names confessions in general. When a religious community applies for inclusion into the Register of Legal Entities with a legal form "traditional religious community or association," it is up to the Ministry of Justice to decide, whether a religious community is really traditional or not. The Ministry of Justice either accepts the claim of the new religious community or rejects it; usually the older traditional religious association is against the registration of the new traditional religious association" (Glodenis 2008, 402).

ISLAMIC LAW IN LITHUANIA? 123

In practical terms, the Ministry has been consulting the Muftiate and seeking its informal *imprimatur* or at least *nihil obstat*. So far, there has been no instance of objection by the Muftiate to recognition of a Muslim religious community as a traditional religious community or refusal by the Ministry to register it as such. However, as noted by Glodenis, the Law on Religious Communities and Associations (or indeed any other piece of legislation) does not explicitly name the Muftiate as the umbrella or supervising Sunni Muslim organisation in the country. So, at least formally, alternative / rival Sunni Muslim muftiates or other organisations may be registered at the Ministry's discretion as Sunni Muslim traditional religious communities. However, on what basis the Ministry is to decide "whether a religious community is really traditional or not" remains unclear, as the criteria implied in the Law, namely that the applicant community is to "comprise a part of Lithuania's historical, spiritual and social heritage," is very vague. On the other hand, both Judaist and Old Believer communities have rival legal persons with the equal vis-à-vis the state status of traditional religious communities. One of the Judaist communities, Habad Lubavich, in fact, has never had historical presence in Lithuania and from the historical point of view hardly qualifies as a community that comprises "a part of Lithuania's historical, spiritual and social heritage." With this precedent in mind, one should not be surprised if, or when, an alternative Sunni Muslim religious community not only applies for the status of a traditional religious community but is eventually granted it.

The second problem is that, arguably, "since the tradition of specific churches and religious organisations in Lithuania is an objective status of relations of churches and religious organisations with the society irrespective of the willpower of the legislator, the legislator may not withdraw the statement of the existence of this tradition" (Ruškytė, 2008, 174). In other words, it is not envisaged in the Law of 1995 or any other piece of legislation that the status of a "traditional" religious community might be needed to be removed. The Constitutional Court, in its 2007 decision stated that "the constitutional confirmation of the institute of recognition of traditional churches and religious organisations means that their state recognition is non-revocable. Traditionality is neither created nor annulled by an act of will of the legislator. The naming of churches and religious organisations as traditional is not an act of their, as traditional organisations, creation but an act of statement of their traditionality – of the state of their relations with the society, reflecting the evolution and state of the society's religious culture, not dependent on the will of the legislator."

This raises the question, under what circumstances, if at all, Sunni Islam in general or a particular officially registered Sunni Muslim religious community may be stripped of its status as a traditional religion / traditional religious community? For instance, if Muslims (and particularly their leadership) claiming to be Sunni (and by extension of a "traditional religious community") start behaving in a manner which does not enjoy the support of the majority of the society and is not (anymore) held by it to "comprise a part of Lithuania's historical, spiritual and social heritage" referred to in the Law.

The Law on Religious Communities and Associations (Article 20) envisions the procedure for the closure of religious organisations by the court. However, it speaks in general terms and does not separately elaborate on the case of traditional religious communities. Apparently, it would be the court's prerogative to decide on the matter; however, like in the case of registration or refusal thereof of an applicant community by the Ministry of Justice, the court would have to come up with more solid evidence than that the religious community or the entire confession does not (anymore) "comprise a part of Lithuania's historical, spiritual and social heritage." In any case, the court would have to deal with the claims and behaviour of the community under question, which, unless they were terrorism-related, very likely would be presented by the community itself as practice required by nothing less than the Islamic law.

Concluding Observations

Discussions on the feasibility of the application of the Islamic law in Europe and its scope is most likely to become even more urgent than is has been hitherto. While some European countries might or indeed have already chosen to integrate some aspects of it into their national legal systems, others are adamant to keep it out. In this regard, Lithuania may be regarded as falling into the first category, as its legal system since practically regaining the country's independence has been accommodating of a number of aspects of the Islamic law, as discussed above.

However, though the potential for its application is there, the actual implementation of the Islamic law in the country lags behind. This discrepancy has been caused, first of all, by virtual absence of demand for the Islamic law among the primary segment of the country's Muslim population, the Lithuanian Tatars. On the other hand, the situation appears to be slowly changing – the emergent segments of Muslims of convert and immigrant background are much more devout and demanding than their Tatar counterparts and have already proceeded with securing their religious rights enshrined in the national legislation.

So far, however, it is the generally thoroughly secularised Lithuanian Tatars who hold key positions in the country's formal Muslim religious organisations, all of which are regarded by the state as traditional religious communities. Muslims of the convert and immigrant backgrounds have so far not made it into positions of power or authority, nor have they yet tried to set up any alternative organisations aspiring to the status of a traditional religious community and rather have chosen the path of formal submission to the Tatar leadership. This, however, in view of the changes in the demographic composition of the Muslim population – with decrease in the numbers of Tatars and increase in the numbers of Muslims of convert and immigrant backgrounds – is destined to change.

But the issue is not so much who will be in charge of the Muslim communities in Lithuania as how those in the power positions will understand the contents of Islam and the place of the Islamic law in the communal and individual life of the country's Muslims. With many of the Muslims of convert background being of revivalist leanings, it may be predicted that if or when their representatives make it into power positions in the local Muslim organisations, they may much more vigorously seek to secure the religious rights of their coreligionists. In the most extreme case scenario some of the country's Muslims might gravitate in the direction of conservatism to the point when their understanding of the contents of Islam and the way of life based on it would clash with the life style of the majority population and it would be not (any more) considered "to comprise a part of Lithuania's historical, spiritual and social heritage." This would put the Muslim community on the collision course with the state, which would have to reconsider its relation with the Muslim community.

From the point of view of the legislation in force and its explication by the Constitutional Court, it appears that while isolated Sunni Muslim religious organisations may lose under exceptional circumstances the status of traditional religious community and even be banned by court, the confession of Sunni Islam itself may never be stripped of this status. If this is the case, the Lithuanian state in the future may face a problem of recurrent re-establishment of Muslim religious organisations that would claim the status of traditional religious community but their activities would be found to be disruptive of the status quo in the social order of the state and society.

On the other hand, there has been a growing support from the side of the Ministry of Justice to overhaul the Law on Religious Communities and Associations to the point where no religious community would be officially recognised as traditional. Though the Catholic Church may vehemently oppose such a turn and even sabotage the adoption of the new edition of the Law, if successfully passed in the Parliament and signed into law by the President, the Law would certainly remove the source of possible future legal tension between the Muslim community or a part thereof and the state. However, at the same time, it would most likely narrow the supply side for the practicing of the Islamic law in the country as many if not most of the safeguards would be simply removed.

References

Articles of the Spiritual Center of the Lithuanian Sunni Muslims – Muftiate (1998-04-18, unpublished document).

Büchler, Andrea. 2011. *Islamic Law in Europe?: Legal Pluralism and its Limits in European Family Laws*, Routledge.

Christoffersen, Lisbet & Nielsen Jørgen S. (eds.). 2010. *Shari'a As Discourse: Legal Traditions and the Encounter with Europe*, Routledge.

Cumper, Peter. 2014. "Multiculturalism, Human Rights and the Accommodation of Sharia Law," *Human Rights Law Review*, 14, 31–57.

Gyventojai pagal tautybę, gimtąją kalbą ir tikybą (*Inhabitants by ethnicity, mother tongue and faith*, in Lithuanian). Department of Statistics 2013.

Lithuanian 2011 Population Census in Brief. Statistics Lithuania 2012.

Karčić, Harun. 2015. "Applying Islamic Norms in Europe: The Example of Bosnian Muslims," *Journal of Muslim Minority Affairs*, vol. 35, issue 2, 245–263.

Kruininger, Pauline. 2015. *Islamic Divorces in Europe: Bridging the Gap between European and Islamic Legal Orders*, Eleven International Publishing.

Law on Religious Communities and Associations of the Republic of Lithuania (1995), available at www.legislationline.org/documents/id/18351 [accessed 2017-01-10].

McGoldrick, Dominic. 2009. "Accommodating Muslims in Europe: From Adopting Sharia Law to Religiously Based Opt Outs from Generally Applicable Laws," *Human Rights Law Review*, vol. 9, issue 4, 603–645.

Mehdi, Rubya & Nielsen, Jørgen S. (eds.). 2011. *Embedding Mahr (Islamic Dower) in the European Legal System*, Djoef Publishing.

Račius, Egdūnas. 2009. "Islam in Lithuania" in Larsson, G. (ed.), *Islam in the Nordic and Baltic Countries* (London and New York: Routledge), 116–132.

Račius, Egdūnas. 2011. "Muslims in Lithuania. Revival at the expense of survival?" in Górak-Sosnowska, K. (ed.), *Muslims in Poland and Eastern Europe. Widening the European Discourse on Islam* (Warsaw: University of Warsaw Press), 207–221.

Račius, Egdūnas. 2018. "(Re)discovering One's Religion – Private Islamic Education in Lithuanian Muslim Communities," in Jenny Berglund (ed.), *European Perspectives on Islamic Education and Public Schooling*, Equinox.

Rohe, Mathias. 2004. "Application of Sharīʿa Rules in Europe: Scope and Limits," *Die Welt des Islams*, New Series, Vol. 44, Issue 3, Sharīʿa in Europe (2004), 323–350.

The Constitutional Court of the Republic of Lithuania. Decision on construing the provisions of a Constitutional Court ruling related with the status of the churches and religious organisations that are traditional in Lithuania. December 6, 2007, available at http://www.lrkt.lt/en/court-acts/search/170/ta1375/content [accessed 2017-01-17].

Vitkauskaitė-Meurice, Dalia. 2017. *Annotated Legal Documents on Islam in Europe: Lithuania*, Brill.

CHAPTER 8

The King, the Boy, the Monk and the Magician: Jihadi Ideological Entrepreneurship between the UK and Denmark

Jakob Skovgaard-Petersen

Two Jihadist Ideologists in Europe

"The East is a career," wrote Benjamin Disraeli in 1847. One hundred and seventy years later it is perhaps more Islam than the East in general that can offer career opportunities. And even in this more narrowly defined field of occupation, there is definitely quite a variety of ways of making Islam one's career. Jørgen S. Nielsen is a fine example of a scholar of medieval Islam who, unexpectedly, found himself in the middle of contemporary politics and concerns. He rose to the occasion, serving both Great Britain and Denmark with relevant and concise knowledge of classical Islamic doctrines and institutions, and how these were appropriated and employed by Muslims in Europe today.

This chapter will look at two other men who have made Islam the basis of quite different careers. They, too, have brought ideas from London to Copenhagen, but ideas of rather a different variety. Their brand of Islamic scholarship is inciting and violent; very much unlike Nielsen and to the point that they have both been sentenced to extradition from Europe. I acted as an expert witness in the court cases in Copenhagen, and the following is an analysis of the books by Abu Qatada which were included in the case against Sam Mansour who was Abu Qatada's publisher.

On July 1, 2015, Sam (formerly Said) Mansour was sentenced to four years in prison, followed by extradition from Denmark, for threats and incitement to terrorist acts.[1] Apart from concrete threats against named figures in Danish society, Mansour was also sentenced for publishing three jihadist treatises by Abu Qatada, a Palestinian Jordanian preacher, who in turn had been forced to leave Great Britain for Jordan in July 2013 after a protracted legal battle, also over terrorism related activities. Legal scholars will analyse the verdicts and general impact of the recent drive to strengthen anti-terrorism legislation. Here, we shall turn our interest towards the jihadist ideologists and the

---

1 Politiken, 2/7 2015, 3.

© KONINKLIJKE BRILL NV, LEIDEN, 2018 | DOI 10.1163/9789004362529_009

works they have produced. In spite of a massive interest in jihadism, and the prominence of Abu Qatada on the European scene, surprisingly little has been written on his actual thought and writings, possibly because the general gist of it is well known.[2] Nevertheless, it seems to me that the three works provide interesting insight into the more recent concerns and arguments of a major jihadist ideologist today, at least for the period prior to the rise of the Islamic State in Iraq and Syria in 2014.

Abu Qatada was born Umar Mahmud Uthman Abu Umar in a village near Bethlehem, in Jordanian controlled Palestine, in 1960 or 1961. The family moved to Amman, where the religiously devout Umar went to school and later obtained a BA in Islamic jurisprudence in 1984. He became a convinced Salafi and after troubles with Jordanian security, he moved to Malaysia in 1990 and later to Peshawar, Pakistan, where he finished his MA degree. In 1993, he arrived in London where he preached, often for veteran jihadist groups, and edited the jihadi magazine *al-Ansar*. In 1995 he issued a fatwa allowing for the killing of relatives of Algerian police officers.[3] He had by then taken the name Abu Qatada al-Filastini. From 2001, British authorities recognised him as one of the most influential anti-Western jihadist preachers in the country. He was imprisoned on several occasions, and legal efforts were spent to extradite him from the country. In the meantime, he wrote prolifically on subjects related to jihad, and published some of them with Said Mansour.

Said Mansour was born in Morocco in 1960 and came to Denmark in 1983. In 1984 he married a Danish woman whom he later divorced; they have four children. He opened an Islamic bookstore, and later began publishing jihadi treatises from his house in the suburb of Brønshøj, benefiting from liberal Danish publication laws. As material from Mansour's publishing activities began to appear with jihadists in other European states (including in the flat of the 9/11 hijackers in Hamburg), the Danish security was alerted to his activities, and charges were raised against him on several occasions.[4] In 2007 has was sentenced to three and a half year in prison on charges of incitement to terrorism. Released in 2009, he continued preaching and publishing, and in 2014, the case was raised that led to his sentence in July 2015 to four years in prison followed by extradition to Morocco. Mansour and his lawyer have vowed to appeal his

---

2   See Lia, Brynjar: *Architect of Global Jihad. The Life of al-Qaida Strategist Abu Musab al-Suri.* London: Hurst and OUP, 2007, 182–189.

    Nesser, Petter: *Abu Qatada and Palestine.* Die Welt des Islams 53, 2013, 3–4, 416–448.

3   Nesser, op. cit., 426.

4   Politiken, 2/7 2015, 2.

sentence to prevent that he will ever be handed over to Moroccan police. In June 2016 his Danish citizenship was revoked.

Three Genres, One Message

The three books of al-Qatada that were presented in court represent different genres. Still, they have a lot in common. They are not simply Islamist in the sense of propagating an Islamic system that would be the most just and appropriate system for Muslims to live under. Rather, they are emphatically Jihadist in the sense that jihad is not seen as a means to an end (the just, God-pleasing society), but as the end itself: in their rendering, jihad, and only jihad, is the single truly God-pleasing act.

All three books are addressed to the already recruited young *mujahidin*, those belonging to the victorious band (*al-ta'ifa al-mansura*) who will ultimately prevail. Abu Qatada considers himself their *shaykh*, the absolute authority on the issue of jihad, who guides them and warns them against false and cowardly interpretations of jihad. Their main fight is against the tyrannical idols (*tawaghit*) who rule the Arab and Muslim world by oppressing the Muslims who have accepted their own weakness (*al-mustada'fin*). These states are unlawful, as are their armies and police, and their media are mendacious. Worst of all, they are supported by the learned men of religion (*al-'ulama*). The task of the latter was to propagate God's law and speak truth to power, but they have let the Muslims down out of fear and greed. And they are not the only ones: also the Islamist movements have opted for collaboration with the tyrants, and many Islamic thinkers have turned out to be hypocrites (*munafiqun*) who did not want to pursue the jihad that is clearly mandated by God. Even some of the *mujahidun* have miserably retracted (*muraja'at*). In the meantime, groups who do not heed God's true message are gaining power: the *zanadiqa* (heretics who adhere to un-Islamic ideologies), the *rawafid* or *safawiyun* (Shi'a) and the *nusairiyun* (Alawites). Behind this deplorable state of affairs, or at least benefiting from it, are the Western infidels (*kuffar*) and crusaders (*salibiyun*).

This age, then, is characterised by its barbaric ignorance (*jahiliyya*) and disobedience towards God (*kufr*). But this is all according to God's will. It is God's great test (*mihna, ibtila*) of the true believers who should only be thankful that He has given them this opportunity to prove themselves. For God has given them a promise (*wa'd*) that they shall inherit and rule the earth (*al-waratha*). They should know in their hearts that God will let them win if they steadfastly follow the program (*minhaj*) He has prescribed for them in the Qur'an. It teaches them to be patient and put their trust in God (*tawakkul*); for in the

THE KING, THE BOY, THE MONK AND THE MAGICIAN 131

end, those who do not fear death but love it, and seek martyrdom for God (*shahada*) cannot be defeated.

The Calamity of the Age

This is the age in which we are living. But recently, something happened. Those who had made themselves weak did in fact rise against the tyrants and overthrew them. The smallest of the books has been published to address the situation after the revolutions of 2011.

Entitled *An Approach to the Calamity of the Age*, this booklet is an attempt to take stock of the new situation and reassure the young *mujahidin* that no victory can be achieved without jihad on God's path. While celebrating the defeat of the tyrants, the book warns against the new forces that have appeared, but also points to new opportunities for jihad in the chaos that has ensued.

Published in 2012, the book appeared more than a year after the revolutions of winter 2010–11.[5] Abu Qatada admits that it has taken some time for the jihadi movement to make up its mind about what to do about these revolutions, and his point is that they can celebrate, but only in the way that the Muslims celebrated when the Byzantines defeated the Persians (11). This was Divine providence, and it may serve the believers, but it was not a victory for God's revelation. Abu Qatada insists that these tyrants had not fallen, had it not been for the jihadis, their true adversaries, who had weakened their capacity for suppression and their legitimacy (34–38). But this is not a time to rejoice; rather this is the time for the mujahidin to prepare for the battle against those Muslims who have rejected true faith. This is the time to call upon people to submit to their Lord (45). The Islamist parties who have won elections must be forced to implement God's law. They must prepare for the elimination of the Jewish state and for the conquest of Rome (46).

But at the time of writing, Abu Qatada can see that the Islamist movements of Egypt and Turkey, although voted into government by the people, are going procrastinate and delay the introduction of God's law, and they are not going to confront Israel and the West. They accept parliamentary democracy and talk about the "sharing" of power with ungodly forces (53), like their brethren in Jordan and Yemen have done for long. So the mujahidin should not take part, but confront. One way of doing this is by rejecting the state courts and set up alternative Muslim ones (*majalis tahkim*) to judge among the believers (60).

---

5 The book, المقاربة لنازلة العصر قدرا وشرعا, can be downloaded at https://archive.org/details/thawrat_al-shou3oub.

Abu Qatada takes heart from the development in Libya and Syria where the state has broken down and chaos and barbarity have emerged. More than the fall of the tyrants, this will provide space for the *mujahidin*. The comfortable life has disappeared, and people no longer fear death. Most promising is Syria: an Afghanistan has risen just next to the Jewish state, the population is armed and mobilised for a jihad that will move on to Palestine (61–62).

Abu Qatada ends with an eulogy to Abu Musaab al-Zarqawi (d. 2006) and his successful jihad in Iraq which brought the biggest tyrant, USA, to defeat. His *mujahidin* have been patient, biding their time. Now it has come. They must fight for God and never expect gratitude for their efforts (63–66).

There are perhaps few surprises in Abu Qatada's assessment of the 2011 revolutions from the point of view of the *mujahidin*. He is right, of course, that the *mujahidin* have been implacable enemies of the regimes, but they, too, have sometimes received support from one regime in its fight against another, not least in the Iraqi jihad. Likewise, his contention that the majority of the Arabs want an Islamic state may have been well founded after the Tunisian and Egyptian elections in late 2011 and early 2012, but later elections have shown that this is by no means a given. Finally, Abu Qatada's cynical remarks on the blessed developments in Libya and Syria, and the need to create chaos to build up an Islamic civilization bear resemblances to those of another Jihadist thinker, Abu Bakr Naji, in his book "The Management of Savagery" from 2004.[6]

An Interpretation of the Prophet's Battles

If the first book is small and written for the political moment, the second book is massive and claims to have lasting, indeed eternal, value. Dated to 2012, it has been written over years in prison and smuggled out in pieces. It is an 800-page exposition of the psychological program that God unveiled for mankind in His directions to the prophet about the wars with the heathen Meccans.[7]

The book takes a chronological view of the major battles fought by the prophet and his supporters against the Meccans, from the battle of Badr in 624 to the battle at Tabuk in 630. While the traditional *maghazi* literature enumerates participants and feats of heroism, and modern Muslim literature concentrates on Muhammad's strategic genius, Abu Qatada's approach is quite

---

6 Lia, Brynjar: Doctrines for Jihadi Terrorist Training. Terrorism and Political Violence, 20: 518–542, 2008, 527–532.

7 The book, محواً ...التخذيل و التراجعات على خُطى الصمد الله صبغة مع, can be downloaded at https://archive .org/details/fadle_live_201504.

THE KING, THE BOY, THE MONK AND THE MAGICIAN 133

different. As stated in the introduction, the *maghazi* literature on the battles is written by human beings, and thus partial and necessarily incomplete. The Qur'an, by contrast, gives a complete and detailed picture of what the battles were really about, namely the forging of the character of the believer. This is due to the fact that jihad is "the culmination of Islam," the decisive moment when the individual is confronted with the ultimate test (7). This is especially true in these days when the *'ulama* are deceiving the Muslims by telling them that jihad is not a duty. These learned men may teach people about their religion, but they are deliberately omitting its most important ingredient. Moreover, to be a Muslim means to engage in a process: in order to build them up as Muslims, a focus on their soul and the will is required; this is what the Qur'an does in its exposition of the prophet's wars (9).

This means that the many skirmishes with the Meccans are of no interest. What matters are the major turns of events: the battles of Badr and Uhud and the trench, the invasion of Banu Qurayza and the treaty of Hudhaybiyya. Of these, the battle of Uhud takes up the most space. The reason is that, not long after the providential victory of Badr, this was a defeat that the believers had not expected, and many defected and became the hypocrites. The battle of Uhud, then, is what resembles the stage of the jihad today.

Abu Qatada stresses the importance of Q 3:139, revealed after the defeat: "So lose not heart, nor fall into despair: For ye must gain mastery if ye are true in Faith".[8] God calls on the Muslims to go on the offensive. Not to conquer this or that, but to be in the state of fighting, as jihad is the only way to avoid being a despised and humiliated human being, the only civilised way of living (115). Muslims must go on the offensive, for the obstacles are veils that God will remove when he witnesses the steadfastness of the believers (248–50). This is the chapter of the book where martyrdom (*shahada*) is discussed and held up as the ultimate goal of the true believer (122–25). To be a *mujahid* is to seek martyrdom, and never meet the unbelievers halfway. Throughout history, God has tested the Muslims with invasions: the crusaders, Tatars and imperialists have ensured that Muslims suffered the defeats necessary for God to build up their character and make the band of true believers prevail in the end. Uhud was the first of those trials, and we are living through yet another of them. Blessed are those who live in an era of martyrdom (250).

After nine years of warfare, Abu Qatada concludes, the "Qur'anic build-up" of the *umma* and the individual believer had come to an end: when Muhammad died, the *umma* was ready for more jihad and conquest, not less. The Muslims obtained their place in history: other peoples envied and feared them (430).

---

8   Qur'an 3:139, Picktall's translation.

Abu Qatada's interest in a Qur'anic "program" (*minhaj*) with the intention of "building up" the character of the believer appears to be inspired by the work of Sayyid Qutb. In his last book, *Ma'alim fi 'l-tariq* ("Signposts") from 1965, Qutb adopts the *minhaji* approach to jihad, claiming that it was revealed in phases, but concentrating on the transition from Meccan to Medinan Suras.[9] Abu Qatada adopts the Qutbian idea of a divine program for the formation of the true believer, but sharpens it by seeing no Islam outside jihad, and loosely applies the different stages of the battles to the contemporary jihad since the 1980s.

The King, the Sorcerer, the Monk and the Boy

Abu Qatada's third book published by Sam Mansour is entitled "Gaining Guidance through Following the Boy".[10] It is perhaps the most intriguing of the three. Once again, it is presented as an interpretation, *tafsir*. This time, however, it is not a reading of our age, or of the battles of the prophet, but a book-length textual reading of a single prophetic hadith, from the collection of Sahih Muslim.[11] And that hadith is extraordinary in itself, and the interpretation is idiosyncratic and loose, to say the least.

The text of the hadith is as follows:

> Suhaib reported that Allah's Messenger (ﷺ) thus said:
> There lived a king before you and he had a (court) magician. As he (the magician) grew old, he said to the king: I have grown old, send some young boy to me so that I should teach him magic. He (the king) sent to him a young man so that he should train him (in magic). And on his way (to the magician) he (the young man) found a monk sitting there. He (the young man) listened to his (the monk's) talk and was impressed by it. It became his habit that on his way to the magician he met the monk and set there and he came to the magician (late). He (the magician) beat him because of delay. He made a complaint of that to the monk and he said to him: When you feel afraid of the magician, say: Members of my family had detained me. And when you feel afraid of your family you should say: The magician had detained me. It so happened that there came a huge

---

9   Qutb, Sayyid: *Ma'alim fi 'l-tariq*. Cairo, Dar al-Shuruq, 11th edition, 1987, 62–66.

10   The book كتاب درك الهدى في اتباع الفتى can be downloaded on http://ia700803.us.archive.org/5/items/abu_qatada_new_1433/DARK_ALHODA.pdf.

11   Muslim book 55, hadith 93. It is also found in al-Tirmidhi, Ahmad ibn Hanbal and others.

THE KING, THE BOY, THE MONK AND THE MAGICIAN

beast (of prey) and it blocked the way of the people, and he (the young boy) said: I will come to know today whether the magician is superior or the monk is superior. He picked up a stone and said: O Allah, if the affair of the monk is dearer to Thee than the affair of the magician, cause death to this animal so that the people should be able to move about freely. He threw that stone towards it and killed it and the people began to move about (on the path freely). He (the young man) then came to that monk and informed him and the monk said: Sonny, today you are superior to me. Your affair has come to a stage where I find that you would be soon put to a trial, and in case you are put to a trial don't give my clue. That young man began to treat the blind and those suffering from leprosy and he in fact began to cure people from (all kinds) of illness. When a companion of the king who had gone blind heard about him, he came to him with numerous gifts and said: If you cure me all these things collected together here would be yours. He said: I myself do not cure anyone. It is Allah Who cures and if you affirm faith in Allah, I shall also supplicate Allah to cure you. He affirmed his faith in Allah and Allah cured him and he came to the king and sat by his side as he used to sit before. The king said to him: Who restored your eyesight? He said: My Lord. Thereupon he said: It means that your Lord is one besides me. He said: My Lord and your Lord is Allah, so he (the king) took hold of him and tormented him till he gave a clue of that boy. The young man was thus summoned and the king said to him: O boy, it has been conveyed to me that you have become so much proficient in your magic that you cure the blind and those suffering from leprosy and you do such and such things. Thereupon he said: I do not cure anyone; it is Allah Who cures, and he (the king) took hold of him and began to torment him. So he gave a clue of the monk. The monk was thus summoned and it was said to him: You should turn back from your religion. He, however, refused to do so. He (ordered) for a saw to be brought (and when it was done) he (the king) placed it in the middle of his head and tore it into parts till a part fell down. Then the courtier of the king was brought and it was said to him: Turn back from your religion. And he refused to do so, and the saw was placed in the midst of his head and it was torn till a part fell down. Then that young boy was brought and it was said to him: Turn back from your religion. He refused to do so and he was handed over to a group of his courtiers. And he said to them: Take him to such and such mountain; make him climb up that mountain and when you reach its top (ask him to renounce his faith) but if he refuses to do so, then throw him (down the mountain). So they took him and made him climb up the mountain and he said: O Allah, save me from them (in any way) Thou likest and the mountain began to quake and they all fell down and that person came walking to the king. The king said to him: What has happened to your companions? He said: Allah has saved me from them. He again handed him to some of his courtiers and said: Take him and carry him in a small boat and when you reach the middle of the ocean (ask him to renounce) his religion, but if he does not renounce his religion throw him (into the water). So they took him and he said: O Allah, save me from them and what they want to do. It was quite soon that the boat turned over and they were drowned and he came walking to the king, and the king said to him: What has happened to your companions? He said: Allah has saved me from them, and he said to the king: You cannot kill me until you do what I ask you to do. And he said: What is that? He said: You should gather people in a plain and hang me by the trunk (of a tree). Then take hold of an arrow from the quiver and say: In the name of Allah, the Lord of the young boy; then shoot an arrow and if you do that then you would be able to kill me. So he (the king) called the people in an open plain and tied him (the boy) to the trunk of a tree, then he took hold of an arrow from his quiver and then placed the arrow in the bow and then said: In the name of Allah, the Lord of the young boy; he then shot an arrow and it bit his temple. He (the boy) placed his hands upon the temple where the arrow had bit him and he died and the people said: We affirm our faith in the Lord of this young man, we affirm our faith in the Lord of this young man, we affirm our faith in the Lord of this young man. The courtiers came to the king and it was said to him: Do you see that Allah has actually done what you aimed at averting. They (the people) have affirmed their faith in the Lord. He (the king) commanded ditches to be dug at important points in the path. When these ditches were dug, and the fire was lit in them it was said (to the people): He who would not turn back from his (boy's) religion would be thrown in the fire or it would be said to them to jump in that. (The people courted death but did not renounce religion) till a woman came with her child and she felt hesitant in jumping into the fire and the child said to her: o mother, endure (this ordeal) for it is the Truth.[12]

This is quite an unusual hadith. It is much longer than ordinary *ahadith*, and without a chain of transmitters (*isnad*), although accepted by Muslim and other collectors. Moreover, the typical hadith lets the prophet make a statement about a subject or act in some real life situation which lends itself to a

---

12   Quoted from http://www.sunnah.com/muslim/55. Chapter no 17. Accessed July 28, 2015.

THE KING, THE BOY, THE MONK AND THE MAGICIAN 137

theological, juridical or ritual interpretation. This one lets him narrate a long and detailed story without any further comment as to its meaning or consequence. The story has the character of a myth or saintly legend, as known for instance from early Christian hagiography.[13] There is a struggle between good and evil characters, and what appears to be a moral lesson, stressing the boy's complete trust in God and decision not to oppose the king, and, of course, the inscrutable workings of the Lord.

In the book Abu Qatada begins by rendering the hadith and then proceeds to comment upon it verse for verse, like a classical *tafsir*. In contrast to a classical tafsir, , however, he soon wanders off in a variety of directions, only taking the line as a point of departure to discuss various issues of concern to contemporary young jihadists. This begins from the very first line: "There lived a king before you and he had a (court) magician." The mere mention of a king who has a court magician gives Abu Qatada the opportunity to explain how tyrants are in need of legitimation, as they don't get it from the people, and therefore rely on experts in legitimacy. In the story this is the magician, but in real life it is the Muslim *'ulama* who were once suitably remote from power, but are now its servants (20). Like the magician, they became the cover of the sultan's power, and like a snake they have cast off their religious skin (22). Another equivalent of magicians is the people of the media who, like Iblis, work through verbal seduction (24). But, according to Abu Qatada, the first line also contains a more ominous message: the quest for legitimacy is due to the fact that the king is in need of a following, and could not rule if he were not supported. It is thus wrong to consider the tyrant as culpable, but not the subjects on whom he relies. Jihad is consequently not only against the tyrants and their soldiers, but also against their acquiescing subjects (15). Their weakness is not an excuse, but a culpable failure on their part (17). Jihad is against everyone, civilians included (18).

"I have grown old. Send some young boy to me". This line allows Abu Qatada to reflect over the good force of youth. He has been accused of seducing the young, but the fact of the matter is that it is the older people who lack depth and understanding, especially if they have been oppressed. Just like the Israelites, the Muslims will have to wait for forty years before a new and liberated generation can take over (30).

"When you feel afraid of the magician, say: Members of my family had detained me. And when you feel afraid of your family you should say: The magician had detained me." This line is taken by Abu Qatada to mean that lies,

---

13   Cook, David. "The 'ashab al-ukhdud': history and 'hadith' in a martyrological sequence", Jerusalem Studies in Arabic and Islam 34 (2008), 125–148, 142.

and even oaths, are religiously acceptable, indeed mandatory, if they serve the believers (32). This leads him to a rejection of those muftis who stress that in the lands of the unbelievers Muslims must follow the laws of the land. On the contrary, says Abu Qatada, they are not allowed to say a word of truth to the police or the courts, even in cases such as theft or homicide which are also punishable according to the Sharia (36).

The *tafsir* continues in this vein, using lines in the story as points of departure for digressions about the character of the young *mujahid*, the blindness of other Muslims, God's signs to the believers, and how to triumph even during torture. It culminates in the protracted self-sacrifice of the boy:

> "He said: You should gather people in a plain and hang me by the trunk (of a tree). Then take hold of an arrow from the quiver and say: In the name of Allah, the Lord of the young boy; then shoot an arrow and if you do that then you would be able to kill me." The boy's remarkable instruction to the evil king in how finally to get rid of him is what fascinates Abu Qatada and other jihadists in this story, and the reason why they refer to it. Abu Qatada announces that Islam shall only prevail through martyrdom (102), and suicide operations are not only allowed but especially pleasing to Allah (104). The faith that the people are converted to is precisely this faith of self-sacrifice (107). And self-sacrifice is needed for, as Abu Qatada points out, the world is at war, and the unbelievers are killing the Muslims in the tens of thousands, while the media are lying, and hypocritically promoting smokescreens such as human rights and humanism (111). This is the eternal war between *kufr* and Islam. And every young Muslim who does not bow to the tyrants must make the young boy's words his own: "you are wishing for my death, and so am I. But know that my death shall turn your lives into a hell" (114).

David Cook has treated this hadith in some detail and identified it as a centrepiece in the recent development of a jihadi legitimation of suicide attacks.[14] This line of reasoning takes its departure in the last chapter of Sayyid Qutb's *Ma'alim fi 'l-tariq*, where the Qur'anic (85: 1-9) story of *ashab al-ukhdud*, the "people of the pit," believers who were tortured and killed for their faith, is taken to mean that martyrdom is the pinnacle of faith and a godly reward, no matter whether an actual victory is achieved.[15] In a modern jihadist literature

---

14   Cook, David "The 'ashab al-ukhdud': history and 'hadith' in a martyrological sequence," Jerusalem Studies in Arabic and Islam 34 (2008), 125–148.

15   Sayyed Qutb (1965), 139.

THE KING, THE BOY, THE MONK AND THE MAGICIAN   139

this has led to attempts at legitimising suicide operations as long as they serve the cause of jihad.[16] As this seems to contradict the Qur'anic injunction (4:29) against suicide, this hadith is employed to demonstrate that God consents in intentionally suicidal acts if they serve the Muslim faith: at the end of the story the boy instructs the king in his own killing, but this very act leads the people to faith. This is interpreted as a covenant between God and the Muslim whereby it is the duty of the true believers to fight and seek martyrdom, and God's reward is paradise.[17] This theme is also prominent in Abu Qatada's interpretation which, as we have seen, is broader, and more idiosyncratic, than previous Jihadist interpretations of it.

There are, however, problems with this employment of the hadith. David Cook points out that it "is still problematic although it is a clear case of a believer dying specifically for his faith (and this is comparatively rare in Muslim accounts), since the boy is not a fighter and he does not kill anyone else (like Samson) when he is killed. Thus, the supportive value of the story is unclear."[18] One could add to this that the story in Muslim's collection is not placed in the book of jihad, but in the (almost contrasting) book on asceticism and the softening of hearts (*kitab al-zuhd wa l-raqa'iq*). In Muslim's time, it appears, it was seen as a testimony to the rightfulness of the pacifist retreat of the faithful when confronted with an unjust ruler. Hence, neither the story itself, nor its early interpretation, seem to support Abu Qatada's understanding of violent jihad as the only acceptable position of the true Muslim.

Conclusion

This chapter has analysed three texts by the contemporary jihadist thinker Abu Qatada, all published by the Danish-Moroccan activist Sam Mansour. The three books are all written as an interpretation (*tafsir*); one of them of contemporary Arab politics, the second of the prophet Muhammad's warfare, and the third of a legend narrated by Muhammad. In all of them, Abu Qatada proffers advice to young committed jihadists about strategy, attitude and self-sacrifice.

---

16   Cook, David (2007) *Martyrdom in Islam*. Cambridge University Press, 149–152. A longer survey of pro and con positions is provided in Shereen Khan Burki: "Haram or Halal? Islamists" Use of Suicide Attacks as "Jihad." *Terrorism and Political Violence*, 23: 582–601, 2011.

17   Cook (2007), 152.

18   Cook (2007), 152.

After all, the enemy is the same, and God's demands and expectations from the believers have not changed, either.

As we have seen, *tafsir*, to Abu Qatada, is an open discipline which allows him to discuss issues of interest to himself and the *mujahidin* and pass judgments on them. In the books on the prophet's wars and the hadith about the boy the connection to the underlying narrative is often the psychological one: the wars, and the legend, illustrate how God works on the character-building of the believer. This interest in the divine *minhaj* (program) for the believer seems to be inspired by Sayyid Qutb who in his *tafsir*, the *Fi Zilal al-Qur'an*, also exposed the underlying divine program in a kind of psychological literary interpretation. But Abu Qatada, who honors Qutb for his martyrdom, goes beyond Qutb in his adoption of the strategy of deliberately spreading barbarism through acts of monstrous violence, as advocated by Abu Bakr Naji.

Recently, these ideas have been overtaken by events: in July 2014 the Islamic State was proclaimed, very much along the line of the books we have analysed. Abu Qatada released a longer article, "The Cloak of the Khilafa," denouncing the Caliphate pretensions of the Islamic State.[19] Siding with the other jihadist militants in Syria (Jabhat an-Nusra and Ahrar al-Sham), Abu Qatada's friend Abu Muhammad al-Maqdisi tried to mediate between Islamic State and the Jordanian state, but was misled by the former. Suddenly they found themselves to be allies of convenience of Jordan's security service, their old enemy.[20]

In September 2014, shortly after the publication of his denouncement of the caliphate of ISIS, Abu Qatada was released from charges of terrorism by a Jordanian court and could settle in Jordan as a free man. The BBC described the eruptions of jubilations coming from his supporters and himself, and his son said the family had always been optimistic about the verdict.[21] The treaty of extradition between Britain and Jordan had included a guarantee that evidence obtained under torture could not be employed. Abu Qatada who had based his defence in Britain on the claim that he would not receive a fair trial in Jordan was thus proven wrong. As were his writings about actively seeking martyrdom. Ironically, Sam Mansour, too, has declared that he will fight hard to stay within the Danish court system that he rejects, arguing that in the Kingdom of Morocco he could be sentenced to death. But was not the king's capital punishment what the boy in the hadith so eagerly sought?

---

19   Available at http://eldorar.net/sites/default/files/klefha.pdf.

20   http://www.economist.com/news/middle-east-and-africa/21629476-todays-jihadists-are -too-extreme-even-leading-ideologues-holy-war-jail.

21   http://www.bbc.com/news/world-29340656.

CHAPTER 9

"ALLAH IS IGNORANCE": An Essay on the Poetic Praxis of Yahya Hassan and the Critique of Liberal Islam

Thomas Hoffmann

Dark Horse of Arab-Muslim Descend

In Denmark, it is rare that poets make headlines beyond the culture sections and spur fierce debate in the broader public sphere, not to mention downright violent reactions. That a Danish poet should cause news articles and column pieces to be circulated in the newspapers like *The Guardian, New York Times, Wall Street Journal, Spiegel, Frankfurter Allgemeine,*and other reputable media outlets is exceptional. That was the fate, however, of Yahya Hassan, a young Danish poet and, from 2015, aspiring politician too. In 2016 his comet-like career was literally speaking arrested as he received a prison sentence (one year and nine months) for gun violence and a number of other offences.

Hassan is of Muslim-Palestinian descent but born (19 May 1995) and raised in Denmark's second largest city, Aarhus, in a part of the city known to the public as a so-called immigrant ghetto.[1] In other words: a poetic dark horse of Arab-Muslim descend. Apparently, Hassan had a fairly traditional religious upbringing, such as participation in the Friday prayer as a regular event. However, as Hassan grew up he became increasingly involved in juvenile delinquency as well as various forms of artistic praxis, mainly rap music and creative writing. Islam seems to have become less and less a factor in his life. During his trajectory of repeated stays at remand homes Hassan's literary talent was noticed and subsequently encouraged and nurtured by the pedagogical personnel. In 2013, at the age of eighteen, Hassan entered in the prestigious *Forfatterskolen* (Writer's School), a two year long state-recognised programme of creative writing. In the very same year, Hassan had his official debut as a full-fledged poet

---

* Title of a poem in *YAHYA HASSAN*, 90.

** This is a revised version of an article published in the Danish literary journal *Kritik*, 2014.

1 The only other Aarhus-based piece of fictional literature that somehow also deals with Islam and religious bigotry is the well-received author and professor of English Tabish Khair, *How to Fight Islamist Terror from the Missionary Position* (Northampton, Mass.: Interlink Pub Group, 2013).

© KONINKLIJKE BRILL NV, LEIDEN, 2018 | DOI 10.1163/9789004362529_010

with a poetry collection displaying his own name in all caps: *YAHYA HASSAN*. This "shouting" and "loud" typography continues throughout the 169 page long work dealing with a bleak list of topics, such as domestic violence, parents and peers' social control, panoptic internal surveillance, juvenile delinquency, substance abuse, sexual abuse, social security fraud, dreary encounters with social service institutions, the plight of Palestine and Palestinians and the widespread religious hypocrisy and bigotry. All articulated in a somewhat artificial Arabo-Danish resembling the ethnolect known in slang as *perkerdansk*.[2] One topic, however, pervades most of the poems, namely that of Islam and Muslims – and always articulated in a derogatory and transgressive language. In short: a work of poetic rage.[3]

The book was released on the 17 October 2013 by Denmark's largest and oldest publishing house, Gyldendal, and it immediately became a huge bestseller with more than 100,000 sold copies during the first three months of its publication. In a country of 5½ million people, where poetry collections usually get issued in maximum 400 copies, and where 3,000 sold copies of a novel turns it formally into a bestseller, the breakthrough of *YAHYA HASSAN* had been unprecedented for decades. It has subsequently been published in Norwegian, German, Spanish, and Italian, but still awaits English publication.

The success of the book was partly prepared by a newspaper interview with Hassan a fortnight prior to the publication. The interview flaunted the headline "Poet: I'm fucking mad at my parents' generation." and it was a scathing critique of his parents generation's utterly social failure, the domestic violence and abuse, the social security scams, and the above mentioned religious hypocrisy and bigotry – even though Hassan admitted that many people from his community actually did manage to take control of their own lives in a productive and beneficial manner.[4] Not surprisingly, the interview provoked sweeping political and cultural debate on issues of failed integration and the collective failure to prevent the rise of a new Muslim underclass right in the midst of a welfare state such as Denmark. In the broader public, the interview was partly taken as an important insider-testimony, as the authentic, almost prophetic, voice speaking unpleasant truths against powerless power. Yet it also garnered

---

2 *Perker* is a racist term for a person with Middle Eastern/South Asian roots and appearance; *dansk* is the word for Danish language. Subsequently, *perkerdansk* is derogatory slang for the special ethnolect spoken among some Danish youths with mainly Middle Eastern background.

3 For the interview *Yahya Hassan: Poems of Rage*, see Louisiana Channel: https://www.youtube.com/watch?v=1HE6ZsH8ldU.

4 "Digter: Jeg er fucking vred på mine forældres generation," *Politiken*, October 5, 2013.

AN ESSAY ON THE POETIC PRAXIS OF YAHYA HASSAN 143

serious criticism from parts of the Muslim communities in Denmark that felt offended and denigrated by Hassan's angry statements and his blasphemous rhetoric in many of his poems.

Thus, along with this exceptional fate among Danish poets, the poems and the person of Yahya Hassan became a veritable cause célèbre with heated public debate, verbal and physical attacks and subsequent legal aftermaths. This included multiple death threats and a number of physical assaults perpetrated by a number of Danish and Palestinian Muslims who apparently had felt offended by the "Islam-critical" contents and comments of the poems and the poet.[5] Given the tense security situation that has gripped the Danish population and state apparatus after the so-called Cartoon crisis, Hassan was granted 24/7 bodyguard protection from the Danish state (which he has subsequently renounced in 2015).[6]

The controversial status of the poems and their poetic persona certainly owed much to the resentful words on the Muslim immigrant community. Hassan's ethnic-religious authenticity as a "witness," emerging from the most underprivileged Muslim classes in a European *banlieue*, was something new to the Danish public. Thus, his whole poetic praxis has been viewed as a radical break with an alleged "law of silence" upheld in immigrant communities in regard to the Danish public sphere and in regard to the repressive behavior of the parental generation. Among pundits and commentators his poetry has not only been identified as the voice of a dissident, but has also been interpreted as a breaker of taboos of political correctness. Indeed, several right-wing and some left-wing commentators took Hassan's poetic outbursts as an indication that the previous national discourse on matters relating to the Muslim communities had been a moral betrayal in regard to the facts on the ground as well as the people living in these environments – despite all the good intentions not to stigmatise a vulnerable community. In the words of the literature editor of Denmark's most influential center-left newspaper, *Politiken*, "The rules of

---

5   "15 year old threatened Yahya Hassan: He abused my god and prophet," *Politiken*, March 7, 2007 http://politiken.dk/indland/ECE2228594/15-aarig-truede-yahya-hassan-han-svinede-min -gud-og-profet-til/; "Yahya Hassan attacked in Palestine," *cphpost.dk*, June 6, 2004 http://cphpost .dk/news14/national-news14/yahya-hassan-attacked-in-palestine.html.   One of Hassan's attackers was a Danish Muslim who had earlier served a seven year prison sentence for attempted terrorism, see "Yahya Hassan overfaldet på Hovedbanegården af tidligere terrordømt," *Information*, November 19, 2013.

6   This included, among other things, an almost fatal attack on the most controversial of the cartoonists, i.e., Kurt Westergaard, as well as a foiled spectacular terror-attack against the shared headquarter of Jyllands-Posten and Politiken in Copenhagen.

political correctness make it so that precisely those people the rules should be protecting end up shut out by them and forced into silence."[7]

Religious Skid Marks in *YAHYA HASSAN*

Hassan's poetry collection is crammed with references to Islam and Muslims. On almost every page of the 169 pages long collection the reader encounters a direct reference or an allusion. However, they cannot be said to draw the lofty and illustrious trajectory that is so often associated with Islam in poetic expression. Rather, all the references and allusions to Islam and Muslims seem to draw a grimy track of skid marks in the reader's mind, constantly blending representation of Islam and Muslims with all the depressing social realities of an ethnic and religious underclass. A casual perusal of the book reveals the first (and most appropriate) Islamic reference in the third poem of the collection, namely that of prayer and Allah ("CHANGED TO DOLLARS AND PRAYED TO ALLAH," 8[8]). In the next poem we come across a reference to the Islamic prayer ritual as well as the category of infidels. In the seventh we read about a mosque. The eighth poem is titled "RAMADAN," and so it continues throughout the collection with more or less direct references to sundry aspects of Islamic, Muslim and Arab culture – yet all set in an explicitly Danish framework, except for a few detours to the Palestinian territories and the proverbial foreign uncle in Dubai, suffering from a heart-condition. To be sure, *YAHYA HASSAN* is a genuine Danish poetry collection, notwithstanding its Arabisms, its pious Arabic idioms (in somewhat loose transcription), and its so-called *perkerdansk*.

Interwoven in this poetic patchwork the reader encounters a number of direct references to Islam's sacred text par excellence, the Qur'an. As far as I can count we come across the first reference in the nineteenth poem, "MORNING PRAYER IN LEBANON." The poem's protagonist describes a visit to Lebanon, during which the protagonist struggles with a bout of diarrhea. The poem closes with the following verses:

> GRANDPA READING THE QUR'AN
> AND WITH FEVER SWEAT ON THE BROW
> I SNEAK DOWN TO THE LAST ROW

---

7   http://www.spiegel.de/international/europe/danish-immigrant-teen-emerges-as-literary
-sensation-a-958515.html.

8   Unless stated, all translations of Hassan are mine.

AN ESSAY ON THE POETIC PRAXIS OF YAHYA HASSAN

> THE MAN WITH THE LARGEST BEARD
> OPENS THE PRAYER WITH ALLAHU AKBAR
> AND THIS IS HOW I SHIT MY PANTS IN GOD'S NAME
>
> *YAHYA HASSAN*, 29

This passage almost amounts to an angst-ridden scatological parody. In classical Islamic theology the believer's proper attitude towards God is that of pious fear of God (*taqwa*), but in this instance the poem's speaker turns this attitude into a most corporeal, transgressive, and embarrassing act. While there is a pun going on with the Danish phrase "to shit one's pants out of fear" there is also an allusion to one of the most used phrases in the Qur'an, namely the so-called *basmala*, in its English rendition "In the *name of God*, the Merciful, the Compassionate." The idiomatic fusion of defecation and God's name is transgressive, bordering to *sabb allah*, "blasphemy" against God. It is doubtful, however, that the passage constitutes a deliberate intertextual reference to the classical Arabic genres of obscene-scatological literature known as *mujūn* and *sukhf*.[9] These works did not sheer away from religious tropes and rhetorical props when they pursued their transgressive literary agendas. We can, for instance, read about the jester Ibn al-Jassas who deliberately misquotes Sura 3, verse 192, replacing the verb *akhzaytahu* "You [i.e. God] annihilated him for good" with the verb *akhraytahu*, "You [God] made him continuously defecate."[10] This example from classical Arabic literature is just but one example among several in which the Qur'an or Qur'anic themes are treated in a highly satirical and deliberately transgressive manner.

There are several references to the Qur'an in the collection (e.g. "A STONE AGE HAND A PAPERBACK-QUR'AN," 103; "AND HIS QUR'AN FILLED HEAD," 109; "YOU YOU CAN NO' GET QUR'AN," 145; "ME FIRST I SWEAR ON THE QUR'AN," 169), but I will not go into the meaning and context of the specific examples here.

All the references, allusions and possible intertextual links to Islam in *YAHYA HASSAN* is one thing, but something quite else is the performative aspect of the poetic work, that is, the very recitation of the poems. Quite a number of people in Denmark (and a select few outside the country) have been

---

9　The major contemporary academic studies on *mujūn* and *sukhf* are, respectively, Zoltán Szombathy, *Mujun: Libertinism in Medieval Muslim Society and Literature* (Exeter: Gibb Memorial Trust, 2013), and Sinan Antoon, *The Poetics of the Obscene: Ibn al-Hajjaj and Sukhf* (New York: Palgrave-Macmillan, 2013).

10　This example is taken from Ulrich Marzolph's article "Humor" in *Encyclopaedia of the Qur'an*, vol. II (Leiden: Brill, 465).

able to listen to Hassan's distinctive recitation style; on national television, in numerous public poetry readings around the country, and on the internet's biggest platforms, *YouTube* and *Facebook*.[11] In these fora the Qur'an turns up again but now as a vague aural frame of reference, namely that of Qur'anic recitation. Yahya Hassan himself has emphasised that the artful form of Qur'anic recitation, such as the artful *tajwīd* (bearing the sense of "beautification"), constitutes an important source of inspiration, just as several of Hassan's listeners have remarked on this perceived connection. A connection which overlaps with another of Hassan's old poetic-performative roots, namely the popular genre of rap (also associated with the musical genre of hip hop), which stylistically, like *tajwīd*, occupies a gray area between speech, prose, poetry, and singing. The question is now if this description holds true, that is, whether Qur'anic recitation *classic* can be detected in Hassan's oral performance or whether it should be construed as a somewhat more intricate construction. Before I try to answer this, a few basic observations on Qur'anic recitation must be interpolated.

Some Notes on Qur'anic Recitation

A close relationship exists between the Qur'an as sacred text and the Qur'an as text of recitations. Unlike the Bible, which claims its title by virtue of its Greek reference *to biblos*, i.e., "the books," the literal meaning of *qur'an* is "declamation," "recitation," or "reading out." Hence, already in its self-referential title the Qur'an signals that it is a text that emphasises orality and *logos,* although there are substantial references to notions of scripture and book culture throughout the Qur'an. An emphatic element of what could be poetic language is also traceable. Of course, this poetic language does not abandon the overarching communicative and rhetorical tenor (e.g., its exhortations, warnings, words of consolation, legal rulings, episodic narratives), but the Qur'anic text frames these communications in a kind of linguistic self-awareness and "playfulness," in which various formalised speech patterns gain an important role, such as varied repetition (e.g., rhyme, alliteration, parallelism), unusual syntax and grammar (e.g., abrupt shifts between the 1st, 2nd, and 3rd person reference), unfamiliar words and *hapax legomena*, puns and sound symbolisms, as well as a striking degree of self-referentiality in regard to language and Qur'an. These immanent oral-poetic features constitute an important factor in the Qur'an genesis, its composition and rhetoric. It is perhaps no surprise that this also spills over in the performative praxis of the Qur'an. Qur'anic recitation is thus

---

11   See e.g. https://www.youtube.com/watch?v=1HE6ZsH8ldU.

an integral part of the Islamic ritual praxis as well as the daily soundscapes of major Islamic nations.

Such emphasis on poetic logos has also left its mark in the highly refined and specialised tradition of Qur'an recitation that can boast of highly equilibristic Qur'an reciters. Some of these reciters are decidedly "stars" who receive high donations for their skills that are demanded for official events and distributed in modern media of cassette-tapes and CDs. A fitting setting for Qur'an recitation is of course the grand halls of Friday mosques, where the acoustic space adds a certain note of reverb and oratorical gravitas to the recitation. The sound of the spacious prayer hall is thus often imitated in many modern recordings where the reverb effect has been exploited to the full.

Without going into the technical details and different styles of Qur'an recitation, the overall impression the specific "oriental" use of vibrato, which endows the sound with a terrace-like contour, which also has the classic oriental touch of plaintive sadness itself.[12] Traditionally, it is stated also that the Qur'an must be articulated with *bi l-huzn*, "with sadness" or "with sorrow"; the many threats and warnings to human beings in the Qur'an are thus granted with a completely different atmosphere as when we read the text in a "mundane" manner. Thus, in live recitations it is not a breach of good form if one among the listening audience breaks into tears. Rather, it can be considered as exemplary pious conduct. Another prominent feature of recitation is the monotony – not to be confused with boredom – due to the fact that the reciter often delivers the text without natural pauses and breaks and without "actor-like" dramatisation of voices. One could perhaps compare the aural expression with arabesque repetitive pattern shapes.

Yahya Hassan and Qur'anic Recitation

Hassan's sudden fame offered many of us the opportunity to get acquainted with Hassan's special reading style; examples can quickly be accessed on the internet.[13] Multiple layers can be identified in his reading style. First, it is characterised by its unmistakable hybrid of Århusiansk (i.e., the typical speech dialect from the city of Århus) and Arabic accent combined with a number

---

12   For the standard work on Qur'anic recitation, see Kristina Nelson, *The Art of Reciting the Qur'an* (Cairo: The American University in Cairo Press, 2001).

13   E.g.   http://www.dr.dk/nyheder/kultur/video-se-yahya-hassan-laese-digte-op-i-vollsm ose#!/;   http://politiken.dk/tv/debattv/ECE2093760/yahya-hassan-fremsiger-digtet-barn dom/.

148   HOFFMANN

of Arabic terms, phrases and names like, for instance, WALLAH, ALLAHU
AKBAR, MASJID SALSABIL, QIYAM ALLAYL. In that sense, the sound of
Hassan's poems can be described as a prime example of the so-called ethnolect
"perkerdansk," which I have already described. Virtually all the Arabic expressions in the poetry collection have Islamic provenance, for example, *WALLAH*,
which is an oath that can be rendered as "I swear by God," and is often used as
an intensifying exclamation when you want to emphasise something in a statement. This expression is perhaps the most used expression in perkerdansk and
its popularity correlates squarely with the significant use of religious formulas
that is typical of spoken Arabic. Besides that, it is my contention that this expression has wandered into Danish when young people in perkerdansk sometimes throw in the phrase "jeg sværger," i.e., "I swear," into their statements.

Second, as already mentioned, several observers of Hassan's reading style
have noted that it shares stylistic features with traditional Qur'anic recitation.
I am, however, skeptical as to this Qur'anic "recognition" among the audience.
Why this skepticism? It is based on several factors. First, I have not yet come
across anyone Arabic-Danish speaking Muslims who have characterised
Hassan's reading style as Qur'anic in terms of style. This may be due to a
reluctance to associate Hassan's at times blasphemous "Islam-critique" – or
rather Muslim-critique – with recitation of the holy Qur'an. It could also be due
to the fact that they do not perceive any connection between his reading style
and that of classical Qur'anic recitation. Hassan himself has time and again declared his veneration for Qur'anic recitation. In an article from the newspaper
Fyens Stifttidende we read that "he uses Qur'anic recitation as a kind of music,
and it is probably the only thing, he says, that he has taken from his religion."[14]
In a short report from a reading at a local high school, we are told that his style is
"a mixture of Qur'anic recitation and gangsta rap, as he called it."[15] In a relatively extensive feature article from the newspaper *Politiken* we read the following:

> JETLAG-ECLIPSE, he says loudly with a deep voice and pronounces ev-
> ery syllable of word distinctly. Chanting at a pace somewhere between
> rap and Qur'anic recitation he recites [...] He shifts weight from one foot
> to the other as a boxer. He rocks back and forth with his upper body and
> prolongs the vowels. The capital letters beat the air out of the crowd.[16]

---

14   Lone Shauman: "Yahya Hassan i Odense: Tag selv ansvar." *Fyens Stifttidende* 24.01.2014.
      http://www.fyens.dk/indland/Yahya-Hassan-i-Odense-Tag-selv-ansvar/artikel/2444223.
15   http://www.roende-gym.dk/nYahya Hassaneder/vis/artikel/farlig-poesi-yahia-hassan/.
16   Sandra Brovall & Peter Hove Olesen: "Da Yahya Hassan blev digter," *Politiken* 09.10.2014.
      http://politiken.dk/magasinet/feature/ECE2169134/da-yahya-hassan-blev-digter/.

What I hear is not so much the typical Qur'anic recitation style, with its modulations and at times extremely prolonged articulation of syllables, the slightly plaintive tone, the extensive use of reverb, and *ghunnah*.[17] Rather, what is heard is a voice with roots in modern European and Danish style of poetry recitation, which coincidentally resembles Qur'anic recitation in its diminishing of dramatised voice and in its increase of an almost ritualistic phonetic flow and rhythm. Language as a tool of communication is put on a par with language as sound and embodiment. In addition to this elite poetic tradition, the echoes of rap and hip-hop rhythms (cf. Hassan's reference to gangsta rap) are quite manifest.

Hassan has repeatedly declared that he treasures Qur'anic recitation. He has called attention to its euphonic character when he for instance announced that he listens to Qur'anic recitation *as if it was music*.[18] Hassan has even staged his own Qur'anic recitation in so far as he has produced a YouTube recording on which he recites surah 33, *al-Ahzab*, "the Companions."[19] As an introduction to his YouTube-recitation Hassan posted the following statement on his Facebook-account: "Qur'anic recitation is my religion" (the statement has a nice rhyming quality).

An Unwitting Critique of Liberal Islam?

One issue remains to be considered. Why this insistence on the Qur'an, especially Qur'anic recitation? Why this insistence on a connection to Hassan's poetic praxis? What is Hassan's project? What does this enfant terrible want to accomplish vis-à-vis those Muslim communities from which he rose and diverged from? It is obvious that the poet engages passionately and actively with the Muslim communities, which he has also polemicised, parodied, and cursed with his poems, interviews and public "stunts" and performances (e.g., several of his poetry readings and debates in the ghettos or his showing up for the opening of a controversial mosque in Copenhagen). Several times we have had the opportunity to read that Hassan does not have an issue with the religion of Islam as such – rather, it is the Muslims (some of them at least) and

---

17   A special technique of nasalisation.

18   "He uses, however, Qur'anic recitation as a kind of music, and that probably the only thing, he says, that he has brought with him from his religion." (my translation) Lone Shauman: "Yahya Hassan i Odense: Tag selv ansvar." *Fyens Stiftstidende* 24.01.2014. http://www.fyens.dk/indland/Yahya-Hassan-i-Odense-Tag-selv-ansvar/artikel/2444223.

19   https://www.youtube.com/watch?v=ZYtciBlKLME.

150 HOFFMANN

their administration of their religion that is problematic. In other words: what is really at stake here?

To a certain respect Hassan's insistence on a liaison between aesthetic praxis and experience on the one hand and the Qur'an on the other is fully in line with a deep current in the Islamic-Qur'anic tradition. The German Qur'anic scholar and essayist Navid Kermani published in 2000 his award-winning work *Gott ist schön: Das ästhetische Erleben des Koran* in which he argued for a close, but in modern times almost supplanted connection between the Qur'an and aesthetic experience – in Islamic dogmatics codified as *i'jâz*, i.e., the inimitability of the Qur'an in both content and style.[20] Kermani demonstrated how the Islamic reception of the Qur'an not only depended on theological, philosophical, and legal arguments, but also aesthetic categories and experiences. Whereas aesthetic has tended to be considered marginal or irrelevant in favour of more truth-orientated claims in the sacred scriptures of Judaism and Christianity, the claim and dogma of beauty in Islam – via the Qur'an's *i'jâz* – was put forward as an argument for the very truth of the Qur'an and of the *dîn*, religion of Islam. It is true because it is beautiful and beautiful because it is true! Based on these analyses Kermani contends that Islam as such stands out as the veritable *Kunstreligion*, that is, the philosopher Friedrich Schleiermacher's (1768–1834) bold *terminus technicus* for the basic religious character of aesthetic experience. We may conjecture that it is this aesthetic-*cum*-religious (in this order) approach which Hassan feels attracted to and nurtured by, while simultaneously feeling challenged by experiencing this aesthetico-religious sensibility as being marginalised and frozen in barren rituals among Muslims today.

To Hassan's *Wahlverwandschaften* of poetry, aesthetics, and Qur'an, adds yet another wild and transgressive component, which probably should be ascribed to Hassan's "risky" past as a juvenile delinquent, partly due to his hyper-controversial role as detractor, "whistleblower," or "prophet" from the ghetto, partly due to his seemingly provocative and blasphemous poems (e.g., the poem ALLAH IS IGNORANCE) and "un-Islamic" behavior where beer drinking and marijuana smoking is flaunted publicly. All of these components led to a prolonged existence under a highly security-driven agenda with bodyguards and frequent threat assessments.

Just as we can identify an aesthetic common denominator between poetry and Qur'anic recitation, so we can recognise certain traditions within Islam in which the transgression of pious behaviour and rhetorical is appreciated in

---

20 Navid Kermani, *Gott ist schön: Das ästhetische Erleben des Koran* (München: C.H. Beck, 1999).

either a very sophisticated or a more vulgar manner; for instance in relation to the traditions regarding wine-drinking and intoxication as cultivated among elite poets and uncouth mystics. Thus, certain radical Sufi sects cultivated provocative inversion of conventional pious praxis by deemphasizing shari'a-prescribed behaviour, for instance by drinking alcohol publicly. On public television[21] Danish viewers could observe how Hassan frequented the famous autonomous neighborhood Christiania of Copenhagen to purchase cannabis, which he subsequently smoked while listening to Qur'an-recitation and now and then join in the recitation. On his Facebook profile Hassan also posted a recording of one of Egypt's most beloved Qur'an-reciters, that is, Abdu l-Basit Abd as-Samad (1927–1988), while commenting the recording with the words: "When Abdul Basit recited the Qur'an in public some listeners would smoke themselves stoned and get drunk before they would attend the recitation session. This is not mentioned to offend anyone, but to illustrate that there is a ritualistic approach to Islam and a more spiritual approach, some possess both in their consciousness, others have only one or the other, and those who only practice the ritual approach must be bored." In this quotation, Hassan seems to call attention to a pre-*Islamist*[22] era as a more pluralistic, paradoxical, and spiritual ideal, an era when the Islamic tradition and the folk traditions had not yet been gripped by the austere moral and political programs of Islamism. When observing Hassan's remarks and praxis his seemingly "wild" project seems quite coherent: it is as if this young poet wants to rehabilitate and promote a past praxis, which was more spiritual, more tolerant towards ambiguity, and resented the massive boredom and social conformity of Islamist life.[23]

It is inevitable, then, to ask if Hassan is pursuing a reformist Islamic project. The answer, I believe, must be in the negative. First of all, Hassan has never addressed his work as such. Second, the writings and "stunts" of Hassan do not seem to reveal a manifest religious agenda. Nonetheless, his work, public statements, performances, and what we might call his total poetic praxis, point in an interesting direction. It is a direction that we have not seen articulated very clearly among Europe's so-called liberal Muslims. They have cultivated a liberal

---

21   The tv-show *Søndag Live* 2013: https://www.dr.dk/nyheder/indland/video-dr-tager-paa -christiania-med-ung-omstridt-digter.

22   The concept of pre-Islamism could perhaps be added to the already well-established concept of post-Islamism.

23   Boredom and social conformity has often been mentioned as a trigger-factor by Islamism- and jihadism-researchers like, for instance, Scott Atran, *Talking to the Enemy: Violent Extremism, Sacred Values, and What it Means to be Human* (London: Allen Lane, 2010) and Olivier Roy, *The Failure of Political Islam* (Cambridge, Mass.: Harvard University Press, 1994).

(and at times highly self-critical) voice on Islam and Muslims in the public sphere. Hassan's combination of passionate poetry praxis, deliberate blasphemous provocations and taboo-busting critique of Muslim communities, and his persistent appropriation and commendation of Qur'anic recitation, in many ways expose the mainstream discourses on liberal, moderate, or reformist Islam, which has been embraced and even promoted by European authorities in the political arena as well as in academia. Hassan's radical praxis indirectly exposes the new liberal and moderate Islam (as voiced by so-called "representatives" or self-appointed religious avant-garde entrepreneurs) as a new orthodoxy. These representatives often position themselves as anti-radicalised and anti-radicalizing voices while simultaneously cultivating and disseminating a relatively conformist, "rationalistic" or rights-based, conservative worldview.

This liberal, moderate and rights-based discourse was in many ways spearheaded by the Swiss academic Tariq Ramadan, whose views became more acute and widespread post-9/11, not least within the academia, but also in mainstream media. At times, it seemed as if the time and energy invested on analysing and discussing Ramadan's version and vision of Islam was almost as massive as that on Islamic fundamentalism.

Recently the historian Zaheer Kazmi, Oxford University, has called for a more critical approach to liberal Islam and has offered alternative versions and visions of late-modern Western Islam that hitherto have been relegated to the margins of research and popular reception. Kazmi has been working on Muslim "anarchism" for a number of years and published a handful of critical articles on liberal Islam.[24] Together with another Oxford historian and expert on modern Islam, Faisal Devji, the two should presently be working on a volume with the title *Beyond Muslim Liberalism.*[25] Kazmi launches a radical critique of the various Muslim liberal attempts, because he finds its liberalism a disguised form of neo-orthodoxy, hegemony that recycles conservative values and inhibits true creative thinking in Islam. Kazmi writes: "Liberal Islam, steeped in orthodoxy, rationalism, and arrogated notions of representation, has lost its vitality and ability to engage constructively with such radical departures. Its modalities are much the same as those of traditional forms of religious authority, engaged as they are in perpetuating threats of 'deviance.'"[26] Instead

---

24   Kazmi, "The Limits of Muslim Liberalism," *Los Angeles Review of Books*, 4th April 2014, https://lareviewofbooks.org/essay/limits-muslim-liberalism; "Is liberal Islam the answer?" *openDemocracy* 4 March 2015: https://www.opendemocracy.net/transformation/zaheer -kazmi/is-liberal-islam-answer; "Automatic Islam: Divine Anarchy and the Machines of God," *Modern Intellectual History* 12, 2015, pp. 33–64.

25   Forthcoming Hurst/Oxford University Press.

26   Kazmi, "The Limits...."

Kazmi calls attention to other voices who are more radical and "anarchist,"[27] for instance:

> [...] the theosophic approach to Islam of French philosopher Abdennour Bidar, which draws on Nietzsche, Heidegger, and Muhammad Iqbal; the counter-cultural anarchistic critiques of Peter Lamborn Wilson (pseud. Hakim Bey) and Michael Muhammad Knight, inspired by discourses of heresy and paganism (a syncretism not alien to Islamic history in India and Africa); the anti-statism of free-market libertarians, such as Imad-ad-Dean Ahmad, who, in an ironic genealogical twist given their associations with American conservatism, draw on Ludwig von Mises and Murray Rothbard to call for a radical Islamic neoliberalism. All trace alternative genealogies of Islamic liberty that, in their own ways, question the premise that the future of Islam lies in its assimilation to the liberal state.[28]

Hassan's artistic and existential praxis aligns very well with some of the "heretical" projects that have been pursued by writers as Wilson aka Hakim Bey and Knight. In their writings, moving between essays, auto-fiction, and the novel, Wilson and Knight (both converts) cultivate pre-modern heterodox Islamic traditions, movements, and practices; for example, Sufism (not least the traditions of anti-social behavior and scandalous exclamations, the latter known as so-called *shathiyât*), syncretism (in which Islam mixes with traditional African, Indian or Javanese religion), heresy, drugs (cannabis, wine, and opium). Knight, sometimes promoted as the Hunter S. Thompson of Islamic literature, also exploits modern subcultural aesthetic movements like the beatniks, the punks, and the rap-artists. A handful of titles from these prolific writers give us a sense of their subjects and approaches, for instance *Scandal: Essays in Islamic Heresy and Sacred Drift: Essays on the Margins of Islam* (Wilson),[29] *Tripping with Allah: Islam, Drugs, and Writing* or *William S. Burroughs vs. the Qur'an* (Knight).[30] Whether we will experience more of that anarchistic and transgressive potential from the fringes of contemporary Islam in Yahya Hassan's writings or witness other radical Muslim free-thinkers and artists is not to be predicted here, but it should certainly be welcomed by the author of this essay.

---

27   Kazmi explicitly excludes the jihadis even though they share some resemblance with classic anarchistic writings, e.g. Bakunin.

28   Kazmi, "The Limits...."

29   Peter Lamborn Wilson, *Scandal: Essays in Islamic Heresy* (no place: Autonomedia, 1988); *Sacred Drift: Essays on the Margins of Islam* (San Francisco: City Light Book, 1993).

30   Michael Muhammad Knight, *Tripping with Allah: Islam, Drugs, and Writing* (Berkeley: Soft Skull Press, 2013) or *William S. Burroughs vs. the Qur'an* (Berkeley: Soft Skull Press, 2012).

PART 3

Multitudes of Muslims in Europe

∵

CHAPTER 10

Human First – To be Witnesses to Each Other's Life: Twenty-one Years of Struggle for Equal Human Dignity

Naveed Baig, Lissi Rasmussen and Hans Raun Iversen

Introduction

An international class on religious dialogue at University of Copenhagen in 2012 had a hard time to find a common ground for a possible peaceful encounter between Muslims and Christians. Especially two Nigerian students who had experienced the killing of a neighbouring Christian family in the Muslim uproar after the Danish Cartoon Crises in 2006 could not see Muslims as more than "evil people." In the middle of the term, the class had a guest lecture by Dr. Johnson Mbillah, at that time director for the *Programme for Christian Muslim-Relations in Africa*, who came along with a friend of his, a Muslim Sheikh. Having introduced his friend and himself as respectively Muslim and Christian and both of them Africans, Dr. Mbillah asked; "So, this friend of mine, is he first an African or is he first a Muslim? And I myself am I first an African or am I first a Christian?" You could hear a needle fall to the ground before Dr. Mbillah answered his own question: "No, my friends, we are first of all human beings, both of us!" Following that visit, a new willingness for religious dialogue spread through our class.

Being is more basic than meaning. Sharing life and recognizing one another as human beings is more important than making meaning systems fit together. Humans have the right to be the ones they are and to strive to become the ones they want to be. The right to cultural and religious identity is what the Danish father of church and nation, N.F.S. Grundtvig (1783–1872) was fighting for, labelling cultural identity *folkelighed* (Iversen 1987). Human beings are, however, not prisoners in iron cages made by their cultures and religions, as it may seem to be indicated e.g. in some sorts of cultural anthropology (e.g. Geertz 1973). Coming closer to the persons behind the meaning systems, you may discover one

---

* The authors, Naveed Baig is vice chairman and coordinator and imam of the hospital project (Ethnic Resource Team), Lissi Rasmussen is center chairman and project leader of the prison project (Katalysator) and Hans Raun Iversen is board member of IKS.

© KONINKLIJKE BRILL NV, LEIDEN, 2018 | DOI 10.1163/9789004362529_011

another as human beings with common basic conditions of life as it is argued e.g. in existential anthropology (Jackson 2012). There are common conditions for human life that precede culture and religion. Human beings work together to interpret, express and preserve their existence and self-understanding.[1] If we meet and mirror one another in our quest for self-understanding we may come to a different encounter with one another compared to the one we may get from comparing cultures and religions in religious dialogues. This requires and promotes mutual trust, as it tends to develop when working together in diapraxis.

This chapter is a report and a reflection on the discovery of common human ground during the 21 years of work at the *Islamic–Christian Study Centre*, in 2016 renamed the *Centre for Co-existence* in Copenhagen. Not only was the work of the centre transformed through this process, in addition, a new road to a better understanding of the existential quest of fellow human beings in serious life crises has been opened.

The Islamic–Christian Study Centre and Jørgen S. Nielsen

The Islamic–Christian Study Centre (IKS) was established in May 1996 in Nørrebro, Copenhagen. Unlike most dialogue centres around the world at the time it was founded jointly by Christians and Muslims. A dialogue group of four Christians and four Muslims had met for two years and decided to share their experiences and friendship with the rest of society. The group convened a briefing to gauge the interest of the various Christian and Muslim organisations. Nearly 50 representatives attended from 10 Christian and 11 Muslim organisations, together with a number of people from the University of Copenhagen, and signed a resolution stating that the time had come to start a joint centre for Christian-Muslim dialogue. Since then, the centre has had an equal number of Christian and Muslim board members and has been supported economically by a number of Christian and Muslim organisations and societies.

The aim of the centre was then, as it is today, to promote constructive relations and improve coexistence between people of respectively Muslim and Christian backgrounds through academic, public and practical work. The centre was to be a place where Christians and Muslims could meet face to face, on an equal footing and in security and mutual respect. This approach was a

---

1   *Human beings are responsive beings. Manifest for an existential anthropology.* http://projects.au.dk/existential-anthropology/researchers/ (visited April 11, 2017).

new point of departure in Denmark and in certain circles very controversial at that time as even today.

The equal approach and the work that the IKS has been carrying out are greatly inspired by the *Centre for the Study of Islam and Christian-Muslim Relations* in Birmingham, directed by Jørgen S. Nielsen. Undersigned author, Lissi Rasmussen, had been studying there over longer periods and worked with Jørgen S. Nielsen continuously since 1977. He became a very important support and inspiration for the IKS from the start and throughout the years. From time to time, Jørgen has visited the IKS and given advice and lectures there. This inspired us to continue the good work, despite the hostility experienced by the centre in society, as well as in certain Christian and Muslim environments. As it turned out, precisely by applying the equal approach, joint ownership made it possible to build and maintain mutual trust despite the highly negative sentiments that have been experienced by Muslims in the Danish society, especially after September 11, 2001, and during the Danish Cartoon Crisis in 2006.

Developments and Experiences

During these years, the IKS struggled to become a recognised partner for ethnic minorities and a number of Christian and Muslim organisations and congregations. Friendships and communities developed across religious and cultural boundaries. Through face-to-face encounters in the IKS, common study groups and study tours and projects, many people gained increased knowledge of each other and thereby revised their prejudiced perceptions of the other, basing them more and more on real knowledge.

Volunteers in the IKS have contributed to opening dialogue around the country, including initiating meeting places, dialogue groups, interreligious councils, conferences, seminars etc. The IKS has also been and still is a resource centre where organisations, institutions and individuals can benefit from the human as well as material resources and experiences of the centre, including the widespread network and the mutual trust among people that the IKS has built over the years. Not least, young Muslims have, through equal cooperation and involvement in the conversation about the common future, gained more self-confidence and surplus of energy to be active in society and in the public debate.

In addition, involvement in international interfaith and development projects in collaboration with, among others, the World Council of Churches and the Lutheran World Foundation, in the Middle East, Pakistan, Indonesia and Nigeria, England and Norway, has provided the centre with inspiration and strength here in Denmark. Also, in these contexts Jørgen S. Nielsen has been an important work partner.

A Turning Point

During its initial years, the goal of the IKS was pursued primarily through smaller dialogue groups, education, information, and advice and open dialogue meetings on Islam, the relationship between Islam and Christianity and common ethical issues. It was important simply to bring people together and demonstrate that it was possible to sit in the same room and talk about religion and faith in a peaceful and constructive way.

Over the years, however, it became increasingly clear that inter-religious dialogue, in the traditional Western sense, focused on faith was not enough.[2] There was a need for joint action in relation to the common challenges we are confronted with as human beings, as Christians and Muslims. Several major events made this clear and at the same time made the work of IKS more urgent and more difficult. The events of September 11, 2001, and the subsequent political campaign in Denmark with Islam and Muslims as the main theme led to a "change of system" in Danish politics, with the Danish People's Party becoming a decisive political power. Other parties were influenced by the nationalist party's pandering to xenophobic voters.

In 2003, the Danish government joined the US "coalition of the willing" and sent troops to Iraq. This had both a negative and a positive impact on relations between Christians and Muslims. It was negative in the sense that some Muslims perceived the operation as an aggression against Islam and Muslims. They therefore turned against the West, including Denmark. In addition, some Danes were confirmed in their enemy image of Muslims and Islam, and fear of terrorism on Danish soil increased. At the same time, Muslims and Christians experienced that the disagreement of the population in relation to the war and the Danish participation in it walked across religious affiliations and cultural backgrounds. Many Danes of Christian and Muslim background stood together in demonstrations against the war.

Later came the Danish Cartoon Crisis (in Denmark labelled the Muhammad Crisis) in 2006. Immediately after the spectacular development of the crisis in the beginning of February, the situation worsened, which also led to polarisation among Muslims and Christians. Christian and Muslim organisations and individuals needed to position themselves in relation to each other within the two communities and were on guard of each other. Alliances and hostilities arose where they had not previously existed. This led to some scepticism and rejection of dialogue activities on each side. Extremist groups on both sides were reinforced.

---

2 For theoretical considerations on this, see Rasmussen 1997.

HUMAN FIRST – TO BE WITNESSES TO EACH OTHER'S LIFE   161

The crisis did not lead to the self-criticism and openness in public debate that many had hoped for. Political populism and the government's arrogant attitude towards its critics continued. The same applied to the media discourse that still focuses on individual imams' statements and behaviour, and not on actual events. At the same time, many dialogue initiatives were taken by individual Muslims and Christians and by various organisations.[3]

Despite good international and interreligious contacts, the IKS faced the risk of becoming a mental reservation for a small group of people somehow isolated from the increasingly nationalist and populist debate in Denmark, where politicians compete in using hard language. Just to mention one expression: refugees without residence permit who cannot be returned to their countries of origin used to be called "people on tolerated stay." Now the slogan is, that "tolerated stay must be as intolerable as possible."[4]

Joint Diaconal Projects

IKS has from its beginning considered it important that Christians and Muslims meet in a common space to deal with social and general human issues and challenges. In 2003 it was decided to go a step further – not only to relate reflectively and dialogically to the issues, not just to deal with each other in relation to "a third challenge," but to interact and engage together in that challenge. Therefore, the activities of the IKS became more and more goal-oriented and practice-related – a tendency that was reinforced by the events transpiring in 2006. Interaction – to work together around common specific tasks with common objectives – increasingly has become the foundation upon which IKS developed relationships and a community, not only internally among the actors in the work, but especially among people in Denmark.

From 2003, IKS focused on three specific project areas, which are closely linked: (1) advocacy for equality; (2) counselling in the health service system from 2003 (*Ethnic Resource Team, ERT*); and (3) work among youth in prisons from 2011 (*Katalysator*). In all three areas, the IKS started to work closely together with relevant partners in state and municipalities and with other NGOs.[5]

From the Christian perspective these ways of working builds on the traditions for diaconal work and pastoral care and counselling among people in

---

3 For further information and analysis of Danish immigration politics and especially the Danish Cartoon Crisis, see Iversen 2010, Martin 2010, Sørensen 2010 and Warburg 2010. See also Rasmussen 2007.

4 Repeated again in Jyllands-Posten November 4 2016 by Minister of Integration, Inger Støjberg.

5 For further information, see the web sites www.ikstudiecenter.dk, http://ressourceteam.dk, www.centerk.dk.

need. Since the emergence of pietism in the 18th century, diaconal work has been seen as a humble Christian work of love for one's neighbour, carried out among people in isolation from society as Christians are challenged to undertake not least in hospitals and prisons (cf. Mt 25:31–46). In recent years a theologically stronger understanding of diaconal work has emerged from the discovery that the New Testament word *diaconia* is a general expression for being sent with a mandate from one (in the last instance God) to another to serve this other in the place of the sender (God), as Jesus himself did it (Collins 1990). In addition, also the modern understanding of pastoral care as accompaniment at a part of a person's life journey provides inspiration for the new kinds of work at the IKS (Grevbo 2006).

In Islam the purpose of almsgiving, rights of neighbours, bringing up children, visiting the sick, feeding the hungry, helping the oppressed all point towards the vast social responsibility that God laid upon people from the Islamic faith pointing towards the viceregency principle (khilafah) (Baig 2007). Likewise the Prophet mentioned that the most beloved to God are those most attending to God's creation (Gilliat-Ray et al. 2013); and after belief in God, the greatest virtue is benevolent love towards one's fellow human.

Below we will focus on *ERT* and *Katalysator*. The two diaconal projects have been important –, not least for the volunteers who are directly involved in the work, and the relationship of trust that arises between them and the people the projects are directed to and who need help and support. The work also has implications for those who in different ways are involved in the projects. What is discovered and recognised is not Muslims and Christians but human beings struggling to respond to the existential challenges of their lives.

Ethnic Resource Team (ERT) – IKS in Hospital

Positions for chaplains working in relation to patients with other than the majority faith (the Evangelical Lutheran Church) are not available at the Danish Hospitals, and no multi-faith chaplaincy work is organised and structured according to official politics in this area. This was the reason why the Islamic–Christian Study Centre in 2003 initiated an inter-religious volunteer corps, Ethnic Resource Team (ERT) for ethnic minorities in hospitals in the Copenhagen area, which later also included chaplaincy services.

The Development of Ethnic Resource Team (ERT)
There were from the beginning ten ERT volunteers. The hospitals and wards themselves could now establish contact with faith communities through the

ERT when needed, and hospital staff, patients and relatives could call upon ERT members if they needed someone to talk to with similar background as their own. Moreover, one of the first activities was to offer a number of courses on "Islam in health service" to staff members, nurses, doctors and students in the health area.

This volunteer corps was extended and its work formalised and developed into a pilot project at the hospitals, running from January 2008 to January 2011. It was partly financed by two hospitals, the national hospital (*Rigshospitalet*) and Herlev Hospital, where it was integrated into the hospital organisation. In 2011 ERT became a permanent partner in the daily function of the hospital, primarily in Rigshospitalet and Herlev Hospital. The project manager (Naveed Baig) was hired as coordinator of ERT in four Copenhagen hospitals with Rigshospitalet as the host hospital for the team. He is now placed within the personnel department and the ecclesiastical function. Naveed Baig who is also a trained Muslim chaplain has also delivered volunteer Islamic chaplaincy services to patients and families alongside giving hospital staff, diversity- and religious management training since 2005. This is the first instance of a semi-formal chaplaincy service in Denmark for a faith denomination other than that of the Evangelical Lutheran Church (Nielsen 2011, Chapter 12).

The Work of ERT

The overall purpose of ERT was and still is to secure that ethnic minorities gain the best possible access to the hospitals and receive optimal care. In addition, it is important that the general care and spiritual care for patients and families with different ethnic backgrounds have an equally high standard of care as that for ethnic Danish patients and caregivers in general. Thus, the team had and still has three main functions:

- to provide visiting and support service to patients and relatives with ethnic minority background
- cultural mediation between hospital staff and patients/relatives
- to offer and conduct training and supervision to staff

From the beginning the resource persons were, and still are, undergoing intensive training and supervision so that they can act as interlocutors, consultants and lecturers and be available for hospital staff.

The visiting task today is handled by more than 60 volunteers from various ethnic, cultural and religious backgrounds who provide care and support to patients and relatives. Almost half of them have a background in healthcare. In total, the team accounts for 25 different languages which by far correlates to the patients' and relatives' language needs. During 2014 ERT had 223 patient related contacts in seven different hospitals.[6] About a third of them were related to chaplaincy services – especially to the Muslim chaplain. Members of the team taught 64 sessions to hospital staff relating to topics such as cultural diversity, communication, bio-ethics and religion.

To Feel at Home

There was a guestbook in the prayer room after it was established at Rigshospitalet in 2006, just opposite the church. In this patients could write their comments and wishes for the future. A patient expressed her content with the new room in the following way: "It is really nice that we got a prayer room. It's so good to feel at home in one's own home and not be left out."[7] One of the words for a hospital in the Danish language is *sygehuset* which translates to "home for the sick." The patients "feeling at home" comment suggests a sense of comfort and warmth that she found in feeling recognised through the acknowledgement of her religion. The Rigshospitalet brochure about the prayer room states: "Rigshospitalet highlights that all patients and relatives can practice their faith and religion. To acknowledge this Rigshospitalet has furnished these prayer room facilities." Spiritual and religious care have been shown to be important to patients and are acknowledged to have a significant and beneficial impact on patient outcomes (see for example "Standards for Spiritual Care Services in the NHS in Wales 2009" and Gilliat-Ray, Sophie et al. (eds.) 2013 and La Cour 2014).

Katalysator (Catalyst) – the IKS in the Prison

Project *Katalysator* (Catalyst) is based on a comprehensive study, *Personal Narratives and Crime. Ethnic minority youth in Copenhagen Prisons.* The research was carried out by Lissi Rasmussen, who also wrote up the report. It was published in June 2010 as a book from the *Centre for European Islamic Thought* that was located at University of Copenhagen from 2007–2013, directed by Jørgen S. Nielsen.[8] The study shows that most of the youngsters with ethnic minority

---

6   "Patient related" here does not necessarily mean physical contact but can also be indirect contact such as for example in an inter-disciplinary meeting at a hospital ward where a patient case is discussed with ERT.

7   Henning Nabe-Nielsen, "Mødet med mennesker af anden tro i sundhedsvæsenet, Magasin om Religionsmøde." Folkekirke & Religionsmøde, May 2012 p. 16.

8   The book can be downloaded freely from www.centerk.dk. See Rasmussen 2010.

(primarily Muslim) background have experienced missing or negative contact to adults, many interrupted processes throughout childhood and youth, combined with experiences of injustice and social exclusion in society (both personal and at the structural level). At the same time, their personal narratives show that these young people are unique individuals who wish to be perceived as such. But many of them experience that they have not been confirmed or recognised as such either through childhood (in the family, in school) or later as young people – personally through education or work and collectively as included equal citizens in society. In the terminology of the German sociologist Hartmut Rosa, they miss resonance, positive response from others leading to reflections on and strengthening of their own identity (Rosa 2016a and b).

In this way, there is a seedbed for political-religious radicalisation in the form of the anger and frustration over lack of recognition borne by many of the young people. Most of them are hardly socialised as Muslims. Their Islam is part of their identity but their knowledge of its content is very limited.[9]

Since 2011, Katalysator has had an official cooperation with the prison authorities and has been able to send volunteer resource persons/mentors (currently 20) into Copenhagen prisons where they mentor youths (primarily from ethnic minorities), who express a wish to leave crime behind. The inmate is allocated a volunteer mentor who will support and guide him/her through the challenges he/she faces in the current situation and help the prisoner become better equipped at taking charge of his/her own life.

Priests and imams who work with young prisoners in study groups make contact with the young inmates in the prisons. Mentors are searched for and selected according to competence, particularly ability to be attentive and able to converse and reflect. They undergo upgrading courses and are supervised by professionals. The mentor follows the young mentee through serving his/her sentence, and when the mentee leaves prison the mentor tries to help him/her to move forward with an education or a job.

Katalysator has had (as of February 1, 2016), since the beginning of 2011, more than 200 mentor arrangements. The project has been shown to have a positive effect on those young people, including several that had been abandoned by both the prison probation authorities and the municipality. This is in accordance

---

9   The respected expert on political Islam Olivier Roy has found the same results when coming to that small segment of Muslims, especially criminals with Muslim background who may become radicalized, prepared to commit terrorism. "It is not Islam that is being radicalized; it is the radicalization and nihilism (belonging to Western society) that is being Islamized" (*Kristeligt Dagblad* January 7, 2016). For Professor Roy's general argument, see Roy 2010.

with recent research pointing to personal relations and new constructive fellowships as needed for preventing radicalisation and furthering reintegration in society (CERTA 2016). Two of the IKS's board members are appointed imam and pastor in Copenhagen prisons, where they work – both through individual conversations and study groups – to build trust with the youngsters. Some of the volunteers have come from lives of crime themselves and have completed or are in the process of completing higher education or work.

In November 2013, Katalysator also was opened as a networking and advisory centre, run by the Islamic–Christian Study Centre aiming to "catalyse" a new development for youngsters who come out of prison. The centre seeks to involve local citizens in its work. It has a large network of volunteers, who in various ways contribute to the project.

After release and during the latter part of the sentence the youths can come to the centre, receive counselling and support leading them towards an education and/or seeking employment. They also receive help to face the challenges that come with having left a life of crime. In Katalysator they can develop a more wholesome network, and participate in activities together with other youths, strengthening their own identity and aspirations for a good life.

The method that is used is to involve the young inmates and ex-inmates in association-life, in activities such as sports, music, social work, conflict resolution and relief work. Through cooperation with a number of volunteer organisations, the centre tries to make the inmates and ex-inmates interested in the work these organisations are doing, for instance raising money for projects in Gaza and Afghanistan, joining an organisation in Lebanon working with Syrian refugees or working in the streets with other youngsters. Many inmates who have decided to leave crime have a strong urge to do something for others. Katalysator tries to give them the opportunity to do so and to do it with other young people, who are involved in this kind of work.

Diaconal Collaboration and Coexistence

The experiences of the IKS have shown that interfaith cooperation in the diaconal sphere has an impact on the coexistence of people in society. Thereby polarisation, conflict, counter-cultures and extreme reactions can be discouraged or avoided. Diaconal cooperation and work for coexistence are linked and conducive to each other. The shared understanding among those who take part in the interaction that equality is an important principle has a significant effect on other Danish citizens. A strongly socializing society like Denmark has to take care of all its citizens equally. This also applies to young criminals and the ill with ethnic minority background who can easily be lost in an individualised society. The common experiences of the cooperation thus can be summed up in six points:

1. The most important point is that a common goal is reached: Counselling is being done. People receive the help and support needed in a crisis. Their strength and quality of life is improved.
2. The citizens who receive help find that their needs (including the spiritual ones) and dignity is recognised and taken seriously in the community they live in. This promotes better self-esteem. They experience what it is to be part of the social community ("to feel at home in one's own home").
3. The interaction affects the people who are involved in the work. The volunteers feel that they are needed and have a function, a positive contribution to make. They are required actors.
4. A better mutual understanding and solidarity is achieved among the participants – because of the shared responsibility, they feel that they have a relation to a common concern. They learn from each other and discover new aspects of both the others and their own tradition.
5. The co-operation has an impact at the grassroots level: Other people in the community see that there is consistency between the words and actions of the people involved. At the same time, they discover that it occurs across cultural and religious differences – that there is togetherness, mutual trust and solidarity between the people involved. The "us" and "them" division – the polarisation between citizens – is counteracted.
6. The common practice – the responsibility Christian and Muslim participants share as believers – leads naturally to reflections on the purpose and meaning of counselling and social ethics in the various religious traditions. Thus, an Islamic care or counselling theology has developed, emerged from the European context and inspired by the Christian tradition and theology.

Through cooperation in hospitals and prisons, Muslims have become more aware of the theology of counselling, as expressed in Islam. In particular, the question of what kind of coping strategies such as rituals, prayer, story-telling etc. the care-giver can use in an Islamic context, becomes very relevant. This has further led to an awareness among young Muslims and university staff of the importance of education in Islamic spiritual care.

Education in Islamic Theology and Practice

In the history of Islam, in Muslim countries there has been no great need for organised care work or for a specific counselling theology. It has been the family's task and responsibility to take care of the sick and suffering. It begins, however, to gain relevance and shape in Western societies where also Muslim citizens are characterised by individualisation and family breakdown and thus often stand alone without a family with the time and ability to live up to its responsibilities.

Thus, Islamic spiritual care is not explicit but implicit in Islamic theology and has not been properly systematised to a discipline such as in the case of the Christian pastoral tradition. However, it is on the way both in the West and in Muslim countries (Gilliat-Ray et al. 2013). This means that the reprocessing of Islamic spiritual care at the theological level is needed also in Denmark. In a Danish context, we need spiritual advisers, both men and women who can perform caring tasks in public institutions such as nursing homes, mental health, prisons, hospitals, universities and military etc.

There is no theological Islamic education at the university level in Denmark, let alone an education in Islamic spiritual care as it is found in a number of European countries (Johansen 2006). Therefore, the undersigned three writers along with a number of imams, academics and other representatives of various Muslim communities have discussed the possibility of setting up an education at the Faculty of Theology at the University of Copenhagen, that may approach an Islamic theological training, but initially is primarily designed to qualify Muslim candidates to handle spiritual care in institutions and mosques.

This can be done by making it possible to put together individual study programmes (flexible master) in the field of "Islamic theology and practices" where seven different courses were planned for 2016 and 2017. Adviser for these courses is the adjunct professor of University of Copenhagen, Jørgen S. Nielsen who was exploring and testing these opportunities during his time as a research professor at the University of Copenhagen. The first course on Islamic spiritual care was implemented in January 2016. This is an important step forward since the work for Islamic theological education at University of Copenhagen has been going on since 2003 (Iversen 2006).

These courses take starting point in parts of the Islamic theological tradition and practice, particularly spiritual care, emphasising that there is an immediate need for in Denmark and whose relevance and content is acknowledged by most of those who know the area. Islam is studied both from the outside and inside: Islamic theology and practices are studied against the background of the historical context in which they were developed, but also current interpretations and portrayals of Islam that exist among Muslims in Europe today are included. This dual approach to the study of Islam is promoted by the participating teachers, including keynote speakers from abroad, and the difference in skills and diversified background of participants expected to participate.

The programme accommodates not only a theological need among Danish Muslims, but may also help to meet the quest for recognition and belonging that many especially young Muslims have.

Concluding Perspective: A Universal and a Danish Human Point

By having a social and human engagement in common, by being engaged in the well-being of other people, religious and cultural differences become secondary and easier to relate to. Prejudice and negative attitudes towards "the other" may be overcome, as respect for the other's equality renders them obsolescent. This is in brief the lesson experienced at the IKS during its 21 years of work, pointing back to a profound universal as well as basic Danish tradition.

Gajus Plinius Caecilius Secundus, the Roman politician who lived approx. 61–113 CE is reported to have said, when he lost a dear friend: "I have lost the witness to my life, I am afraid that I will begin to live less carefully." We all need witnesses to our lives. This is how it is for ethnic minority citizens – many of them with Muslim backgrounds – who fall severely ill and are hospitalised in Denmark. They need somebody to be with them in their difficult situation, a person who can listen to them and who understands them, and they need to be reminded of who they are as Muslims in their dependency of God. Moreover, this is not least how it is for ethnic minority youth who during their upbringing have taken some of the bad things from the Danish society and only very little of the good things from their parents' Muslim tradition. They have a strong need for a mentoring witness who can tell them and the rest of society who they really are: unique human beings created in the image of God, as Muslims and Christians believe it to be.

The work of the IKS reminds us all of the universal human need to have witnesses to our lives. It also reminds us of another universal tradition, which may have had its strongest expressions in the authorship of N.F.S. Grundtvig, who always emphasised his "Human first, Christian next" (Cf. Hall et al. 2015). All of us are born equal as human beings. We need to feel at home where we are. On that background and in the culture we happen to live in, we may become Muslims, Jews and Christians e.g. First and always, we are human beings before and hopefully after anything else.

Literature

Baig, Naveed. 2007. *Den Muslimske Patient*. Islamisk-Kristent Studiecenter, Copenhagen.

Baig, Naveed. 2015. *Islamic Spiritual Care*. MA-dissertation, Copenhagen University.

CERTA Intelligence & Security. 2016. *Modstandskraft mod radikalisering og voldelig ekstremisme: et eksplorativt studie af modstandskraft i udvalgte danske lokalmiljøer.* Virum: Trygfonden.

Collins, John N. 1990. *Diaconia. Re-interpreting the Ancient Sources*. Oxford, Oxford University Press.

Geertz, Clifford. 1973. *The Interpretation of Cultures. Selected Essays.* New York: Basic Books.

Gilliat-Ray, Sophie et al. (eds.). 2013. *Understanding Muslim Chaplaincy.* Surrey: Ashgate.

Grevbo, Tor Johan S. 2006. *Sjelesorgens vei: En veiviser i det sjelesørgeriske landskap – historisk og aktuelt.* Oslo: Luther forlag.

Hall, John A. et al. (eds.). 2015. *Building the Nation. N.F.S. Grundtvig and Danish National Identity.* Copenhagen: DJØF-Publishing.

Iversen, Hans Raun. 2010. "Background of the cartoon Crises in Danish mentality." *Religion in the 21st Century. Challenges and Transformations.* Surrey: Ashgate, 191–206.

Iversen, Hans Raun. 1987. *Ånd og livsform. Husliv, folkeliv og kristenliv hos Grundtvig og sidenhen.* Århus: Anis.

Iversen, Hans Raun. 2006. "Preface," in: Birgitte Schepelern Johansen, *Islam at the European Universities, Report II.* University of Copenhagen.

Jackson, Michael. 2012. *Lifeworlds. Essays in Existential Anthropology.* University of Chicago.

Jenkins, Richard. 2011. *Being Danish. Paradoxes of Identity in Everyday Life.* Copenhagen: Museum Tusculanum Press.

Johansen, Birgitte Schepelern. 2006. *Islam at the European Universities, Report II.* University of Copenhagen.

La Cour, Peter. 2014. "Tro og alvorlig sygdom – om forskningen i nordisk kontekst," in: L. Danbolt, L. Engedal, H. Stifoss-Hanssen, K. Hestad og L. Lien (eds.) *Religionspsykologi.* Oslo: Gyldendal Nordisk.

Martin, David. 2010. The Settled Secularity and Happy Denmark. *Religion in the 21st Century. Challenges and Transformations.* Surrey: Ashgate, 183–190.

Nielsen, Jørgen S. (ed.). 2011. *Islam in Denmark.* Lexington Books.

Rasmussen, Lissi. 1997. *Diapraksis og dialog mellem kristne og muslimer. – i lyset af den afrikanske erfaring.* Aarhus University Press.

Rasmussen, Lissi. 2007. *"Bridges instead of Walls."* Christian-Muslim Interaction in Denmark, Indonesia and Nigeria. Minneapolis: Lutheran University Press.

Rasmussen, Lissi. 2010. *Livshistorier og kriminalitet.* Centre for European Islamic Thought, University of Copenhagen. A summary in English, Personal Narratives and Crime: http://centerk.dk/wp-content/uploads/2013/10/Summary-of-a-report.pdf.

Rosa, Hartmut. 2016a. *Resonanz: Eine Soziologie der Weltbeziehung.* Berlin: Suhrkamp Verlag.

Rosa, Hartmut. 2016b. "Resonance: Towards a New Conception of the Good Life." Paper from the conference *In-Between: The Protestant Heritage of Existential Thought.* Aarhus University.

Roy, Olivier. 2010. *Holy Ignorance. When Religion and Culture Part Ways.* Oxford University Press.

Sørensen, Anders Berg 2010. "The Politics of Lutheran Secularism: Reiterating Secularism in the Wake of the Cartoon Crises." *Religion in the 21st Century. Challenges and Transformations.* Surrey: Ashgate, 207–214.

Warburg, Margit 2010. "Globalisations and Religious Diasporas: A reassessment in the Light of the Cartoon Crises." *Religion in the 21st Century. Challenges and Transformations.* Surrey: Ashgate, 215–228.

CHAPTER 11

Muslims Accused of Apostasy: An Ahmadi Refutation

Göran Larsson

The followers of the Ahmadiyya movement have suffered from discrimination, violence and attacks since Mirza Ghulam Ahmad (1835–1908) issued his first religious messages in the 1880s in the village of Qadian in India. With the Partition of India and Pakistan in 1947, the attacks on his followers became more intense. For example, since 1974 it has been forbidden and punishable for Ahmadis to identify themselves as Muslims in Pakistan, and several research reports have documented the heavy persecution that Ahmadiyya Muslims suffer in many countries and regions of the world.[1]

Regardless of the fact that the Ahmadis are both an example of a Muslim reform movement and have played a key role in the early history, establishment and spread of Islam in both Europe and North America,[2] the movement has not been much studied. By downplaying the minority positions that exist among and within Muslim groups, it is easy for researchers that focus on Islam and Muslim affairs to come to the wrong conclusion that a "correct" interpretation of Islam is only found among the majority Sunni population.[3] Internal differences, minority positions in opposition to majority positions

---

* This study was prepared within the framework of a larger research project, "Leaving Islam: Apostasy, Freedom of Religion and Conflicts in a Multireligious Sweden," funded by the Swedish Research Council (Vetenskapsrådet).

1 See, for example, *A Beleaguered Community: On the Rising Persecution of the Ahmadiyya Muslim Community* (International Human Rights Committee, 2015).

2 On the role of the Ahmadiyya movement in the early history of Islam and Muslims in Europe, see, for example, G. Jonker, "A Laboratory of Modernity – The Ahmadiyya Mission in Inter-war Europe," *Journal of Muslims in Europe* 3 (2014), 1–25, G. Jonker, *The Ahmadiyya Quest for Religious Progress: Missionizing Europe 1900–1965* (Leiden: Brill, 2016) and B.A. Jacobsen, G. Larsson and S. Sorgenfrei, "The Ahmadiyya Mission to the Nordic Countries," in *Handbook of Nordic New Religions*, (eds). J.R. Lewis and I.B. Tøllefsen (Leiden: Brill, 2015), 359–373. For the significance of the movement in North America, see, for example, E.E. Curtis IV, *Muslims in America: A Short History* (Oxford: Oxford University Press, 2009).

3 This problem is, for example, partly addressed by A. Lathan, "The Relativity of Categorizing in the Context of the Ahmadiyya," *Die Welt des Islams*, 48: 3(2008), 372–393.

© KONINKLIJKE BRILL NV, LEIDEN, 2018 | DOI 10.1163/9789004362529_012

MUSLIMS ACCUSED OF APOSTASY

and struggles over questions of legitimacy and authority are present in both history and the present day when it comes to the study of religions in general and Islam and Muslims in particular. While this chapter is only devoted to a debate about accusations of apostasy from Islam, it serves as a reminder that Muslim groups are seldom united in their thoughts or actions when it comes to how to interpret and apply Islam.

The chapter opens with a brief outline of the history and theology of the Ahmadiyya movement. This background is important because it will give the reader a backdrop to the text that is the focus of my chapter, namely *The Truth about the Alleged Punishment for Apostasy in Islam*.[4] This specific text is an apologetic work rejecting the common idea that Muslims should be allowed to kill anyone accused of leaving Islam. The text was originally delivered by the fourth Caliph of the Ahmadiyya movement, Mirza Tahir Ahmad (1928–2003), at the annual Jalsa Salana held in Tilford, UK, on 27th July 1986. The speech was delivered in Urdu, but was published in an English translation in 2005. Ahmad's text illustrates that the debate over apostasy and how to treat individuals who are accused of leaving Islam is an open one, showing that it is possible to find different answers among Muslim theologians in both history and today.

By paying attention to internal conflicts over how to define who is and who is not a Muslim, it is easy to show that the definition of a Muslim is not a static or self-evident category – on the contrary. Authority over interpretation and the laying down of categories and typologies is always related to issues of power. Categories like orthodoxy and heresy are not natural, but are constructed and closely related to whoever has the authority and power of decision.[5] In both history and today we find abundant examples showing that Muslims have conflicting opinions about Islamic dogmas and about how to live and practice Islam. As demonstrated by Ahmad's text, the question of apostasy is not an exceptional case, and even though a large number of Muslims strongly believe that it is wrong to leave Islam and that apostates should be killed,[6] it is

---

4   H.M.T. Ahmad, *The Truth about the Alleged Punishment for Apostasy in Islam* (Tillford: Raqeem Press/Islam International Publications Ltd, 2005). The text can be retrieved from https://www.alislam.org/library/books/Apostasy-in-Islam.pdf (accessed 2015-07-17).

5   On the importance of considering classifications and power when studying religions, see, for example, M. Craig, *A Critical Introduction to the Study of Religion* (Sheffield: Equinox, 2012).

6   See, for example, R. Peters and G.J.J. De Vries, "Apostasy in Islam," *Die Welt des Islams* 17: 1/4 (1976–1977), 1–25. See also *The World's Muslims: Religion, Politics and Society* (Pew Forum on Religion and Public Life, April 30, 2013), 55. Retrieved from: http://www.pewforum .org/2013/04/30/the-worlds-muslims-religion-politics-society-exec/ (accessed 2015-08-08).

174

important to stress that other Muslim theologians have also come to different conclusions about this important issue.[7]

A Short Historical and Theological Background

The Ahmadiyya movement is often portrayed as a messianic and prophetic reform movement dating back to the end of the 19th century. At this time this was one of several reform movements that were being shaped by modernity and British dominion on the Indian subcontinent. Theologically the movement's roots are found in the thoughts of the medieval mystic Muhyi al-Din ibn al-ʿArabi (1165–1240), who "postulated an uninterrupted succession of non-legislative prophets following Muhammad."[8] This idea is close to those of the founder of the Ahmadiyya movement, Mirza Ghulam Ahmad (d. 1908), who claimed to be a "divinely inspired religious thinker and reformer."[9]

Contrary to the great majority of Sunni and Shiʿa Muslims, the Ahmadiyya community of Qadian, for example, believe that Jesus died a natural death and that he was not taken up to heaven as most Muslims believe.[10] Besides this doctrinal belief, Ahmadis also promote a non-violent interpretation of the doctrine of *jihad*.[11] This interpretation made them several enemies and has been seen as indicating an unwillingness to fight the British colonial system, meaning that they were viewed as a Trojan horse within the Muslim community.[12] Even more controversially, they also believe that "a follower of

---

7   See, for example, A. Saeed and H. Saeed, *Freedom of Religion, Apostasy and Islam* (Farnham: Ashgate, 2004); A.A. Na-Naʿim, *Islam and the Secular State: Negotiating the Future of Shariʿa* (Cambridge, Massachusetts: Harvard University Press, 2008); and T.J. Alalwani, *Apostasy in Islam: A Historical and Scriptural Analysis* (London and Washington: The International Institute of Islamic Thought, 2011). Also the influential and often quoted Internet portal Onislam.net (earlier named IslamOnline) contains a fatwa that condemns that apostates from Islam should be killed, see "Should an Apostate Be Killed? (reply date 2014/12/21." Retrieved from: http://www.onislam.net/english/ask-about-islam/faith-and -worship/islamic-creed/166989-should-an-apostate-be-killed.html (accessed 2015-09-08).

8   Y. Friedmann, "Ahmadiyya," in *The Oxford Encyclopedia of the Modern Islamic World*, (ed.) J.L. Esposito (Oxford: Oxford University Press, 1995), 54.

9   Friedmann, "Ahmadiyya," 55.

10 For an overview of different Muslim beliefs about the death of Jesus, see, for example, T. Lawson, *The Crucifixion and the Qur'an: A Study in the History of Muslim Thought* (Oxford: Oneworld, 2009).

11 On Ahmadiyya opinions about Jesus, see Mirza Bashir-Ud-Din Mahmud Ahmad, *Invitation to Ahmadiyyat* (Tillford, Surrey: Islam International Publications Ltd., 1997), 12–24.

12 See, for example, A. Latham, "The Relativity," 378–379.

MUSLIMS ACCUSED OF APOSTASY

the Holy Prophet has appeared amongst us as the Promised Messiah."[13] To come to this conclusion, it is necessary to make a distinction between law-bearing prophets (i.e. those who have been sent with a new law) and so-called secondary prophets (*zilli nabi*), who are to guide the believers back to the true faith.[14] According to the followers of the Qadiani branch of the Ahmadiyya movement, Mirza Ghulam Ahmad belongs to the second category, and it is he who is the promised Messiah.

> The claim of Hazrat Mirza Ghulam Ahmad (upon whom be peace) is that God has raised him for the guidance and direction of mankind; that he is the Messiah foretold in the Traditions of our Holy Prophet and the Mahdi promised in his Sayings; that the prophecies contained in the different religious books about the advent of a Divine Messenger in the latter days have also been fulfilled in his person; that God has raised him for the advocacy and promulgation of Islam in our time; that God has granted him insight into the Holy Qur'an, and revealed to him its innermost meaning and truth; that He has revealed to him the secrets of a virtuous life. By his work, his message, and his example, he has glorified the Holy Prophet and demonstrated the superiority of Islam over other religions.[15]

These claims have made the followers of Mirza Ghulam Ahmad a hated and despised group among many Muslims around the world.[16] But the movement has also been divided over its theological message, and today it is necessary to distinguish between the so-called Qadiani and Lahori branches. The first is commonly referred to as the Ahmadiyya movement; it follows the theology outlined in the quotation above and is the largest group. In comparison, the Lahori group is closer to mainstream Sunni Islamic opinion and stresses that Ghulam Ahmad should be seen as a "renewer" (*mujaddid*) and not as the Mahdi.[17]

As long as the Indian subcontinent was under the British domination, the Ahmadiyya community attracted mainly doctrinal disputes among Muslims, though Hindu and Christian leaders also expressed strong opinions about

---

13   Mirza Bashir-Ud-Din Mahmud Ahmad, *Invitation*, 24–25.

14   Lathan, "The Relativity," 376.

15   Mirza Bashir-Ud-Din Mahmud Ahmad, *Invitation*, 58.

16   See, for example, A.N. Burhani, "Hating the Ahmadiyya: the place of 'heretics' in contemporary Indonesian Muslim society," *Contemporary Islam* 8 (2014), 133–152. See, also Latham, "The Relativity," 372–393, and *A Beleaguered Community*.

17   Friedmann, "Ahmadiyya," 54–55.

the movement.[18] With the ending of the colonial system and the Partition of India and the establishment of Pakistan in 1947, the Ahmadiyya community became a source of conflict. The Pakistani *Jama'at-i-Islami* movement and the *Majlis-e-Ahrar* especially insisted that the Ahmadiyya community and its followers should be labelled as heretics and apostates from Islam. After several conflicts and with the growing tension, the National Assembly of Pakistan came to the conclusion that the followers of the Ahmadiyya movement were not Muslims. The decision of 1974 reads:

> [A] person who does not believe in the absolute and unqualified finality of the prophethood of Muhammad (peace be upon him), the last of the Prophets, or claims to be a Prophet, in any sense of the word or of any description whatsoever, after Muhammad (peace be upon him), or recognises such a claimant as a Prophet or a religious reformer, is not a Muslim for the purpose of the Constitution or Law.[19]

In April 1984, the Pakistani president, Muhammad Zia ul-Haq (1924–1988), issued yet another decree that made it punishable to follow Ahmadiyya religious observances and to propagate either Qadiani or Lahori beliefs.[20] Because of these measures and other persecution, the main body of the Ahmadiyya community went into exile in the United Kingdom, but the movement is also well established in most parts of Europe, North America, Australia and Africa. In these continents, the tension between different Muslim groups is often limited to doctrinal disputes, but in many parts of the Middle East, the Persian Gulf region and Asia, Ahmadiyya Muslims face persecution and even legal penalties.[21]

As documented by Jørgen S. Nielsen and other scholars who have worked on the history of Islam and Muslims in Europe, it is an established fact that the Ahmadiyya movement is one of the earliest Muslim missionary organisations in the West. Both in Europe and North America, Ahmadi missionaries were among the first Muslim organisations that opened mosques and presented Islam to a non-Muslim audience. For example, the first Ahmadi missionary came to Scandinavia already in 1956 and they opened mosques in both Denmark and Sweden in the 1960s and 1970s. For example, in Denmark, which

---

18   Some of these debates are documented and analysed in S. Lavan, "Polemics and conflict in Ahmadiyya History: The *'Ulama,'* The Missionaries, and the British (1898)," *The Muslim World*, 4(1972), 283–303.

19   Quotation taken from Friedmann, "Ahmadiyya," 55.

20   Friedmann, "Ahmadiyya," 55 and Lathan, "The Relativity," 385.

21   See, for example, Burhani, "Hating the Ahmadiyya" and *A Beleaguered Community*.

MUSLIMS ACCUSED OF APOSTASY 177

is the home country of the jubilar of this Festschrift, it was the Ahmadiyya movement who built the first proper mosque in Denmark. Already in 1966–67 the Nusrat Djahan mosque was opened in Copenhagen.[22] However, Denmark is not an exceptional case, a similar pattern is found in many other European countries. But even though the Ahmadiyya movement plays a leading rule for the establishment of Islam in Europe, the movement remains a strangely understudied group. If this has to do with the fact that the Ahmadis have been stamped as heretics by many Muslim groups, or if this disengagement just shows a lacuna in the research is an open question, but no matter of how we reply the Ahmadiyya movement merits serious attention from researchers that are interested in both the religious landscape of Europe in general and the establishment of Islam and Muslims in Europe in particular.

Mirza Tahir Ahmad's Views of Apostasy

Within the limited space of this chapter, it is not possible to go into great detail in analysing Mirza Tahir Ahmad's rejection of the view that apostates from Islam should be killed, and I therefore only focus on the major points in the text. The main arguments in *The Truth about the Alleged Punishment for Apostasy in Islam* are derived from a comprehensive and critical discussion of terminologies and categories that can be related to apostasy in both Islamic sources (i.e. Qur'an and *Hadith*) and Islamic debates (especially *fatwas*).

Already in the first section of Ahmad's text it is clear that the refutation is related to the fact that Ahmadiyya Muslims have been condemned as heretics from Islam and that it is legal to discriminate against them in Pakistan. According to Ahmad, the Muslim community has been harmed by the fact that some Muslim theologians are influenced by socio-political conditions when they interpret Islam. Because of this he laments and says:

> The sword of the Islamic world is being drawn against the world of Islam, and the daggers of the Islamic world are being used to stab the world of Islam in the chest. Whether it is the conflict between Iran and Iraq, or between two rival factions of Palestinian Mujahidin; whether it is the contention between Syria and Jordan, or that between Libya and Egypt, whichever way you look at the Islamic world the forces of Islam are locked in combat against each other.[23]

---

22   See, for example, Jacobsen, Larsson and Sorgenfrei, "The Ahmadiyya mission."
23   Ahmad, *The Truth*, 5.

To remedy this problem, it is necessary to stop the killing of innocent people and return to the Qur'an and the sayings of the Prophet Muhammad. In this way a "true" understanding should emerge, and Muslims should learn that neither the Qur'an nor the Sunna support the death penalty for apostasy from Islam according to Ahmad. Without going into any details, this conclusion is contrary to the majority of Muslim theologians who are convinced that the hadith-literature contains reports that support that Muhammad commanded that apostates should be killed.[24] However, it is less common to find Muslim theologians who argue that the Qur'an contains an explicit recommendation for the killing of apostates. Passages in the Qur'an seem to indicate that apostates should be punished in the next life. In pursuing his line of argument, it is also important for Ahmad to oppose the claim that Ahmadi Muslims are heretics or non-believers (*kafir*). Accordingly, if one notes how the Prophet Muhammad defined a Muslim, it is clear that Ahmadis also should be seen as Muslims according to Ahmad. Ahmad quotes three prophetic sayings to support his claim, the first of which reads:

> The Holy Prophet[sa] said: "Write down for me the name of every such individual who claims to be a Muslim by the word of his own mouth."[25]

A person who declares that he or she is a Muslim is a Muslim according to the quotation above, but according to the second example from the *hadith* literature it is also necessary to observe the requirement to pray, follow the same *qibla* and eat the slaughtered meat as "we do" (i.e. the Prophet and the first Muslims).[26] The third prophetic saying quoted by Ahmad relates to a military episode in the early days of Islam. When the Prophet Muhammad is informed that a member from the Juhaina tribe has been killed after reciting the *kalima* (La ilaha illAllah), he mourns and says:

> "O Usama! Did you kill him despite his reciting *La ilaha illAllah*?" I [Usama] submitted, "O Messenger of Allah! But he recited *La ilaha illAllah* due to his fear of the weapons and for fear of getting killed." The Holy Prophet[sa] exclaimed, "Why did you not cut open his [chest to look at his] heart so that you could ascertain whether he had recited it due to fear or whether it was a heartfelt recital?"[27]

---

24   Cf., for example, Peters and de Vries, "Apostasy."
25   Quoted by Ahmad, *The Truth*, 10.
26   Ahmad, *The Truth*, 12.
27   Ahmad, *The Truth*, 14–15.

MUSLIMS ACCUSED OF APOSTASY

This quotation should be interpreted to the effect that defining a Muslim is a matter between the individual and God. Consequently, Ahmad holds that every individual who is sincere and says *La ilaha illAllah Muhammadur Rasulullah* is a Muslim. According to Ahmad, this definition is based on the words of the Prophet and does not state that any Muslim theologian who came after the Prophet Muhammad should be denounced. Consequently it is wrong for the Pakistani authorities to state that all Muslims should denounce Mirza Ghulam Ahmad (the founder of the Ahmadiyya movement) in order to be a Muslim.[28] This addition to the *kalima* (i.e. that it is necessary to denounce Mirza Ghulam Ahmad) was not used in the case of earlier so-called prophets, like, for example, the Musaylima,[29] who was a rival to the Prophet Muhammad in the 7th century. Furthermore, if this were put to practice, what does it imply for those who were Muslims before the Pakistani state made this addition to the law obligatory in 1974?[30] This way of putting the argument can be understood as an Ahmadiyya strategy to show that the Pakistani state does not follow the words of the Prophet Muhammad but makes up its own laws for socio-political reasons.

To prove his case, Ahmad also discusses the terms and categories that are used for apostasy. According to Ahmad's understanding, it is impossible for a Muslim to declare another person a heretic or apostate from Islam as long as he or she testifies that they are Muslims. Consequently, the only way to say that a person has left Islam is if the individual declares this openly and if the decision is based on free will. Ahmad writes:

> The word "*irtidad*" is exclusively used in the *active* sense, and it can never be used in the passive sense. That is, only such a person is called a *murtad* [i.e., an apostate] who *himself* announces that he is relinquishing the faith.[31]

Based on this and other verses from the Qur'an, Ahmad concludes that there are no passages in the holy text that actually permit a Muslim to call another human a *kafir* as long as he or she follows Muhammad's definition of a Muslim

---

28   Ahmad, *The Truth*, 18.

29   According to early Muslim sources, Musaylima was a rival to Muhammad and claimed that he was destined to share Muhammad's mission, and he also received revelations from the angel Jibril. Musaylima never denied Muhammad's prophecy, but he claimed that he also was given prophecies. On this rival to Muhammad, see Kister, M.J. "Musaylima," *Encyclopaedia of the Qur'ān*, Vol. 3 General Editor: Jane Dammen McAuliffe, 460–463. See also Ahmad, *The Truth*, 99–100.

30   Tahir, *The Truth*, 19–20.

31   Ahmad, *The Truth*, 26.

(as set out by Ahmed above). To him the Qur'an states that a belief should be based on freedom, there being no compulsion in religion (Q 2:257; cf. also Q 5:93 and Q 10:100). As stated in Q 88:22–25:

> [O Muhammad], Admonish, therefore, for you art but an admonisher; You are not a warden over them; But whoever turns away and disbelieves, Allah will punish him with the greatest punishment.[32]

This verse is interpreted in such a way as to say that Muhammad should give guidance to all mankind, but this duty does not give him (or any other Muslim) the right to use compulsion.[33] This interpretation is obviously not supported by, for example, the Pakistani theologian Allama Shabbir Ahmad Uthmani (1887–1949), whom Ahmad addresses in his text. This theologian claims that the Qur'an gives believers the right to kill apostates. Uthmani bases this understanding on Q 2:55, which reads in his translation: "O nation of Bani Isra'il! You wronged your souls by making a calf an object of worship. You should now turn toward God and, then *murder your own people*."[34]

To come to a proper understanding, at least in Ahmad's interpretation, it is important to highlight the context of this specific verse, which is related to the Mosaic Law and not the followers of Muhammad. According to Ahmad, the only way to understand how Uthmani came to his conclusion, i.e. that it is proper to kill apostates from Islam, is that "he had learnt it from the Bible" or that "Uthmani has invented himself and has attributed his invention to the Qur'an."[35] Ahmad argues that, instead of applying an established approach to Islamic sources, Uthmani has interpreted the Qur'an to serve the aims of the Pakistani state.

When discussing polemical debates concerning apostasy from Islam, Ahmad holds that most Muslim theologians base their opinions on either weak *hadith* traditions or medieval *fatwas*.[36] As has been pointed out by several academics,[37] Ahmad stresses that most theologians who argue that apostates should be killed base their arguments on the fact that apostates were often

---

32   Unless otherwise stated, all quotations from the Qu'ran are taken from Ahmad.

33   Ahmad, The Truth, 34.

34   Quoted from Ahmad, *The Truth*, 35.

35   Ahmad, *The Truth*, 44. On Jewish and Christian opinions and debates about apostasy, see, for example, Stephen G. Wilson, *Leaving the Fold: Apostates and Defectors in Antiquity* (Minneapolis: Fortress Press, 2004).

36   Ahmad, *The Truth*, 49.

37   See, for example, J.L. Kraemer, "Apostates, Rebels and Brigands," *Israel Oriental Studies*, x (1980), 34–73.

MUSLIMS ACCUSED OF APOSTASY 181

rebels against the Muslim community.[38] Those put to death were primarily (if not only) killed because they were rebels who threatened the social order, a punishment that had nothing to do with their theological beliefs. Consequently it is wrong to argue that they were killed because of their apostasy – it was rather their rebellion that was considered punishable by death.

Looking more closely at the *hadith* literature, Ahmad argues that the reports that seem to support apostates being killed are based on weak traditions. However, in this chapter I am not able to go into any details about the science of *hadith* (*ilm al-hadith*). For the sake of the present argument, it is only relevant to know that many Muslims who argue that apostates should be killed base their opinions on *hadith* reports and not on the Qur'an.[39] To solve this problem, it is necessary for Ahmad to demonstrate that these reports depend on weak traditions and are of a category that Muslims should not follow.[40] Some of them are classified as *gharîb*, i.e. they are only reported by one narrator, some of whom are viewed as unreliable, like, for example, 'Ikrima [written as 'Ikrama in Ahmad], one narrator of prophetic traditions whom Ahmad does not trust.[41] But more importantly, it is fundamental for Ahmad to stress that "we cannot make a Hadith to overrule the Holy Qur'an. That was exactly the inviolable principle adopted by the Holy Prophet."[42]

Finally, Ahmad stresses that those Muslims who believe that it is right and legal to kill apostates are supporting an inhuman system, thus violating the human rights that all individuals are entitled to. This aggressive interpretation of Islamic sources also conflicts with Mirza Ghulam Ahmad's message of peace and love for everybody. He writes:

> Those who are in favour of the death penalty for apostasy do not take into account the ill effects of their inhumane and innovative view on mutual relations with other nations and religions. Why don't they understand that if their view is valid then it would mean that the followers of other religions will be allowed to change their faith, but a Muslim will not have the same right to leave his religion! Islam would appear to have the right to change other people's religion, but other religions will absolutely have

---

38 Ahmad, *The Truth*, 66–67.

39 See, for example, Peters and De Vries, "Apostasy."

40 Ahmad, *The Truth*, 92–93.

41 Ahmad, *The Truth*, 114–115. On the unreliability of 'Ikrima,' see, for example, Ahmad, *The Truth*, 116–120. For an academic analysis, see J. Schacht, "'Ikrima," *EI²* (online edition, University of Gothenburg).

42 Ahmad, *The Truth*, 86.

no right to invite Muslims to change their religion! What a dreadful face of Islam they are painting to show to the world?[43]

Even though Ahmad does not use the term Islamophobia, his way of arguing demonstrates that those who claim that apostates should be killed are contributing to anti-Muslim attitudes and thus giving non-Muslims a reason to hate Islam.[44] This inhuman behaviour is a violation of the principle of freedom of religion, and because of this attitude many people in the world think that Islam is "an ignorant faith belonging to the dark ages."[45]

Conclusions

As demonstrated by Ahmad's refutation, *The Truth about the Alleged Punishment for Apostasy in Islam*, there are many different ways of reading and interpreting the Qur'an and the *hadith* literature, and there is no consensus among Muslim theologians regarding apostasy. In analysing Ahmad's text, however, it must be stressed that, although both Ahmad and his critics are selecting verses and passages from the same Islamic sources, their respective selections and interpretations are very different. In order to understand their varying conclusions, close attention should be paid to conflicting political and theological intentions, it being clear that the proposed suggestions and interpretations always serve different purposes. For the Ahmadiyya community, it is necessary to defend Mirza Ghulam Ahmad's interpretations and to show that the violence against and persecution of the followers of the movement is illegitimate and contrary to Islamic sources. For his opponents, however, the aim is to demonstrate and convince fellow Muslims that it is legitimate and proper to criticise and even fight the Ahmadiyya movement. From this point of view, the debate about apostasy and how to interpret Islam is a classic example of the insight that interpretations of religions are closely related to the prevailing political, social and historical contexts. How to define orthodoxy and heresy is therefore a battle over authority, legitimacy and power.

---

43   Ahmad, *The Truth*, 122–123.

44   Cf., G. Larsson, "'Most Muslims are Like You and I, but "Real" Muslims...': Ex-Muslims and Anti-Muslim Sentiments," *Journal of Muslims in Europe*, 5(2016), 205–223.

45   Ahmad, *The Truth*, 151.

CHAPTER 12

Marginalised Islam: Christianity's Role in the Sufi Order of Bektashism

Emil B.H. Saggau

Introduction[1]

On a warm spring day in May 2009, Professor Jørgen S. Nielsen and I, along with a group of fellow researchers crossed a busy marketplace in the Northern Macedonian town of Tetovo. At the end of the marketplace, we found the monastery (*tekke*) of Harabati Baba belonging to the Bektashi Sufi order (*tariqa*). We were invited in and were seated side by side with the local leader (*Baba*) and an initiated disciple (*dervish*). Surprisingly, in the hour-long conversation the like of Mother Theresa was mentioned in the same breath as Ali, Prophet Mohammad's son-in-law. On the wall hang pictures of Ali, the twelve holy Imams and one of Mother Theresa, with the latter being the object of worship. She was emphasised as one the order revered.

The conversation with the Baba of Tetovo illustrated one central question this Sufi order has posed to both Islamic studies and studies of religion in South East Europe, and that is the place and role of Christianity in Bektashism.[2] Studies have emphasised Bektashism as a syncretistic blend of Islam and Christianity or labelled it as a bridge between the two religions.[3] These descriptions of Bektashism have often only fleetingly touched upon the nature of the two religions' meeting in Bektashi belief, rituals or especially the holy texts.

Therefore, this article sheds light on the subject through an analysis of the role Christianity plays. The focal point of the analysis are two central holy Bektashi texts, known as the Velayetname and the Makalat. The two texts are very different in content, structure etc., but seem to draw on a common

---

1 I wish to thank Jørgen S. Nielsen for taking me along on his travels to the Bektashi tekkes and thereafter having several enjoyable discussions on this subject.

2 Irene Melikoff, *Hadji Bektach, un mythe et ses avatars: Genese et evolution du soufisme populaire en Turquie* (Leiden: Brill, 1998) & *Sur les traces du soufisme turc – recherches sur L´islam populaire en anatolie* (Istanbul: Les Éditions Isis,1992).

3 Antonina Zhelyazkova, *The Spread of Islam in the Western Balkan Lands under Ottoman Rule (15-th–18-th Centuries)*, (Sofia, BAS, 1990), 141–150.

© KONINKLIJKE BRILL NV, LEIDEN, 2018 | DOI 10.1163/9789004362529_013

understanding of Christianity. The two texts do not seem to depart from the broader Islamic or Sufi tradition in their use of Christianity, but rather they do deploy Christian figures, beliefs or stories in a new Bektashi context. Christianity is used as a stepping-stone for the Bektashi towards the Divine, which only can be reach in its fullness through the teaching of the Bektashism.

Christianity plays a central role in these texts due to a unique combination and dialectic between social-geographical, religious and historical factors. Christianity's role is based on a complex development of a pragmatic logic, in a special historical frame of religious interaction from where the order emerged and where it did preserve its attitude and traits. In that aspect, Bektashism is a kaleidoscope into the interlacing between Islam and Christianity in the Balkans and in Anatolia through the long centuries of the Ottoman Empire. Bektashism's use of Christianity opens a window into what happens when religions meet and new forms of those religions are born and stabilised, and reveals, how Christianity and Islam intertwine on a theological, historical and social level.

The Rise and Fall of Bektashism

A few central elements in the history of Bektashism are crucial to understand in order to discuss and analyse the role of Christianity. Bektashism has not always existed as an established Sufi order and at times the order has been under extreme external pressure. In the 14th century, Bektashism was founded by a Türkmen Baba, Haji Bektash Veli, and his life is portrayed in the holy text *Velayetname*. His ideas quickly spread amongst the Ottoman and especially to their janissary corps. Later, the movement became established as a *dervish tariqa* around the 16th century and the order found its current form under Sultan/sheikh Baba Balim (d. 1516).[4] The order was also affected by the so-called *Hurufism*, a highly sophisticated numerological belief system, which has had a great impact on the sacred Bektashi text called *Makalat*.[5] Bektashism reached its height in the 17th century and was spread across the Ottoman Empire, and especially in the Albanian-speaking regions.[6]

---

4   John Kingsley Birge, *The Bektashi order of Dervishes* (London: Luzac Oriental, 1994), 33–40, 51, 71, 74–76.

5   Emil Hilton Saggau, "Bektashi-traditionen: En folkelig sufisme," Tidsskriftet for Islamforskning, Volume 8, nr. 2, (2013), 81–113.

6   It is in general believed that the Bektashi order never penetrated the Balkan further than the Northern part of Kosovo, but a few recent studies suggest that they might have been active further north in Ottoman controlled Bosnia, see Eric Cornell, "On Bektashism in Bosnia," in *Alevi Identity: Cultural, Religious and Social Perspectives*, Tord Olsson, Elisabeth Ozdalga, Catharina Raudvere (ed.), (London: Routledge, 1996), 11–18.

CHRISTIANITY'S ROLE IN THE SUFI ORDER OF BEKTASHISM   185

The established religious Bektashi authorities were attacked in 1826 and in 1925 by especially the Sunni authorities. Following these attacks in the early 19th and 20th centuries, the organisation of the Bektashi order in Turkey began to dissolve. Here, Bektashism only survived as such as a local practice and belief system amongst the Alevis and Kizilbash.[7] The order survived in the Balkans, but was heavily decimated after the Balkan Wars and the First World War. In the 1940s, the order could only be found amongst Albanians, and under Albanian communism this remaining part of the order was dissolved and forced underground for almost fifty years.[8] Today, Bektashism is scattered across the South East Europe and has only partly survived in small communities, where the revived order remains primarily in Albania, slowly rebuilding since the end of communism.

Studies of Bektashism reflect its rise and fall and can be divided into sections that focus on various parts of Bektashism – both historically and geographically: (1) anthropological or ethnographic studies that were undertaken from 1900–1950. The most well-known of these are John Kingsley Birge's *The Bektashi Order of Dervishes* from 1937, which has become the standard work on classical Bektashism;[9] (2) within the last thirty years a series contemporary studies of Alevis and Kizilbash communities throughout the former Ottoman space has been made;[10] (3) a number of shorter articles present Albanian Bektashism, mostly conducted by Albanian speaking academics;[11] (4) A few modern studies has been conducted on the history of Sufism, Bektashism or the Ottoman janissary corps, in the former Ottoman space.[12] In addition to these academic studies, the still surviving institutionalised form of Bektashism

---

7   Irene Melikoff "Bektashi/Kizilbash; historical Bipartition and Its Consequences," in *Alevi Identity: Cultural, Religious and Social Perspectives*, Tord Olsson, Elisabeth Ozdalga and Catharina Raudvere (London: Routledge, 1996), 1–10.

8   Robert Elsie, "Der Islam und die Derwisch-Sekten Albaniens. Anmerkungen zu ihrer Geschichte, Verbreitung und zur derzeitigen Lage," Kakanien revisited,(2004), 1–12.

9   See for example Birge, *The Bektashi order of Dervishes*; F.W. Halsluck, "Geographical Distribution of the Bektashi," The Annual of the British School at Athens, Vol. 21, (1915/16).

10 See for example David Shankland, *The Alevis in Turkey – the emergence of a secular Islamic tradition*, (London/New York: Routledge, 2007); Jørgen S. Nielsen and Antonina Zhelyazkova (ed.), *Ethnology of Sufi Orders: Theory and Practice*(Sofia: IMIR, 2001).

11 See for example Albert Doja,: "Spiritual surrender: from companionship to hierarchy in the history of Bektashism," Numen, Brill, 53. (2006), 448–510; Cecilie Endresen, "Med Gud og verdenskart: Folk og steder i geislig diskurser i Albania," Chaos, nr. 55 (2011), 107–134.

12 See for example Riza Yildrim, *Dervishes in early Ottoman society and politics; A study of Velaytenames as a source of history,* (Ankara: Bilkent University, 2001).

in Albania has begun publishing works of their own.[13] Most valuable are Huseyin Abiba's recent translation of two of the central sacred Bektashi texts.[14]

A significant challenge to Bektashism today is the rise of both conservative Islam and its more radical variants, such as Wahhabism and jihadi-salafism.[15] Islam in the Balkans has in general been characterised as a local variant of Islam, which had its own distinct form.[16] In the post-communist era, several national Islamic communities have become much more coherent and centralised under new educated leadership. A focused effort from these communities has been put into the separation of the so-called "true" Islam – often the same as orthodox Hanafi Islam – from the more popular "heterodox" or Sufi forms of Islam. Such leadership often argues that Bektashism is something else than Islam due – in their opinion – to the prominence of Christian elements in Bektashism.[17] What role Christianity plays in Bektashism has therefore become a critical question to explore. Most of the mentioned Bektashi studies have not focused in detail on the relationship between Christianity and Bektashism, mainly because they are occupied with other issues. There is therefore a blind spot, when it comes to addressing the role Christianity plays in this Sufi order.

Islam, Popular Beliefs or Syncretism?

The description of Bektashism as "heterodox," "syncretistic" or even "extreme" has been used to explain, why it has incorporated Christian traits.[18] Such labels are highly problematic and presuppose that there is a centre or essence in

---

13   See for example Huseyin Abiva, "The Long Night of Communism (1945 to 1990)" (1990) (http://bektashiorder.com/era-ofcommunism, retrieved 23.05.2012).

14   Huseyin Abiba (trans.), *The Makalat of Haji Bektashi Veli – the discourse of a 13th century Sufi Master*, (Babagan Books, 2006); *The Saintly exploits of Haji Bektas Veli – Manakib-I Haci Bektas-I Veli "Velayetname,"* (Babagan Books, 2006).

15   Stephen Schwartz, "Islamic Fundamentalism in the Balkans," Partisan Review (2000). http://www.islamicpluralism.org (retrieved 25.05.2012).

16   Darko Tanaskovic, "Islam in the Balkans, Islam within the Balkans," in Dragoljub Djordjevic (ed.), *On religion in the Balkans* (Nis: Yugoslav Society for the scientific study of religion, 2013), 33–38.

17   See Jørgen S. Nielsen *et al.* (ed.), *Yearbook of Muslims in Europe* I–VIII, (Leiden: Brill, 2009, 2010, 2011, 2012, 2013, 2014, 2015). Noticeably, this trend has affected most countries in South–East Europe after the fall of communism.

18   Matti Moosa, *Extremist Shiites: The Ghulat Sects* (Syracuse New York: Syracuse University Press, 1988); Harry T. Norris, *Popular Sufism in Eastern Europe, Sufi brotherhood and the dialogue with Christianity and "Heterodoxy"* (London: Routledge, 2006).

CHRISTIANITY'S ROLE IN THE SUFI ORDER OF BEKTASHISM 187

Islam that can be used as a dogmatic standard to assess the tradition. Understanding the Bektashi tradition in Southeast Europe today, rather, requires a socio-religious perspective. According to Samim Akgönül, such an approach investigates how the Bektashis "believe behave and belong."[19]

Bektashism is popularly expressed in poems, short stories, local rituals and celebrations of venerated places and persons. Beyond these, it exists as a more sophisticated and abstract belief-system within the Albanian order. Here, the Bektashi belief is practiced in inauguration rituals, teaching of disciples and education. In both the popular and more learned form does the modern Bektashi use the Qur'an, the Hadith, and many other texts. They follow key Islamic figures, such as Muhammad, Ali, and many of the imams, and practice a number of common rituals and festivals, such as the commemoration of Ali's death.[20] Throughout, the Islamic features of Bektashism are ever present and in that sense the Bektashis belong to Islam. More specifically, they describe themselves as belonging to the Shi'a tradition, and they honour the twelve imams.

The description of the Bektashism as something different from orthodox Islam – be it heterodox or syncretistic – is therefore not based on the lack of Islamic features. Rather, the identification of difference is primarily based on the Bektashis' use of other non-Islamic religious traditions, significantly Christianity. In the following analysis, therefore, the key question remains of how the Bektashis reuse Christianity and whether this transforms them into something non-Islamic?

Convergence with Christianity

Prof. Jørgen S. Nielsen used to illustrate the relationship between Christianity and the Bektashism with an anecdote from the World Council of Churches (WCC). The WCC paid a visit to the Bektashi headquarters in Tirana in the early 90s and was guided around by the grandmaster – the *dede* – of the order. The dede repeatedly asked the WCC leaders how one could become a member of the WCC. Finally, the WCC leader replied that they would like to know, who it was that wanted to become a member. The dede answered, "Our Christian side."

The anecdote illustrates that the Bektashis are themselves well aware of the prominence of Christianity in the Bektashi tradition, broadly speaking. This

---

19   Samim Akgönül, "Muslim as minorities," in Ednan Aslan; Ranja Ebrahim; Marcia Hermansen (ed.), *Islam, Religions, and Pluralism in Europe* (Vienna: Springer VS, 2016), 143–152.

20   Elsie, "Der Islam und die Derwisch-Sekten Albaniens. Anmerkungen zu ihrer Geschichte, Verbreitung und zur derzeitigen Lage."

was already highlighted in John Kingsley Birge's early study. Birge describes that the Bektashis reused elements from six out of the seven Eastern Orthodox Christian sacraments. One of them was drinking wine and eating bread echoing the Divine Liturgy and another one was the reinterpretation of baptism.[21] These similarities are intended by the Bektashis and they are given new meaning within the Bektashi context.

Other studies have observed other forms of similarities, noting that it is only elements or structures that seem to be alike.[22] Nathalie Clayer discusses the Bektashis' use of Christian saints, such as Mother Theresa, and argues that this reuse is based on the prominence of Albanian Nationalism.[23] As mentioned, the Baba in Tetovo made the same connection between the saints and Bektashism, but in his explanation the connection between them was far more complicated than the nationalistic simplification, Clayer suggests. The linking was only partly based on the nationality of saints. In Baba Mondi's view, the Christians were close brothers and sisters in faith as well. According to Bektashi belief, the Christians have received a revelation, which was limited and did not reach its full meaning without being understood through Bektashism.

Such an understanding of the relationship between Bektashism and Christianity seems to be in line with the general description of Christianity within other Islamic traditions.[24] Christianity, as a religion of the book, contains partial truths, which need to be unfolded in the Islamic context. Another example of this is the so-called Bektashi "trinity," which is used as a description for the frequent Bektashi referral to "God, Mohammed and Ali," making them equal, but at the same time different.[25] This structure of three persons' oneness seems to correspond with the Christian trinity, but noticeably it is not a concept of Father, Son and Holy Ghost. In this example, the Bektashi notion, that there is a mystical connection between the three monotheistic religions of Islam, Judaism and Christianity plays a central part. The latter traditions have only

---

21   Birge, *The Bektashi order of Dervishes*, 16.

22   Doja, "Spirtual surrender: from companionship to hierarchy in the history of Bektashism," 456; Erik Cornell, "A surviving Neoplatonisme," Islam and Christian-muslim relation, Routledge, vol.17 nr.1, 1–20 (2006), 15.

23   Nathalie Clayer, "The Bektashi Institutions in Southeastern Europe: Alternative Muslim Official Structures and their Limits," Die Welt des Islams, Volume 52, Number 2 (2012), 183–203.

24   Oddbjørn Lervik, *Images of Jesus Christ in Islam*, (Uppsala: Swedish institute of Missionary Research, 1999), 84–90; Hugh Goddard, *Muslim Perceptions of Christianity*, (London: Grey Seal, 1996).

25   Birge, *The Bektashi order of Dervishes*, 133.

CHRISTIANITY'S ROLE IN THE SUFI ORDER OF BEKTASHISM 189

partial, but not full, access to the revelation. The full revelation can only be accessed through Mohammed, Ali and finally Haji Bektash Veli.

The Bektashis' use of Christian saints, symbols and ritualistic elements is an unfolding of this interpretation of Christianity. According to the Bektashis, Christianity is recycled and put to good use. The so-called Christian behaviour of the Bektashis seems to be based on an Islamic interpretation of Christianity.

Christianity's Places in the Religious Texts

The central and holy Bektashi texts (the Velayetname and the Makalat), in contrast to the Bektashi practices and general beliefs, have not been analysed to the same extent. This makes it more difficult to make the same argument about the Bektashi relationship between Christianity and Islam in these two texts. These texts are often only available in old Turkish, and remain understudied. Shortly after the fall of communism, the Albanian order published the texts in an edited English versions. Even though the textual tradition is not strong in Bektashism, this certainly provides a new opportunity to explore Bektashi thought and practice.

An analysis of Christianity's role in these texts is based on two overall observations: a sociological one and a textual critical one. The basic assumption is that Bektashism, as a religious movement, evolved in similar phases as Christianity. In Max Weber's analysis and sociological theories, Christianity transformed from being a charismatic religion driven by charismatic authorities into an established one with authorities based on traditions, based on written sources.[26] Christianity went through this process in the first centuries CE. It transformed from being a movement based on Jesus' charismatic authority into one based on traditional religious authorities.

The sociological observation is that Bektashism transformed in a similar manner from a nomadic charismatic Sufi movement into a religious order based on tradition. In this light, Haji Bektash Veli, the founder of Bektashism, could be interpreted as a charismatic authority in similarity with Jesus, whose charismatic power is preserved in the textual – and oral – traditions of Bektashism. This tradition became institutionalised in the Bektashi order based on a hierarchy of dervishs and babas. The babas became the religious authorities and based their power on their access to the tradition carried among other things in the holy Bektashi texts.

---

26   Max Weber, *Udvalgte tekster*, vol. 1–2, Heine Andersen, Hans Henrik Bruun og Lars Bo Kaspersen (red.), (Copenhagen: Hans Reitzels Forlag, 2003) vol 1, 359–370, vol. 2, 7–356; Thomas Ekstrand, *Max Weber in a Theological Perspective*, (Leuven: Peeters, 2000).

190   SAGGAU

This sociological observation provides the framework for the text-critical observation, because textual analysis reveals elements of this kind of transformation. Regarding Christianity, the Gospels are understood as the early Christians' attempt to "capture" the charismatic authority in a written tradition creating medium.[27] The Gospels are, so to speak, keeping Jesus' charismatic power alive in a tradition creating medium – the text. A similar development happened in Bektashism, because the Bektashi holy texts were written during a similar transformation period as the Gospels. The Bektashi holy texts are also a tradition creating medium, in which Haji's charismatic power becomes a tradition. The religio-sociological contexts look comparable between the two, and therefore the two sets of texts can be said to have been based on the same religio-sociological circumstances. This compatibility might be due to similarities in circumstances, because both movements were born around a charismatic and ascetic preacher. Alternatively, the institutionalisation of Bektashism might have been modelled on Christianity by the reformer, Baba Balim. There is some evidence that the Christians at least inspired Baba Balim, and he purposely used some elements, such as celibacy, in the institutionalisation of the order.[28] The Bektashi holy texts might also have been intentionally modelled on Christian texts.

These overall observations are a point of departure into the analysis and discussion of the relationship between Christianity and Islam in the Bektashi texts.

Velayetname

The most central Bektashi text centres on the founder Haji Bektashi Veli and is called Velayetname. It is composed of various sections of accounts of his miracles, biographical notes, stories of conversions and longer stories of "historical" events. Velayetname's form bears resemblance to the Gospels, because it is a combination of miracles and sayings from Haji, as are the Gospels for Jesus. The text seems to be compiled from several orally transferred accounts, which were written down at a later point in time by an unknown author. The author sometimes makes the reader aware of his presence through his comments on Haji's actions. The text could be dated to the 15th century, which is based on

---

27   Geert Hallbäck, *Om Markus, analyser og fortolkninger*, (Frederiksberg: Anis, 2002).

28   Doja, "Spirtual surrender: from companionship to hierarchy in the history of Bektashism."

CHRISTIANITY'S ROLE IN THE SUFI ORDER OF BEKTASHISM   191

the mentioning of Sultan *Bayezid* (1354–1403).[29] This is roughly the same time, when the Bektashi movement was turned into a Sufi order.

There is a whole series of shorter sections, which seems to draw on Christian materials. These sections are not direct quotations from the biblical prototype, but rather thematic rewritings of them or intertextual references/comments. The miracles or events in Velayetname are to some extent the same as in the Bible, but in the Bektashi text it is no longer a biblical figure who performs the miracle, but Haji instead. The most obvious ones are the following:

- Two episodes where Haji cures infertility by Allah's help, which is similar to the help the biblical God provides the childless and old Sara, Abraham's wife, in Genesis 17, and Elisabeth, the mother of John the Baptist, in Luke 1,5-25.[30]
- A long section is devoted to Haji's family tree, which is traced back to the prophet Muhammad, just as Jesus' family tree is traced back to Abraham and David, Matthew 1.
- In one episode, Haji resurrects a child, as Jesus does in the three synoptic Gospels (Mark, Matthew and Luke), e.g. Mark 5:35-43.
- In several episodes, Haji brings forth a source of water various times with his stick, just as Moses does in Exodus 17:1-17.[31]
- There are several accounts of how Haji transforms water into blood, just as Aaron transform the river Nile to blood in Exodus 7:14-25.
- Both Haji and his main disciple Sari Saltuk glide on a prayer carpet over the sea in the same manner as Jesus walks on the sea, e.g., John 6:16-21.[32]
- On three occasions, Haji saves a ship, as Jesus saves a ship in a storm in the synoptic Gospels, e.g. Mark 4:35-41.[33]

As described, the miracles Haji performs are not word-by-word the same as in the Bible, but the resemblances are close. Each of the above-mentioned miracles has more or less the same point, which is that Haji or Jesus can control the sea, death, fertility, water and so on. Each miracle is a display of charismatic power.

---

29   *The Saintly exploits of Haji Bektas Veli – Manakib-I Haci Bektas-I Veli "Velayetname,"* Huseyin Abiba (trans.), 14–15, 178.

30   Ibid., 23, 86.

31   Ibid., 40, 75, 96.

32   Ibid., 71, 103–104.

33   Ibid., 142–145, 156–157.

It can be argued that the resemblances between the two texts serve the same purpose – the portrayal of a charismatic religious person. From this perspective, the Bektashi text does not differ from other "Velayetnames," which portray other Anatolian Sufi Master according to Riza Yildrim.[34] It is therefore difficult to distinguish, if this reuse of biblical prototypes derives directly from the biblical material itself or if both texts simply belong to the same sort of narrative genre. The Bible itself never seems prominent in the Velayetname; neither does the Bektashi text reveal any kind of real knowledge of Christianity and its tradition, like celibacy amongst monks.[35] It might therefore have more to do with communality in genre.

It seems much more likely, that the Velayetname's rewriting of biblical miracles comes from a reuse of the hagiographies of saints in the Eastern Orthodox tradition.[36] These hagiographical texts – or simply their stories – might have been known by the author and they are as well built on elements and themes from the Bible. The Velayetname and hagiographies seem to belong to the same form of genre for religious texts. They are both portrayals of a powerful religious person and stories of how their power is manifested. In that respect, they are closely bonded to the Gospels, which also belong to that sort of genre of religious texts.

The central style for composing hagiographies was the so-called *Imitatio Christi*, where the saint was portrayed as an imitation of Christ.[37] The hagiographies were often filled with miracles or episodes that in some way were variation of a biblical prototype. An example is the hagiography of the Slavic Jovan Vladimir of Duklja (d. 1116) from the 13th century, in which a longer episode is devoted to how the Bulgarian Emperor betrays him. The betrayal of Jovan is a rewriting of Judas' betrayal of Jesus.[38] The hagiographic genre could account for the biblical similarities in the Velayetname. If the depiction of Haji is influenced by the Christian hagiographic genre, it is likely that the biblical themes therefore became the background for the narrative of Haji's life through this hagiographic filter. The communality in genre between the

---

34 Riza Yildrim, *Dervishes in early Ottoman society and politics; A study of Velaytenames as a source of history,* (Ankara: Bilkent University, 2001).

35 Abiva, *Velayetname*, 92–98.

36 Birge, *The Bektashi Order*, pp. 35, 48–50; Doja, "Spiritual surrender," 455.

37 The name for the style comes from the medieval text *Imitatio Christi* by Thomas á Kempis, see Kempis, Thomas a, *The Imitation of Christ*, Aloysius Craft og Harold Bolton (trans.), Susan L. Rattiner (ed.), (New York, Dover Thrift edition, 2003).

38 Norman W. Ingham, „The Marthyrdom of Saint John Vladimir of Dioclea, "*International Journal of Slavic linguistics and poetics*, vol XXXV–XXX (1987).

CHRISTIANITY'S ROLE IN THE SUFI ORDER OF BEKTASHISM   193

Gospel, the hagiographies and the Velayetname might explain the use of biblical materials in the Velayetname.

Christians are often present in the text as well, and they appear in short stories depicturing Muslim-Christian common life, some miracles and a few conversion stories. The text is imprinted with images from a Christian milieu. In the Velayetname, the Christians are never enemies of Haji Bektash Veli, unlike Muslim Sunni scholars.[39] This might indicate that the author and the Bektashi community at the time had contact with Christians but without knowing the Christian religion in depth. The massive presence of Christians in Velayetname's many conversion narratives could be a historical relic, suggesting Christian conversions to Bektashism occurred at an early stage in the movement's development. Velayetname contains stories of a missionary journey into the Balkans, which could be a mythical rewriting of these historical events. Such historical "residue" suggests that there must have been some conversions of Christian groups in the Balkans.[40]

Makalat

The other central Bektashi text is called Makalat. The text was, according to the Bektashi tradition, translated from Haji's original Arabic version in 1459. The Makalat draws on extensive knowledge of the Qur'an, as well as the Bible, and the text is filled with direct and correct quotes from both.[41] This is in stark contrast to the Velayetname and it is therefore rather unthinkable to be by the same author. The Makalat seems to have been written under great influence from the Hurufi speculation in arithmology, which is much more alien for the author of Velayetname.[42] In Velayetname the word "Makalat" is mentioned, but the word itself only means a collection of discourse and therefore does not refer specifically to this text.[43] While, the Makalat does pretend to be Haji's discourse and teaching, it is clearly not written in the same religious context as Velayetname. The Makalat is much more coherent and sophisticated in its style. It was probably written later and in a scholarly context. In addition, the text refers to a hierarchical structure in the Bektashi order, which Velayetname

---

39   Abiva, *Velayetname*, 121.

40   Ibid., 147–153.

41   *The Makalat of Haji Bektashi Veli – the discourse of a 13th century Sufi Master*, Huseyin Abiva (trans.), (Babagan Books, 2006), 49, 57.

42   Ibid., 69.

43   Abiva, *Velayetname*, 89–90.

only leaves to conjecture. It is therefore possible to date it to after Baba Balim's reform in the 15th century, where the hierarchy was established.[44] This puts around a hundred years between the texts.

Rather than using biblical narratives, the Makalat tells new stories in which biblical figures play a prominent role in order to prove a Bektashi point. One example is a story about Jesus, the Judaic tribes and the prophet Mohammad. In this story a mountain waits for the full revelation and is not satisfied with Judaism or Jesus, but waits until Mohammad appears. Any trace of an original Judaic or Christian context is removed.[45] The story underlines that Judaism and Christianity are only a partial revelation of the truth. The biblical persons here are integrated into the Bektashi context in order to prove a point. They play no other significant role. Another example is a longer section on Adam.

In this section it is explained where the dirt that Adam was made of came from. It comes from various parts of the world in a strict numerological order.[46] Such discourse about Adam seems to be inspired from the Hurufi speculation in numbers and from the Sufi concept of the perfect man (al-insan al-kamil), which was originally a part of the Sufi master Ibn al-Arabi's (d.1240) teaching. Both depictions of Adam and Jesus are affected by the picture of them in the Qur'an, as well as Ibn al-Arabi's interpretation of them.

Moses, Abraham, Joseph and the Pharaoh from Exodus are also mentioned in the Makalat, which supports the notion that the author must have had some knowledge of the biblical text.[47] The biblical persons in the text are integrated into the Bektashi cosmology as holy persons. The Makalat uses more space to write about the biblical characters than on its portrayal of Ali and Mohammad.

The Makalat is, however, not very innovative in the way it uses the Christian material, but does rather build on an already established Sufi tradition. The Makalat is clearly a sort of Sufi instruction and does therefore belongs to the wide genre of Sufi texts all written as instructions.

In this genre, many of the early Sufi masters, such as al-Muhasibi (d. 857), already alluded to and used Christian images and persons in his sayings and teaching. The Sufi masters were in general critical towards Christianity, but used its rich sources of imagery in their own teaching and especially in their instructions. Jesus played a central role for many Sufi masters, because he was an ideal figure to illustrate an esoteric and ascetic relation to God. An example of this is the Sufi master al-Ghazali (d. 1111) use of Jesus in the text *Ihya ulum*

---

44   Abiva *Makalat*, p. 55.

45   Ibid., pp. 18–20.

46   Ibid., p. 81.

47   Ibid., p. 43, 49, 53.

CHRISTIANITY'S ROLE IN THE SUFI ORDER OF BEKTASHISM   195

al-din, where he is portrayed as a true ascetic. Perhaps the best known Sufi use of Christianity is Ibn al-Arabi. In his work, Jesus has access to the cosmic principles of the world and a part of the revelation, because he is a man created by the spirit (*ruh*). These Sufi masters all had an impact on Bektahism, but the most influential one seems to have been the poet Jalal al-Din Rumi (d.1273), who frequently used Jesus and other biblical personas in his poems.[48] It seems clear that the Makalat draws on its predecessors within this Sufi genre when it portrays or uses biblical characters. The text might have been modelled on, for example, Ibn al-Arabi's work, which also explains the reappearance of both Jesus and Adam as the *al-insan al-kamil*.

The major difference between Makalat and other similar Sufi texts is a more detailed discourse on the relation between Christians and Bektashis. The Makalat mentions *Iblis* (Satan) and those whom he has misled within Islam, as greater enemies than the infidel himself. The infidel does not possess any threat, because one will become a martyr if one kills one or is killed by one. The inner enemy is a much greater threat, because that one can pollute the pure belief.[49] In other words, the Christians are not direct enemies and do not pose a challenge to Bektashism, unlike other Muslims. This theological logic also seems to be present in Velayetname's neutral description of Christians, in stark contrast to the Muslims, who do not embrace Haji Bektash as the true descendant of the prophet. These Muslims are presented very negatively and even cursed at times. Especially educated Sunnis are targeted and ridiculed. This does perhaps also highlight the fact that the texts must have been directed towards a Muslim rather than Christian public. They are meant to be read or heard by fellow Muslims that could be convinced to leave Sunnism and join Bektashism. The stories in Velayetname try to persuade Muslims rather than Christians, and Makalat's Qur'anic elaboration seems to presuppose educated Islamic readers rather that Christians. The two texts are both written by and for Muslims and not meant for missionary activities amongst Christians.

Conclusion: Christianity's Role in Early Bektashism

Both texts bear resemblance to the biblical texts and reuse its themes, but it is clear that the Velayetname and Makalat were written specifically for a Muslim audience. It is therefore highly unlikely that these texts, their authors and the community they reflect, had a clear missionary strategy against the Christians

---

48   Lervik, *Images of Jesus Christ in Islam*, 86.

49   Abiva *Makalat*, 89–90.

in the Balkans. The Velayetname would have been used in uneducated and rural contexts to persuade people of the sainthood of Haji Bektash Veli, where it played on an echo of Christian hagiographic teaching. The text is therefore not a "blend" of Christianity and Islam, but instead the Christian tradition has simply survived as a historical memory in the text. This might reflect that both the author and the intended reader lived in close contact with Christians and that the community at an earlier stage converted some Christians. This early conversion of Christians might have something to do with the conversion of the Janissary corps to Bektashism. The janissary corps partly comprised of enslaved Christians.

Christianity plays a role as a sacred tradition, which both texts draw on and transfigured their message, teaching and portrayal around. In a subtle way, the Velayetname resembles a rewritten Gospel, and it draws on many of the same remedies and many of the same miracles, perhaps through an Eastern Orthodox hagiographical filter, although never in a direct way – a similarity that links the early church and the Bektashis movement, which might be based on the communality in genre between the Gospels, hagiographies and the Velayetname. The Bektashis might have intended this, but there is no clear evidence that they were – or are – aware of this similarity and used it strategically.

By contrast, the Makalat is an entirely different kind of religious text. The Makalat is written for and by highly religious scholars to use within the order's religious practice and teaching, and its content shows a reuse and knowledge of Christianity and the biblical texts. It is an instruction to the initiated members of the order and is in its structure and content similar to other Sufi instructions. It belongs to the same genre and therefore bases its use of Christianity on its predecessors. Makalat's use of Christianity is based on Sufism's generally and extended use of Christianity, where especially Jesus plays a key role.

This rewriting and binding together of the tradition – the syncretizing – is linked with the charismatic sect and its transition from a charismatic to an established and traditional order. It seems that during the 15th century, the Bektashi had standardised their tradition, thereby combining the traits of the Safavid Shi'a, Sufism and Christianity in one. The prominence of Christianity in the Bektashi teaching, sacred texts and rites must be ascribed to the time of the hierarchical foundation of the order under Balim, where it has been necessary to formalise the Bektashi tradition upon the orally transferred stories and the religio-social interaction with Christians. This has a historical and outwards expression in Baba Balim's reform, where many of the Christian-shaped rituals were introduced on a formal level. Balim's reform expresses on a formal level a kind of integration of Christianity. If the reuse of Christianity in the

Bektashi texts was intentional and not due to the similarities in socio-religious circumstances, it might have been due to Baba Balim's reforms.

Lastly, it must be noted that pragmatic religiosity is a central trait in the Bektashi order and to a great extent the "trademark" of their religious practice. Antonina Zhelyazkova argues that the modern Albanian Bektashi order must be seen as a middle ground between Sunni Islam and a pragmatic everyday lived Christianity. She argues that this trait has been established because of the interaction, and thereby development, caused by a historical and social common background in the Balkans.[50] Christianity played in this perspective only a role as the basis for further development of the religious tradition. The Bektashi order interacted and absorbed the Christian tradition.

The religious logic of the esoteric Sufi teaching, where Christianity is ascribed a partial religious truth, seems to be the theological basis for the use of Christianity's myths, figures and rites within the Bektashi teaching. The undogmatic and pragmatic religiosity in the early movement and its presence in the modern order have made it possible to continue this reuse of Christianity in their belief system. Christianity then becomes just another mode of expression for the order.

---

50   Antonina Zhelyazkova, *The Spread of Islam in the Western Balkan Lands under Ottoman Rule (15-th–18-th Centuries)*, (Sofia, BAS, 1990), pp. 141–150; "Islamization in the Balkans as a Historiographical Problem: the Southeast-European Perspective," *The Ottomans and the Balkans. A Discussion of Historiography*, (Leiden, Brill, 2002), pp. 223–267.

CHAPTER 13

Islamic Literature in Bosnian Language 1990–2012: Production and Dissemination of Islamic Knowledge at the Periphery

Ahmet Alibašić

Opening Remarks

Two developments in the past two decades have brought Islamic literature among European Muslim communities to the centre of scholarly attention. The first one was the awakening of local Islamic identities in the wake of global outreach of Salafi and Reformist groups who have often used books as a vehicle to spread their ideas. Literally, tons of Arabic and occasionally English books were imported into Eastern Europe after 1990. Dozens of titles have been translated, occasionally written, printed and distributed gratis in thousands of copies. Salafi books enumerating major "errors" in the local understanding and practice of Islam have regularly been followed by counter-literature, original or translated, defending the local practice. This debate often led to examination of Islamic education institutions curricula, textbooks and required reading lists.

The second factor is the securitisation of all things Islamic. Although the process of radicalisation has not been fully understood yet, it is common to presume that Islamic literature plays a major role. In addition to that, some countries, like the Russian Federation, have established extensive lists of forbidden books.[1] Others have desisted from such medieval practices but have been equally concerned. A few months ago I sat with a couple of Western diplomats at their request to examine several books they brought with themselves which apparently were collected from booksellers in front of Bosnian mosques. Books carrying any sign of Saudi support were particularly suspicious.[2] This

---

1   As of 7 June 2017 the "Federal List of Extremist Materials" contained 4146 items, many of them Islamic books and audio-visual materials. http://minjust.ru/ru/extremist-materials?field_extremist_content_value=&page=20, accessed 10 June 2017.

2   Interestingly literature was not in focus of a major collection of studies on production of Islamic knowledge in Western Europe. See Martin van Bruinessen and Stefano Allievi (eds.), *Producing Islamic knowledge: transmission and dissemination in Western Europe*, Routledge, 2010.

© KONINKLIJKE BRILL NV, LEIDEN, 2018 | DOI 10.1163/9789004362529_014

ongoing debate has motivated a closer examination of Islamic literature in Bosnian language as it has often been at the centre of various debates about foreign influence on local Islamic practice. The most recent example is the translation and free distribution of Ibn Abi al-Izz al-Hanafi's commentary on *al-Tahawi's creed*. The book was sponsored by the Saudi Embassy and was met with fierce response.[3]

Islamic literature in Bosnian language since 1990 could be examined from a number of angles. First, it can be compared in quantitative terms to the period before 1990 as well as to the literature in languages of other native European Muslim communities (e.g., Albanians, Tatars, Pomaks). Second, one could compare publications of the major Islamic organisation in the country, i.e., the Islamic Community (*Islamska zajednica u Bosni i Hercegovini*, hereafter the IC) with those of private publishers, both commercial and non-profit ones. Three, it can be analysed according to the topics covered and orientations of its authors. When doing that, noting absent themes, authors and schools of thought is as important as identifying the most frequently published authors. Four, one may talk about general characteristics, problems and perspectives of publishing Islamic literature in Bosnian.

Introduction

This article examines Islamic literature in the Bosnian language between 1990–2012 in quantitative and qualitative terms. In terms of quantity, the fall of Communism and reintegration of Bosnian Muslims into the global Muslim community in the wake of the Bosnian war in the 1990s, resulted in a relative

---

3   Hamza, Ridžal, "Vjerska učenja vehabijskog islama u izdanju Islamske zajednice: Knjiga koja narušava temelje vjerovanja bosanskih muslimana" (Wahhabi Theology published by the Islamic Comunity: A Book that Ruins the Foundations of Bosnian Muslims' Beliefs), http://www.faktor.ba/vijest/stav-vjerska-ucenja-vehabijskog-islama-u-izdanju-islamske-zajednice-knjiga-koja-narusava-temelje-vjerovanja-bosanskih-muslimana-19274i; Dževad Gološ, „Profesore Begleroviću, Komentar tahavijske akide nije vehabijsko djelo, jer je napisano nekoliko stoljeća prije Muhammeda ibn Abdul-Vehaba" (Professor Beglerović, The al-Tahhawi's Creed Commentary is not a Wahhabi book; it was written centuries before Muhamad Ibn Abd al-Wahhab), http://saff.ba/profesore-beglerovicu-komentar-tahavijske-akide-nije-vehabijsko-djelo-jer-je-napisano-nekoliko-stoljeca-prije-muhammeda-ibn-abdul-vehaba. For a more general discussion see: Harun Karčić, "Islamic Revival in Bosnia and Herzegovina 1990–2010", *Context: Journal of Interdisciplinary Studies* 1: 1 (2014), 112-128; Kerem Öktem, *New Islamic Actors after the Wahhabi Intermezzo: Turkey's Return to the Muslim Balkans* (2010), https://wikileaks.org/gifiles/attach/126/126845_Oktem-Balkan-Muslims.pdf, accessed 7 June 2017.

abundance of Islamic literature. During the Socialist period, the Islamic book was a rarity and primarily addressed issues related to rituals followed by doctrinal and apologetic works. After 1990, religious textbooks continued to dominate Islamic publishing but were also joined by far more books on Islamic thought, culture, Prophetic Tradition (Sunna), Islamic economy, Sufism, children's literature, genocide studies, and Islamic law, often by foreign authors. The list of Islamic publications in Bosnian since 1993 contains some of the most important names of classical and contemporary Islamic scholarship, as well as titles that are obviously the result of various compromises mainly caused by the financial incentives of donors. The quality of work is often a problem as peer review is considered a formality by many.

The key aim of the paper is to explore how the freedom to produce Islamic literature in Bosnia and Herzegovina has resulted in myriad engagements with wider Islamic literature. By doing this the paper explores one facet of how post-Communist Bosnia relates to the broader Islamic "umma" and its implications for Islam in Europe. For the purpose of this paper only printed books were considered because the book in Bosnian language, in addition to personal contact through mosque and *mekteb*,[4] still remains the most important medium of Islamic education. That is especially true of informal religious textbooks (basic introduction to Islam – *Ilmihal*, somewhat more advanced textbook called *Ta'limu-l-islam,* introduction to Qur'anic script – *Sufara*, readers of appropriate didactic texts, prayer guides, and collections of supplications). More recently, the Internet has become a popular medium of Islamic education,[5] including among the radical groups, but years back Internet penetration was quite low. Of significance here is also the fact that sufficient knowledge of foreign languages is still marginal.

As for the consumers of Islamic literature, they are primarily pupils and students attending Islamic religious education in public schools, mektebs, madrasas, faculties of Islamic studies. In addition, there are about 1500 active imams in Bosnia, some 800 Islamic religious education teachers and a couple of hundred of teachers and officials in other Islamic institutions. Beside these,

---

4   These days *mekteb* (ar. *maktab* or *kuttab*) in Bosnian usage refers to the informal basic Islamic education attended mostly by children between 7 and 16 year olds. Nowadays such education usually takes place during weekends in the mosques or at an adjacent simple building also called *mekteb*.

5   For instance, two titles that this author helped produce were put online; one illegally and another one legally. The one on marriage was downloaded over 8,000 times, while the one on preventing radicalisation was downloaded over 6,500 times from one website alone. A few if any Islamic books other than the textbooks would reach such a print-run.

individual believers buy Islamic books to satisfy their own needs for religious guidance. However, it would be wrong to presume that all Islamic books are bought and collected in order to be used. Some will collect and buy books because it is still seen as a highly esteemed, even venerated practice. Others will collect them simply to support the publisher or the author. To the best of my knowledge, no study has assessed the impact of Islamic literature in the Bosnian context or its importance relative to other means of transmission of Islamic knowledge such as mosque attendance, informal networks or new media. One could reasonably presume that the younger generations use Internet resources more often than printed materials.

The future of Islamic literature in Bosnian is at stake, especially in diasporic Bosnian communities where new generation born or brought up in their new homeland tend to understand everyday but not the scholarly Bosnian. Bosnian imams in diasporic congregations already have to teach Islam to Bosnian children in the local language, be it German, English, Norwegian, or Slovenian. In such contexts, the only factor that may prolong the validity of Islamic literature in Bosnian in diasporic communities is the sense of belonging and institutional support, which the Islamic Community in Bosnia and Herzegovina still provides to its members. How much of that allegiance the older generation will manage to transfer to their youngsters remains to be seen. Anecdotal evidence provides mixed signals. The failure of West European Muslims to institutionalise Islam in their societies through a single community may offer some more time for the validity of Bosnian Islamic literature.

Quantitative Analysis

The early 1990s witnessed a significant increase in the production of Islamic literature in the Bosnian language.[6] Two processes were behind this relative abundance of Islamic literature. One was the fall of Communism, which brought about freedom including the freedom to publish on Islam with little if any restrictions. Almost simultaneously, the 1992–1995 war set the stage for reintegration of Bosnian Muslims into *Ummah*. That, among other things, meant significant quantities of Islamic literature flowing into Bosnia. Soon, the quantity brought new qualities, the primary among them being Islamic intellectual pluralism. (This was in line with the general pluralisation of Islamic

---

6   The author is grateful to Azra Hadžić and Amela Lepir for helping prepare a bibliography of books published in Bosnian between 1990–2012, which has served as the basis for this analysis.

religious practice. Prior to 1990 Bosnian Muslims were not very religious but had maintained unified religious practice).[7] Finally, unlike the other areas of Islamic work, the Islamic Community has not tried to monopolise this aspect of Islamic life. As a result, private Islamic publishing has been very active since 1990.

During the Socialist period and war years of 1992–95, the lack of freedom and insecurity affected publishing. In the period 1945–75 Islamic books were rare. For instance, in 1972 a group of young men under the penname hadži Salih Sulejmanović[8] published a prayer instruction book *Namaz: svrha, značaj i obavljanje* (87 pp.) because, according to the authors, no such book had been published in the previous 15 years.[9] That book was an indication of a slight improvement in the field in the early 1970s. During the 1980s, due to the economic crisis and regime crackdown on Islamic intellectuals, Islamic publishing all but ceased. In 1983 and 1985 the IC published only two and three titles respectively. In 1992, El-Kalem, the Publishing centre of the IC, published two reprints. Even worse in 1993 not a single book was published by the IC.

The situation changed significantly after the end of the war in 1995. Since then, the annual average has been a hundred titles. The IC has published between 30 and 70 new titles annually. A similar number of books has been published outside the IC. According to a bibliography of Islamic literature in Bosnian for the period 1990–2011, a total of 1,700 new Islamic titles were published,[10] out of which 900 came from inside the IC (not counting reprints after 1993). The basic Islamic textbook *Ilmihal* by Naim Hadžiabdić was published 19 times. An advanced textbook *Ta'limu-l-islam* by Redžep Muminhodžić, as of today has 18 editions. The prayer guidebook (*Zašto i kako se klanja namaz-salat*) by Halil Haverić and introduction to Qur'anic script (*Sufara: uvod u kur'ansko pismo*) by Idriz Demirović were printed 17 times. During the 1994–2011 period, El-Kalem printed 1,300,000 copies of religious

---

7   Former rector of the International Islamic University Malaysia, Abdul Hamid Abu Sulayman visited Sarajevo back in the 1970s. One of the lasting memories he kept was the almost military discipline and unity with which local Muslims performed their prayers in those days (personal communication). No such unity could be observed today.

8   Aziz Kadribegović, Hilmo Neimarlija, Rusmir Mahmutćehajić, Husejn Živalj and Dževad Hodžić (different from current professor at Faculty of Islamic Studies in Sarajevo).

9   There were cases of pennamed books afterwards as well (e.g. late Munir Gavrankapetanović, member of Mladi muslimani movement was Ismet U. Šehibrahimović).

10   During 1992–2008 26,302 titles were published in BiH (Nevenka Hajdarović, "ISBN: Petnaest godina Centra za ISBN BiH," *Bosniaca*, 14/2009, 11). This means that Islamic literature represents 5–6% of all book production in BiH, which is – by international standards – a significant percentage.

ISLAMIC LITERATURE IN BOSNIAN LANGUAGE 1990–2012

education textbooks and religious instruction manuals. The almanac of the IC *Takvim* was printed in 857,000 copies. Individually the most printed textbooks and manuals have been *Ilmihal* by Bilal Hasanović (145,000 copies) and *Sufara* by Idriz Demirović (110,000 copies), followed by elementary religious education textbooks for public schools (*Vjeronauka*). The most productive years of El-Kalem were 1998 (180,000) and 2008 (169,000 copies).[11]

As for the periodicals, those published by the IC tend to last and have significant print-runs. The official journal of the Islamic Community, *Glasnik Rijaseta Islamske zajednice u BiH* has been published since 1933. Yearbook and prayer timetables *Takvim* has been around for decades and is currently being printed in 40,000 copies. The fortnightly newspaper *Preporod* has been published since 1970 and enjoys a relatively wide readership. The education journal *Novi Muallim* has been published since 1910 with several long interruptions. However, even within the IC some periodicals ceased to appear for a combination of reasons including lack of funding and internal politics (*Islamska misao* and *Hikmet*).

Outside the IC, periodicals are irregular and have no lasting power. Like the organisations publishing them, they represent "shooting stars" that shine bright but fizzle fast. Examples are Salafi magazine *Saff* (now appearing online only), reformist *Novi Horizonti,* and Sufi *Šebi Arus*. Since 2000 the most enduring are journals published by Iranian organisations such as *Znakovi vremena*, journal for "philosophy, religion, science and societal practice" published by Ibn Sina Institute in Sarajevo since 1997.[12]

Dominant Themes and Authors

Prior to 1990 the IC published mainly ritual-related books penned by local authors (*ilmihali*, prayer instruction books, animal sacrifice guides, hajj guides,

---

11 An anecdote may also illustrate the change that has occurred in the two decades since 1990. In the last years of Socialism, a local Muslim scholar started giving Hadith lectures in the second most important mosque in Sarajevo. In preparation for the lessons he used to translate chapters from *Sahih Muslim*. Those pages would then be copied with whatever primitive technology was available then for those purposes. Young people used to flock to the lectures and to make sure they could get a hold of those pages. About two decades later, the same scholar was assigned to give similar lectures in the central mosque hoping that he will have the same success. Alas, only a few old men used to come and listen. The lecture series was soon discontinued.

12 http://www.ibn-sina.net/index.php/casopisi/znakovi-vremena, visited 18 Sept. 2016.

collections of supplications, *Ja Sin* translation, Muslim names, translations of the Qur'an, etc.). These were followed by doctrinal and apologetic works (mainly translations from Arabic or English), works on ethics (*w'az*), pious poetry, stories and novels, biographies of the Prophet and other Islamic personalities, Arabic language textbooks and dictionaries, Qur'anic studies, academic studies on local Islamic heritage, and contemporary Islamic thought (R. Garaudy, M. Iqbal). Rare were books on Prophetic Tradition (Sunna) and Islamic jurisprudence. For example, between the 4th edition of *Fikhu-l-ibadat* (1968) penned by local Islamic scholar Muhamed Serdarević and *Halal and Haram in Islam* by Yusuf al-Qaradawi (1997) little was published on Islamic law.

After 1990, religious textbooks continue to dominate the IC publishing but now there are far more books on Prophetic tradition (including translation of almost all major *hadith* collections), Islamic thought, culture, Islamic economy, Sufism, children's literature genocide studies, and Islamic law but not by local authors. The print-runs of non-textbook literature have significantly decreased due to smaller territory that the IC now covers, more accountability, and perhaps availability of digital resources. Unlike private publishers, the IC has resisted temptation of populist literature on eschatological themes, conspiracy theories, occultism, etc. The same cannot be said of the so-called "scientific" interpretations of the Holy texts.

The list of Islamic publications in Bosnian since 1993 contains some of the most important names of classic and contemporary Islamic scholarships and important scholarly projects (e.g., Teufik Muftić's world-class Arabic-Bosnian Dictionary), as well as titles that are obviously result of various compromises mainly caused by the financial incentives of donors. The vast majority of authors are men but there are women as well. About one third of titles published by the IC (295 out of 906) are translations, mainly from Arabic (ca 200), English (58) and Turkish (13). There are 16 titles translated into Arabic, German, English and Roma. Local authors wrote the remaining 595 titles. This ratio between local and foreign authors seems to be inversely related to privately published books. Significantly, authors of all religious education and madrasa textbooks are local authors. The situation is very different with "teach yourself" manuals and university-required readings, which are often written by foreign authors. This is not surprising, as a good Islamic university textbook is a rare commodity even throughout the rest of the Muslim world.

Few books are available on (re)interpretation of Shari'ah in contemporary societies, methodology of Islamic jurisprudence, Islamic political thought, history of Islam after the four caliphs, woman and family, child upbringing/education, contemporary religious movements, religion in the life of contemporary man, relationship with non-Muslims, human rights and freedoms, and good governance. Knowledge about the Muslim world is very general and does not allow for building quality economic and cultural relationships with that world. Literature addressing youth concerns or assisting imams in the performance of their duties is scarce too.

The following notable contemporary Islamic authors are missing from the list of Islamic literature in Bosnian or are underrepresented: Abd al-Karim Zaydan, Abd al-Wahhab al-Masiri, Ahmet Davutoglu, Ali Mazrui, Fahmi Huwaydi, Fathi Osman, Gai Eaton, Louay Safi, Muhammad Salim al-'Avva, Muhammad 'Imara, Rashid al-Ghannushi, Sa'id Hawwa, Salman 'Awda, Taha Jabir al-'Alwani, Tariq Suwaydan, Abdulhakim Murad (Tim Winter), Umar Chapra, Wahba Zuhayli, Wahiduddin Khan, Khaled Abou El-Fadl, European Council for Research and Fatwa, and Fiqh Academy of the OIC in Jeddah. The reasons for their absence or underrepresentation vary. Some are probably too academic or not very relevant for the Bosnian context to be picked by commercial publishers while there was no one to sponsor the publication of their work (e.g. Murad, OIC Fiqh Academy or Mazrui). Politically active intellectuals are sometimes hesitant to give copyright for their works while they are in government. For some there could be no explanation except that did not have Bosnian students and since nobody in Bosnia does systematic "market research" for important literature in order to make it available in Bosnian they were simply left behind (e.g. Ghannushi or Osman). There is no reason to suspect any systemic boycott of any of these authors.

As for the ideological orientation Islamic pluralism is the norm. Practically all Islamic trends are represented. Traditionalists are represented by S.H. Nasr, F. Schuon, T. Burckhardt, M.M. al-Sha'rawi, M.S.R. al-Buti, and F. Gulen. The most frequent Sufi authors are Abu Hamid al-Gazali, J. Rumi, A. al-Qushayri, A. al-Iskandari, A. al-Sha'rani, J.W. Morris, Abd al-Halim Mahmud, Abu Layth al-Samarqandi, and A. Jilani. Reformists are represented by works of M. Asad, M. Hamidullah, I.R. al-Faruqi, Y. al-Qaradawi, Muhammad al-Ghazali, M. Hofmann, T.J. al-Alwani, Tariq Ramadan, S. al-Awdah, Abu al-Hasan Ali al-Nadawi, A. al-Mawdudi, Sayyid Qutb, and Muhammad Qutb. The most published religious modernists are M. Abduh, M. Iqbal, Fazlur Rahman, Khalid M. Khalid, M. Haykal, Mustafa Mahmud, Z. Sardar, and R. Garaudy. Salafi authors are rarely published by the IC but often by others. The list includes A. al-Jazairi, M.S. al-Qahtani, S. al-Mubarakfuri, M.N. al-Albani, and M. Ibn 'Uthaymin. Generally, the Islamic Community has been trying to protect Hanafi School of law at least in rituals. Because of such concern, it desisted from publishing the translation of *Fiqh al-Sunnah*, a comparative Islamic law work by Sayyid Sabiq, it initially procured. However, the work was published in 2008 by a commercial publisher without much noise.

Abu Hamid al-Gazali is by far the most translated classic with 20 books in 47 editions published in Bosnian, including two full and one abridged translation of his *Ihya' 'Ulum al-Din*. Of those 90% have been published since 1994 and they represent three-quarters of all al-Ghazali translations into Balkan languages; 14% of all translation of theological works from Arabic into Bosnian since 1990 and 5% of all translations from Arabic in the period.[13] He is followed by Ibn Qayyim al-Jawziyyah (who is, interestingly, published by both Sufis and Salafis). The following classics are also fairly frequently translated: Imam Malik ibn Anas, Abu Hanifa, al-Bukhari, Muslim, al-Tirmidhi, al-Nasai, al-Baqillani, Ibn Kathir, al-Qurtubi, al-Nawawi, al-Tahhawi, Ibn Khaldun, al-Suyuti, and al-Shawkani. Egyptian popular preacher Amr Khalid and Saudi scholar Aid al-Qarni are reportedly the best sellers with 30 and 10 titles to their names in Bosnian respectively in the observed period.[14] While Yusuf al-Qaradawi is popular among scholars his books are not always the best-sellers.

Although most authors are Sunnis, Shi'a scholars are too on the list of both the IC and Iranian supported independent publishers such as Mulla Sadra Foundation, Ibn Sina Institute, and Cultural Centre of the Iranian Embassy (Akbar Eydi, M. Tabatabai, M. Khatami, M. Mutahhari, M.R. Muzaffar, M.T. Falsafi). Polemical or critical works such as those criticizing Wahhabis (Stephen Schwartz, Hasen Ali al-Thaqafi, Ihlas waqf), Shi'a (Halid Tulić), or conservatives (M. l-Ghazali and S. 'Awda) or Orientalists (e.g. Bernard Lewis) are occasionally published. Of the non-Muslim authors Annemarie Schimmel, John L. Esposito, Karen Armstrong, and Henry Corbin are favourites. Of local authors the best selling are popular imam Sulejman Bugari, Islamic Studies professors Šefik Kurdić and Safvet Halilović, imam Husein Čajlaković, and self-taught preacher Sanin Musa. Absent from this bibliography are radical (post-)modernists Arkoun, Abu Zayd, Bassam Tibi, and Abdullahi A. An-Na'im while Khaled Abou al-Fadl is fragmentarily translated.

The intellectual Islamic pluralism is probably the most important feature of Islamic literature in Bosnian. In some ways it is a precondition (some may say price) of the unity of the IC in Bosnia and Herzegovina because every excluded trend would in all probability attempt to establish its own community, as has happened in Serbia. In this context, pluralism does not necessarily mean fragmentation. The IC continues to be the undisputed religious authority for the

---

13 Emina Ćeman i Azra Hadžić, "Pogled na prijevode djela imama Ebu Hamida Muhammeda el-Gazalija objavljenih na području Balkana do 2011. godine, sa posebnim osvrtom na prijevode na bosanski jezik," Dec. 2011, manuscript.

14 Amr Khalid's reputation has suffered because of his support for the 2013 military coup in Egypt.

vast majority of Bosnian Muslims. That is so for various reasons, including the institutional stability and longevity of the IC, the presence of properly trained Islamic scholars in the Community (e.g. Current Sarajevo Mufti Dr. Enes Ljevaković), the Community's patience with Salafis, and self-evident nihilism of radical discourses. According to a recent Pew Research Centre survey, 75% of Bosnian Muslims believe that there is only one interpretation of Islam (85); only 2% belong to Sufi tariqas (31); 38% self-identify as Sunnis while 54% say they are "just Muslims" (35).[15]

Qualitative Analysis

Today Islamic literature is available in the Bosnian language to the extent that one could be a decent Islamic scholar without knowing any other language. In addition to the freedom and outside support, one of the factors contributing to this phenomenon is the significant Islamic scholarly/clerical capacity of Bosnian Muslims. Prior to 1990 there was a severe lack of educated imams and other Islamic leaders. Today the situation is very different with many graduates of Islamic studies pursuing different carrier paths or remaining unemployed. What the significance of this is remains to be seen.

Relative freedom of thought is the main advantage of the Bosnian context while small market and limited resources are the main disadvantages. Coupled with the absence of merit based reliable research and publishing funding those put restrictions on serious scholarly works and give leverage to interest groups. As a result, much of Islamic literature in Bosnian is supply driven. That explains the plethora of books on the market. Demand-driven literature is often anthropocentric, not theo-centric, focusing on self-help, spirituality, marriage, Prophetic medicine, and understanding and protection from magic.

Among the publishers, the IC is here to stay. Many independent publishers are short lived. Similarly websites appear and disappear frequently. Publications enjoying the backing of the IC one way or the other last. In addition, the impact of many supply-driven publications is questionable at best. Overall, the content of a book is only one of several factors at work when making the decision to publish. Sometimes money is the decisive factor. In other cases, circumstances and even boredom may play a role. All that results in pretty strange and otherwise confusing situations. For instance, one of the current

---

15   Pew Research Centre's Forum on Religion and Public Life, *The World's Muslims: Unity and Diversity*, Washington, released on 9 August 2012, available at http://www.pewforum.org/uploadedFiles/Topics/Religious_Affiliation/Muslim/the-worlds-muslims-full-report.pdf.

top leaders of the Islamic Community and former mufti translated a book on Islamic doctrine by an Ahmadi scholar while in prison in the 1980s. To add to the confusion, two local professors recommended it to the readers. It does not mean that they approve of the content but that they have not read it at all or at least not carefully enough.[16] Another leading mufti organizing the biggest Traditional Islamic manifestation in Bosnia translated a booklet on doctrine by former Saudi chief mufti Abd al-Aziz bin Baz (d. 1999). All that happened during the 1990s war probably for very specific reasons.[17] In yet another instance a pro-Iranian, pro-Sufi professor critical of everything coming from Saudi Arabia wrote an afterword for the Bosnian edition of Muhammad Qutb's book analysing the contemporary Muslim world. Personal relations with translator or publisher probably played a role.

For those and other reasons, in most cases the tendency to (over-)analyse what is being published is unjustified. Contrary to some expectations, there is hardly any publishing policy even within the IC. Quality is often a problem. Reviews are still considered a formality by most authors and editors. Therefore, to take every publication very seriously would be a methodological mistake.

The content quality of Islamic literature in Bosnian varies widely from the world class books of Professor Fikret Karčić to poor ones. For instance, one madrasa textbook starts with a wrong definition of its subject matter. Translators often censor the text without even notifying the reader. Some books cause strong reaction in the community (*Shvatanja koja trebamo ispraviti* / Attitudes that need to be corrected by an Egyptian missionary Imad al-Misri) or in other religious communities (*Christianity* by Mustafa Šahin or Maurice Bucaille's *The Bible, the Quran and Science*). Some books caused reactions by foreign embassies (e.g. Bani Sadr's book on Human Rights, S. Schwartz's *Two Faces of Islam*). Quality of translations vary from the excellent translations of Prof. Enes Karić to many unreadable translations. Often a lot of meaning gets lost in translation.

Intellectually, local authors have not been very creative. A few new ideas could be identified. One exception would be professor Fikret Karčić with his exposition of Shari'ah as primarily code of ethics with most of its norms not requiring state authority for its application and therefore being very compatible with the secular state and the freedom of religion legal framework.[18] Another example again could be Professor Enes Karić, who has been exploring

---

16   Muhamed Ali, *Islamsko vjerovanje*, trnsl. Husejin Smajić. Sarajevo, Sejtarija, 1995.

17   Shaykh Bin Baz, *Al-'Aqidah al-Sahiha wa ma yudaddiduha*, Visoko: Jam'iyyat Ihya' al-Turath al-Islami, 1993.

18   Fikret Karčić, "Secular State and Religion(s): Remarks on the Bosnian Experience in Regulating Religion and State Relations in View of the New Law on Freedom of Religion," in

the dialectic between religion and culture as well as many other theological themes in a series of novels he has written so far. For instance, his first novel *Songs of Wild Birds* deploys arguments against conservatives. Several factors may explain this lack of creativity despite previous experience with new interpretations offered by Husein Đozo (1912–1982) and President Alija Izetbegović (1925–2003), who remain the best known local Islamic authors abroad. Perhaps it would be reasonable to presume that intellectual creativity has been hampered by the huge inflow of new Islamic knowledge which will take time to internalise and digest.

Local intellectuals are now expected to compete with international Islamic scholars without the opportunity to acquire the same education in classical Islamic sciences. Perhaps the most telling example of local Islamic authorities confronting international Islamic scholarship was the case of Shaykh Yusuf al-Qaradawi giving a different opinion about the permissibility of slaughter of Qurban outside the Islamic Community program for those who cannot perform the duty themselves. The Islamic Community is of the view that Qurban is one of its exclusive areas of competence while some charities would like to organise its collection too. Dissatisfied with the official Islamic Community position some locals procured a fatwa from Shaykh al-Qaradawi who in his opinion justified the action of Islamic charities. That provoked a very public reprimand by the then Grand Mufti Mustafa Ceric, otherwise a friend of the shaykh. Although the debate did not stop Islamic charities from organizing the collection of Qurban, it did assert the authority of local scholars vis-à-vis that of foreign ones. However, in many cases local Islamic scholars have simply not yet been prepared to enter specific theological and juridical debates with their international counterparts. It seems reasonable to expect that this will eventually happen after local scholars again attain the international standards of scholarship they once possessed. In other words, eventually Bosnia may be expected to produce another Hasan Kafi Aqhisari (d. 1616).[19]

Finally, without pretending to be conclusive solely on the basis of a survey of al-Ghazali's works in the Balkan languages, one can conclude that Bosnian Muslims are by far the most active European native Muslim community in Islamic publishing despite the fact that Tatars and Albanians are more populous.[20]

  Stefan Schreiner (ed.), *Religion and Secular State* (Zurich and Sarajevo: European Abrahamic Forum and Interreligious Institute in B&H, 2008), 15–24.

19 For a detailed review of the growth of mainstream scholarship in Bosnia as well as its alternatives see A. Alibašić, "Bosnia and Herzegovina," in Jocelyne Cesari (ed.), *The Oxford Handbook of European Islam* (Oxford: Oxford University Press, 2015), 429–474.

20 See: Jorgen S. Nielsen et al., *Yearbook of Muslims in Europe*, Leiden, Brill, 2015.

The Future of Local Islamic Literature in Bosnia and Herzegovina

Throughout most of the 20th century local Islamic knowledge was in demand due to the isolation of Bosnia from the rest of the Muslim world and because of very limited knowledge of foreign languages in the region. Reintegration of the Balkans into the Ummah in the 1990s and better language skills coupled with the development of Internet temporarily reduced this demand and enabled the translation of hundreds of books without much contextualisation. However, the reemergence of local Islamic tradition and security concerns have given local authors a new, yet limited, window of opportunity. Limited because the significant market for Islamic books in Bosnian is in fact among the Bosnian diaspora, which, as time passes, is expected to grow less and less interested in Bosnian literature and more in the literature of the countries of migration. The exception might be countries where Bosnians continue to migrate to this day, such as Germany. But then that means less demand from ever more depopulated parts of Bosnia.

In such circumstances, the production of Islamic knowledge for the European context in other languages presents itself as an opportunity. That seems to be a prospect more realistic than ever before for at least two reasons. First, there is an increasing demand for such knowledge both from European Muslims and non-Muslims. Second, there are more and more Bosnian Islamic scholars in Bosnia and outside who are comfortable writing especially in English and German but also in Arabic and some other European languages. Young Bosnian scholars of Islam are members of teaching and research institutes in Australia, Malaysia, Germany, Austria, Sweden, Norway, and the USA. Whether they will be able to make original contributions to the nascent field of European Islamic thought and to what extent that contribution will be informed by Bosnian Islamic tradition, it is too early to say.

References

Emina Ćeman i Azra Hadžić. 2011. "Pogled na prijevode djela imama Ebu Hamida Muhammeda el-Gazalija objavljenih na području Balkana do 2011. godine, sa posebnim osvrtom na prijevode na bosanski jezik," Dec. 2011, manuscript.

Hadžić, Azra. „Bibliografija islamistike 1990–2011" (Bibliography of Islamic literature 1990–2011, *manuscript*).

Hasani, Mustafa, ed. „Bosanski indeks islamikus knjiga objavljenih izvan institucija Islamske zajednice u periodu 1997–2009. godine". Sarajevo, Fakultet islamskih nauka, 2010.

ISLAMIC LITERATURE IN BOSNIAN LANGUAGE 1990–2012

Isanović, Amina i Mirnes Duranović. „Translations from Arabic in Bosnia and Herzegovina, 1990–2010: a study by the Next Page Foundation", novembar 2010a.

Isanović, Amina i Mirnes Duranović. „Translations from Turkish in Bosnia and Herzegovina, 1990–2010: a study by the Next Page Foundation", decembar 2010b.

Kapa, Berina. „Arabistika u Bosni i Hercegovini 1990.-1999.: prijevodi monografskog karaktera sa arapskog jezika na bosanski jezik", diplomski rad, Filozofski fakultet u Sarajevu, 2001.

Karić, Amir, ur. *Islamska literatura u BiH: trend i perspektiva (zbornik tekstova sa okruglog stola)*. Tuzla, Medžlis IZ, 2009.

Lepir, Amela. „Konačni spisak svih izdanja Izdavačkog centra Islamske zajednice u Bosni i Hercegovini El-Kalema od 1979. godine do 2004." (rukopis)

Sulejmanović, Salih. *Namaz: svrha, značaj i obavljanje*. Sarajevo, 1972. i Islamabad, 1993.

Van Bruinessen, Martin and Stefano Allievi, *Producing Islamic Knowledge: Transmission and Dissemination in Western Europe*.

CHAPTER 14

European Islam in the Light of the Bosnian Experience

Safet Bektovic

Conceptualisation of Europe, Islam and European Islam

An understanding of European Islam primarily depends on how one understands the concepts "Europe" and "Islam." Both Europe and Islam cover a complexity that includes historical, cultural, political, ideological and religious elements. Although being without fixed boundaries, Europe is initially a geographical notion, but it is also, and perhaps even more so, a historical, political and cultural notion, which again does not constitute a homogeneous entity. Far from it, Europe is an entity with many different faces and an entity which is characterised by continuous change.

So it is difficult, if not impossible, to define a core or substance of European identity. Still, many Europeans would argue that it makes sense to talk about a European identity, emphasising Europe as an idea, a vision people feel they can identify with.

By comparison, although Islam is initially a religion, it also expresses a history, a worldview, an ideology, and very similar to Europe, it is made up by different cultures. The differences between e.g. Indonesian and Arab Muslims, or African and Balkan Muslims, are evident and manifold. Muslims in Europe belong to different national and ethnic groups. With the exception of Balkan Muslims, Tatars and small indigenous Muslim communities in Southeastern and Central Europe, the majority of European Muslims have an immigrant background from Asian and African countries. They may share the same religious background, but have different theological orientations and very different degrees of religiosity which range from strong conservativism to resolute atheism. Furthermore, the first generation of Muslim immigrants do not have a common language, as they either speak the language of their country of origin and/or the language of the country of residence, and thus many Muslim immigrants are either not able to communicate with each other due to linguistic barriers or are unwilling to communicate due to differences in personal politics.

The concept of Euro-Islam has been introduced in the context of Muslim integration into European societies. Thus, the background for the concept is

© KONINKLIJKE BRILL NV, LEIDEN, 2018 | DOI 10.1163/9789004362529_015

originally political, dealing primarily with the question of the relationship between Islam and a modern secular society. It should also be noted that the concept of Euro-Islam was introduced by non-Muslims and secular Muslims, including its first formulation by Swedish writer and politician Ingmar Karlsson. He defined "Euro-Islam" as a "flexible and open Islam," in contrast to a closed – "ghetto Islam," represented by the segregated Muslim immigrant groups. His point was that only a "depoliticised and liberal Islam" can be integrated into Europe (Karlsson 1994).

At the same time, the Syrian-born social scientist Bassam Tibi argued for "Euro-Islam" as a "liberally designed Islam," which has separated culture, religion and politics. His point was that in order to establish a harmonious coexistence with the Other, Muslims in Europe have to adopt individual human rights and accommodate the laïcité-type of secular society (Tibi 1995). However, European Islam is not only about politics and socio-economic integration but also about understanding the dynamics of the Muslim identity in Europe and rethinking Islamic theology in the context of the Muslim response(s) to the new challenges (Rasmussen 2002). In the words of Enes Karic, European Islam should not be designated as a matter of politics and ideology, but also as a matter of culture and coexistence in Europe (Karic 2004).

A proper understanding of Islam in Europe requires systematic theological and historical reflection. This relates to the understanding of the Christian-Muslim inter-religious relationship and coexistence in the European context (Leirvik 2006) but also to the understanding of the entire history of relations between Islam and Europe (Nielsen 1999). Jørgen S. Nielsen distinguishes between four phases of Muslim presence in Europe: (1) Muslim presence in Spain and Sicily ending with the Reconquista in 1492; (2) the permanent presence of Muslim groups in the Volga basin north of the Caspian Sea as a result from the Mongol spread in the 13th century; (3) the permanent presence of Muslim groups in the Balkan region following the Ottoman expansion in the second half of the 14th century; and finally, (4) the contemporary presence of Muslims in Europe, where both European societies and Muslims have been challenged by integration and coexistence (Nielsen 1999, 1–10).

In this regard, it makes sense to investigate the historical, theological and political background of the Islamic presence in Europe, including the everyday lives, attitudes, feelings and expectations of Muslims. Islam and Muslims are two mutually dependent categories, but they are not synonymous. "Homo islamicus" does not exist, and Muslims are also more than just Muslims. As pointed out by Nadia Jeldtoft (2012), research on Muslims and Islam in Europe needs to take into account not only the organised, practicing and politically active Muslims, but also the "non-organised" and "invisible Muslims," who express their identity and their sense of belonging to society in different ways. The general picture of Muslim minorities in both research and public representations leaves an image of Muslims as religiously practicing, devout, vocal and active and as having Islam as their primary identity. By contrast, there are Muslims practicing their Muslim identity in a "highly privatised and individualised" way, stressing "personal autonomy and individual choice." They have an inclusive and pluralistic attitude to religion and try to organise their social lives by their dual sense of belonging, i.e. to both Islam, understood as a minority, and secular society – as defined by the majority (Jeldtoft 2012, 207–208; 215–218; 259–260).

Knowing this, it becomes extremely important then to discuss the conceptualisation and presentation of Muslims. Birgitte Johansen and Riem Spielhaus highlight methodological challenges in relation to the production of knowledge about Muslims in surveys and opinion polls, which, according to them, helps to create a "statistical invisibility of certain Muslims, for instance those without immigration background, as well as Muslim with national background other than Muslim majority countries" (Johansen and Spielhaus 2012, 81–82). Particularly in the last decades, administrations, politicians, scholars, media and NGOs have been interested in obtaining and providing so-called "factual knowledge" about Muslims, giving a picture of how they live, what they think, their interests and concerns, how they are integrated etc. However, this quantitative research, which is undoubtedly relevant and important, is turning Muslims into a political category as well as conceptualizing Muslim identity (what Muslims are) on the basis of what Muslims think and do (ibid.).

This means that Muslim identity should not be interpreted exclusively from one particular interest or theoretical-methodological angle, for example, from the social and political sciences approach (as has been the case in the past decades). This is due to the fact that Muslim identity, both in collective and in individual terms, is also conditioned and determined by a spectrum of different factors, including language, education, profession, gender, environment etc. In this sense, their identity (or rather identities) is not monolithic and static but rather multi-layered and dynamic – no different from other people's identity.

This then brings us to the argumentation put forward by Nielsen (2007), in which he points to the fact that since there is more than one way of being European, in terms of culture, religious practice and identity, one should then come to the conclusion that there are more ways than one for Muslims to become European. According to Nielsen, if you only maintain one particular way of being a European Muslim, as e.g. Bassam Tibi does, you ultimately reduce the possibilities for development of Muslim identities in Europe. On the other hand, if you consider European identity in the light of religious and cultural diversity, you open up a diversity of Muslim identities in Europe, which at the same time provides more opportunities for integration (Nielsen 2007). By analysing Muslim perspectives on European Islam, Mohammed Hashas arrives at the same conclusion. Accordingly, European Islam could be seen as a comprehensive process of "humanisation-historisation-rationalisation," initially starting with Islamic modernism that puts the question of Islam's relationship to modernity on the agenda. However, this process has no consistent theological doctrine or corresponding political program (Hashas 2013).[1]

Keeping that in mind, one must conclude that the categories of European Islam and European-Muslim identity are far from being homogeneous and ready-made. They are rather open and multifarious, and as such, they require a multidisciplinary approach.

Conditions, Possibilities and Perspectives

The majority of the so-called first generation of (economic) migrants, coming from rural areas of North Africa, Anatolia, and Central Asia did not have much experience with modernity nor with secular society. They did not experience living as minorities in a non-Muslim society and were not interested in creating a new identity; rather they focused on preserving the home brought identity as well as passing it on to their children. In addition, they lacked the resources to understand European modernity as well as Islam's relationship to modernity.

Although they have respect for European societies, appreciating the social and educational system as well as structures of legal protection, they are sceptical of the European lifestyle and morality, especially in a situation where they do not have appropriate cultural and religious institutions that could help

---

1 Hashas: *The Idea of European Islam.* 2013. As part of his research, he spent time at the Centre for European Islamic Thought (CEIT) during 2011–2012. My cooperation with him allowed us to share our experiences, particularly on Muslim theological-philosophical reflections on European Islam. Being part of CEIT, and participating in numerous seminars and informal discussions with colleagues, I gained much inspiration and learned new ideas about the conceptualisation of European Islam, which I was able to use in my own research. For this, and much more, I owe a heartfelt thanks to them all. First and foremost, my gratitude goes to the head of CEIT, Professor Jørgen S. Nielsen, who, with his experience, knowledge and vision created a fantastic research climate and a great team of highly engaged and professional colleagues, including: Riem Spielhaus, Nadia Jeldtoft, Niels Vinding, Thomas Hoffmann, Gina Smith, Birgitte Johansen, Emil Saggau, Line Stæhr, Karen Giødesen and Fahreta Ajanovic.

them define themselves as a minority. Many of them are therefore careful and guarded towards the concept of Euro-Islam as a new form of Islam, as they tend to consider it as Europeanisation and assimilation. They therefore prefer to speak about Islam in Europe rather than Euro-Islam, although, one could argue, this does not say anything specific about the interpretation of Islam in a European context.

In fact, research shows that a new interpretation of Islam, one more relevant and applicable to the European context, is primarily sought by second and third generations of immigrants, who are educated and have adapted to a more modern lifestyle. This new generation of Muslims tends to be reflective in regard to the challenges of being a modern Muslim, and as such they are more critical of their parents' traditions and understanding of Islam.

One such example from this new generation is Tariq Ramadan, a philosopher and theologian who has made a great effort to discuss and define Muslim identity in Europe. However, he is careful with using the concept European Islam and prefers to speak on European Muslims. His point of departure is a theological reformation from below, and he is arguing that Islamic principles can be reconciled with European values. Ramadan does not see any obstacles for practicing Islam in Europe and he encourages Muslims to seek ways to combine their religiosity with an active participation in democratic life. Social integration of Muslims is also a way for the Europeans to begin to perceive Islam as a European religion (Ramadan 2002).

In similar fashion, the German convert Murad Hofmann advocates for the compatibility of Islam and European culture. However he focuses on Muslims' self-criticism, relating to conservative political and cultural patterns, as an important prerequisite for developing a new identity. This self-criticism implies e.g. a contextual interpretation of the Qur'an, changing the traditional view on women, liberation from formalism and opening up to critical thinking and practical rationality (Hofmann 1989).

The late Professor Mohammed Arkoun went one step further and emphasised a structural analysis of Islamic orthodoxy as a precondition for openness to new interpretations of Islam that could be relevant in a European context. Arkoun considered a historical-anthropological approach the most fruitful method and he also advocated for a comparative study of Judaism, Christianity and Islam, as three religions which have a common geographical and historical background, and have a distinguished role in European history. It would help to deconstruct the dominating essentialist interpretation of those three religions, and open to a better understanding of their actual coexistence, including the understanding of their humanistic potentials (Arkoun 2006).

It is interesting, however, that all of the above-mentioned – like many others, who deal with the issue of Muslim identity in Europe – exclusively relate to Muslim immigrants, thus presenting European Islam as a new phenomenon. They fail to take Balkan Muslims and other indigenous Muslim groups into consideration, who, unlike immigrants, have a long presence in and a different experience of Europe.

The Bosnian Experience

Bosnia and Herzegovina is a European region whose entire history is marked by religious pluralism. In Bosnian society Muslims, Christians and Jews have lived together for more than 500 years under the rule of different regimes with varying ideologies and through countless historical events and conflicts. Although Muslims have been the largest individual group for most of the time, they were not the majority, as they were outnumbered by the joint Orthodox Christian and Catholic populations.

Bosnia and Herzegovina is the perfect example of both coexistence and conflict. In other words, Bosnian history has shown that coexistence between different religions is possible, even when people have a relatively strong religious identity. However, it has also shown that ethnic-religious conflicts can easily arise, even when people do not take their ethnic-religious identity too seriously.

A quick review of Bosnian history shows that Bosnian Muslims have been a part of the vast Ottoman Empire (from the middle of the 15th century to the end of the 19th century), the Austrian-Hungarian monarchy (1878–1918), the Kingdom of Yugoslavia (1919–41), communist Yugoslavia (1943–92) and of an independent Bosnia and Herzegovina (since 1992), and as such they have more than 100 years of experience living in a non-Islamic, secular society. Throughout these historical periods, with all that it entails, Bosnian Muslims have developed a specific identity based on a harmonisation of Islamic principles with European humanistic values. As a religious minority, Bosnian Muslims managed to balance maintaining Islam as an identity element and opening up to other identities, thus always balancing between tradition and renewal. In this sense they can be considered the first modern example of European Islam. According to Xavier Bougarel, Bosnian Muslims particularly contributed to "the building of a European Islam," by "creating autonomous institutions and integrating them into a modern national state" (Bougarel 2005). They have developed a national consciousness, in line with other European nations, which is not determined (limited) by religion, and they do not problematise the western type of modern democracy.

The modern history of Bosnia begins with great political changes resulting from the Turks' withdrawal from the Balkans and the decision of the Berlin Congress to make Bosnia a part of Austria-Hungary. Immediately after the annexation of Bosnia-Herzegovina by Austria-Hungary, the local Muslim population was subjected to radical cultural and political reforms. The initial reaction to the new regime and the reforms introduced by Austrians was rejection, but gradually they adopted a number of socio-political changes. The relations between religion and state in the monarchy were based upon the concept of recognised religious communities (adopted in 1874). According to this concept, the state guaranteed freedom of religious belief and practice, and the recognised religious communities became corporations of public law.

There is no doubt that the reorganisation of the Islamic community in Bosnia, designed in the image of the Austrian administration, served a strategic objective – to reorient Bosnian Muslims away from Ottoman influence. Many Muslim intellectuals were educated in Vienna, Graz, Budapest and other Austrian-Hungarian intellectual centres, and they were promoters and advocates for modernisation of society. At the same time, a part of the religious elite preferred theological education in Cairo and Istanbul, which already functioned as two of the most important centres of Islam. Borrowing inspirations from the progressive movements in Egypt and Turkey but also from the modern Austrians, Bosnian Muslim scholars managed to establish a new terminology, which served to transform the legal language of classical Islam into a new language of religious and ethical norms which corresponded with a more secular terminology.[2]

Another very influential historical period which proved to be determining in regards to the identity of Bosnian Muslims is the period of Socialist Yugoslavia (1943–92). In the popular discourse among Muslims, it is considered as a period of a "de-islamisation" of Muslims (referring to the adoption of non-Muslim behaviour regarding alcohol, dress, sexuality, and so on). Quite concretely, Islam – and religion in general – was removed from the public political

---

2 As pointed out by Fikret Karcic, this development was clearly evident within the legislative thought (Sharia interpretation). Apart from codification of Islamic personal law following the model of Ahmad Qadiri-pasha's codex in Egypt, the most important reforms were incorporations of Shariah courts into the court system of a non-Muslim country; the adoption of the system of appellation; adoption of many technical features of Austro-Hungarian procedural law-representations of parties by lawyers etc. (Karcic 2007).

EUROPEAN ISLAM IN THE LIGHT OF THE BOSNIAN EXPERIENCE

life and religious practices were relegated to the private sphere, only marked in public by the celebration of religious holidays. The influence of religion was downplayed in the bigger cities, whereas it continued to have a significant role in the rural areas.[3] As a consequence, leading Muslim theologians such as Hussein Djozo and Ahmed Smajlovic were engaged with interpretations of Islam in relation to the secular socialist context. And a group of Muslim activists, known as Young Muslims (Mladi Muslimani), inspired by Islamist movements in the wider Muslim world, began to act against the regime's anti-religious restrictions. They were considered Islamic fundamentalists and a threat to the regime, and were therefore arrested in 1983 in what famously came to be known as the Sarajevo process. Among the accused was Alija Isetbegovic (imprisoned until 1988), who later founded a political party (Stranka Demokratske Akcije) and was elected as the first president of the independent state of Bosnia and Herzegovina.

During the 1990s, Bosnian Muslims went through a very turbulent political process that also affected their attitude to Islam. There is no doubt that the war, which was a consequence of ethnic nationalism and political abuse of religion and culture, has contributed to an increasing Islamisation of the Bosnian Muslim society. Nevertheless, one can still claim, that the majority of Bosnian Muslim are dedicated to a secular democratic society. For most of them the discussion does not revolve around choosing between the Islamic (religious) and the modern (secular), but rather around which model to choose in order to inspire the integration of the religious and ethical elements of Sharia within the existing legal system (Karcic 1999, 2007). Most importantly, this is an attitude which is generated by the official Islamic institutions in Bosnia and Herzegovina and educational institutions that played a crucial role in creating a Bosnian Muslim self-understanding.[4]

---

3   In this regard it is particularly interesting to look at how the Islamic identity was preserved in the families and at the pivotal role that women played in this process. This is described by Norwegian anthropologist Tone Bringa, who spent almost two years in the late 1980s in a village in central Bosnia studying Muslim religious practices. She managed to establish a trust-relationship with the local people and her work resulted in a deep and comprehensive analysis, not only on religious practice and customs, but also about the social structures of village life, about women and, indeed, about modernisation too. Her book has been well-received both in academic circles and by the broader Bosnian audience (Bringa 1995).

4   The Bosnian Islamic community is hierarchically organised. It is led by *Rijaset* (central council of *ulama*) as the main authority, and it is divided into different *Muftiat*s – some larger district areas – and any *muftiat* is further divided into *majlis* and local mosques – lesser organisational devices. In Sarajevo there is the Faculty of Islamic Studies that traditionally educated Muslim theologians/imams, and there are also three Islamic academies (in Zenica,

It should be noted that the ethnic name for Bosnian Muslims is "Bosniak." This is in fact an old name that Bosnian Muslims resumed using in 1992, in order to mark themselves as an ethno-cultural entity, unlike the name "Muslimani" (Muslims) which was adopted in the former Yugoslavia and which indicated that they only belong to a religious group. As pointed out by Noel Malcolm, in the past, the term Bosniak was sometimes used to include all who defined themselves as Bosnians regardless of their religious affiliation. However, since the Orthodox and the Catholics in BiH, during the last centuries gradually began to define themselves as, respectively, Serbs and Croats (rather than Bosnian), the term Bosniak today includes all those who have a Bosnian Muslim background, whether they are religious or not (Malcolm 2002, 126–127; 148–152).

However the Bosniak identity is not free from difficulties, tensions and misunderstanding. Some extreme secular Bosniaks tend to minimise the importance of Islam for their identity and ultimately look towards the pre-Islamic Bosnian heritage as a crucial factor for their identity. According to them, the Bosniak identity has its roots in the old middle-age Bogumil culture which basically was determined by a dualistic religious learning but had a religious practice that resembled Islam. As a contrast, others tend to glorify Islam as the essence of Bosniak-identity and according to them "bosniakness" (Bosnjanstvo) is not only shaped by Islam but outside Islam the Bosniak identity has no meaning. The greater majority of Bosniaks, who consider themselves representatives of so-called Bosnian traditional Islam,[5] insist that they both belong to the Bosnian-European culture and the wider Islamic civilisation, as the two lines historically did determine the development of their identity.

Misconceptions of Bosniaks are related to the ways in which they are perceived by others. They are not always accepted and understood, neither by Europeans nor by other Muslims. In the Europeans eyes generally speaking, they are seen as less European, because they are Muslims; while in the eyes of other Muslims they are viewed as less Muslim because they are Europeans.

Bihac and Mostar) that educate school teachers in Islam. These institutions are integrated into the country's school system.

5 In the last decades, it has been relevant to discuss the meaning and content of the Bosnian Muslim tradition. This is especially due to the presence of various Muslim missionary movements that have been active since the war (1992–95) which would ultimately create confusion among ordinary people. The Islamic religious community organised several seminars and launched campaigns in order to highlight the relevance of maintaining the authentic Bosnian Muslim tradition. In 2006, it also adopted a resolution on Islam interpretation (*Rezolucija islamske zajednice u Bosni i Hercegovini o tumacenju islam*) as a way to prevent infiltration of new and strange interpretations and practices.

The latter has been especially topical in relation to the Islamic mission in Bosnia-Herzegovina run by various Salafi and Wahhabi groups and organisations during the war and in the post-war period. Aside from propagating an Islamist ideology, these groups /organisations, which have gradually established an influence in Bosnia (and more generally across the whole Balkan area), work towards promoting the so-called pure Islam beyond cultural, national and ethnic particularities.

Concluding Remarks

The development of European Islam is not a new project to be initiated or constructed. Rather, it has already manifested itself as a result of the interplay existing between Muslims and the respective European societies they find themselves in. Also, as I have tried to show throughout this article, European Islam has had a long history in the Balkan countries and in that respect one can argue that experiences from this part of Europe are of particular importance for considerations on Muslim identity in Europe.

As an example, the dynamics of the institutionalisation of Islam in Bosnia-Herzegovina can be useful in relation to the institutionalisation of Islam in Western Europe. As pointed out by Niels Valdemar Vinding, the process of institutionalisation of Islam within the established socio-political structure of European societies seems to be one of the main strategic tasks for Muslim communities in Europe (Vinding 2013).

As a new religious and cultural minority in Western Europe, Muslims must seek to answer the following questions:

a) How – in practical terms – will Christians and Muslims live together in a modern society?
b) What is the potential of Islam in relation to modernity, democracy and secular society?
c) How can the relationship between religion and culture in a modern European context be understood?

Clarification of these issues and a readiness to find solutions will surely help in accommodating the Muslim inhabitants of European societies. However, the process of Muslim identification with Europe depends not only on Muslims themselves, i.e. whether they wish to identify themselves as European Muslims and/or whether they assume a reflective stance in terms of their belief and tradition. Rather, it equally depends on the surrounding majority populations, i.e. whether they want to maintain Muslims as a foreign element in society, meeting them with suspicion and social exclusion, or whether they are ready to include them so they can feel sufficiently at home to be both Muslims and respected citizens.

The development of a contextual theology that relates Islam to specific internal and external conditions and challenges that may arise should be a priority. The contributions of Bosnian theologians to this development, with an experience-based interpretation, will surely be unique, regardless of whether we recognise and acknowledge the existence of a specific Bosnian Islam or not.[6] However Bosnian theologians do not agree on the interpretation of all aspects of Islam. There are also internal discussions on the interpretation of Islam as well as of Bosnian Muslim culture.[7]

This brings us back to the question of whether a European Islamic theology (currently debated by politicians and others who seek and demand a new interpretation of Islam) can be developed or not. In order to answer the question, one must first consider the content and profile of such a theology. What do we expect from it? Besides being an expression of theological reflection on the aforementioned issues, many would expect, I suppose, that a European Islamic theology should live up to modern methodological requirements, such as contextual and hermeneutic interpretation of texts, analytical and critical approach to religious phenomenon etc. Thankfully, such a development is already taking place within Muslim theological thought.[8]

---

6 For example, Oliver Leaman denies the existence of a specific Bosnian or Balkan Islam. According to him, Bosnian Muslim tradition developed under the influence of the Turkish Ottoman tradition, and modern Bosnian Muslim theological thinking also developed under the influence of Islamic modernism. He also problematises the concept of European Islam as something that is in tension with Islamic universalism (Leaman 2014, 60–70).

7 This is reflected in a very timely public discussion in 2016 on the ban on wearing religious symbols – including the headscarf – in Bosnian courts. An interesting aspect of this discussion is not the differing views of the secular and religious representatives who generally disagree on this matter, but in fact the internal debate amongst Bosnian Muslim theologians, who have engaged themselves in a public debate of their conflicting views. Some are against the ban and argue that the wearing of the headscarf is not just a symbol but an Islamic duty (e.g. Dzemaludin Latic) whilst others argue that the headscarf is not an essential value of Islam (e.g. Resid Hafizovic).

8 Examples of this are: rethinking of Sharia and Muslim identity in a secular context (A. El-Fadl, B. Tibi, A. An-Naim, F. Karcic); rethinking of Islamic political theories, and Islam's relationship to democracy (W. Hallag, A. Soroush); Qur'anic hermeneutics and re-interpretation of Islamic orthodoxy (M. Arkoun, N.H. Abu Zayd, E. Karic); rethinking Islamic normativity within a European context (T. Ramadan).

When it comes to the profile of the European Islamic thought, no one can expect it to be monolithic. In reality, it should be seen as an open and multiplex process of reactions, adaptation, responding and interactions (just like the development in Bosnia), through which Muslims find their place in the European societies.

Bibliography

Arkoun, Mohammed. 2006 [2002]. *Islam: To Reform or to Subvert*, London: Saqi Essentials.

Bougarel, Xavier. 2007. "Bosnian Islam as 'European Islam': Limits and Shifts of a Concept," in *Islam in Europe. Diversity, Identity and Influence*, eds. Aziz al-Azmeh and Effie Fokas. Cambridge and New York: Cambridge University Press, 96–124.

Bougarel, Xavier. 2005. The role of Balkan Muslims in *Building a European Islam*, EPS Issue Paper Nr. 43. Brussels: European Policy Centre.

Bringa, Tone. 1995. *Being Muslim the Bosnian Way: Identity and Community in a Central Bosnian Village*. Princeton and London: Princeton University Press.

Hashas, Mohammed. 2013. *On the Idea of European Islam. Voices of Perpetual Modernity* (Ph.D. Dissertation). Rome. LUISS Guido Carli University of Rome.

Hofmann, Murad. 1989. "Wir und die Islamische Welt," in *al-Islam. Zeitschrift von Muslimen in Deutschland*. 1989/4. München.

Jeldtoft, Jul Nadia. 2012. *Everyday lived Islam* (Ph.D. Dissertation). Copenhagen: Faculty of Theology – University of Copenhagen.

Johansen Birgitte and Spielhaus Riem. 2012. "Counting Deviance: Revisiting a Decade's Production of Surveys among Muslims in Western Europe," in *Journal of Muslims in Europe 1* (2012): 81–112. Leiden: Brill.

Karcic, Fikret. 1999. "Administration of Islamic affairs in Bosnia and Hercegovina," in *Islamic Studies*, 38:4, 535–561.

Karcic, Fikret. 2007. "From Law to Ethics: the Process of Modernization and Reinterpreting the Shari'a in Bosnia," in *Bosnischer Islam für Europa*, Akademia der Diözese Rottenburg-Stuttgart, pp. 1–6.

Karic, Enes. 2004. *Essays on our European never-never Land*. Sarajevo: OKO.

Karlsson, Ingmar. 1994. *Islam og Europa. Sameksistens eller confrontation*. Copenhagen: Det lille forlag.

Leaman, Oliver. 2014. *Controversies in Contemporary Islam*. London and New York: Routledge.

Leirvik, Oddbjørn. 2014. *Islam og kristendom. Konflikt og dialog*. Oslo: Pax Forlag A/S.

Malcolm, Noel, 2002. *Bosnia. A short history*. London: Pan Books.

Nielsen. S. Jørgen. 1999. *Towards a European Islam*. London: Macmillan Press LTD.

Nielsen. S. Jørgen. 2007. "The question of Euro-Islam: restriction or opportunity?" in *Islam in Europe. Diversity, Identity and Influence*, eds. Aziz al-Azmah and Effie Fokas. Cambridge, New York.: Cambridge University Press, 34–48.

Ramadan, Tariq. 2002. *At være europæisk muslim*, København: Hovedland.

Rasmussen, Lissi. 2002. "Forord til den danske udgave" (= preface to the danish edition), in Tariq Ramadan: *At være europæisk muslim*, København: Hovedland.

Rezolucija Islamske Zajednice u Bosni i Hercegovini o tumacenju islama i drugi tekstovi. 2006. Sarajevo: El-Kalem.

Tibi, Bassam. 1995. "Les Conditions d'un Euro-Islam," in *Islams d'Europe: integration ou insertion communautaire?* eds. Robert Bistolfi and Francois Zabbal: Paris: Éditions de l'Aube, 230–233.

Vinding, Valdemar Niels, 2013. *Muslim Positions in the Religio-Organisational Fields of Denmark, Germany and England* (PhD thesis). Copenhagen: Faculty of Theology – University of Copenhagen.

Index

ADR, *see* Alternative Dispute Resolution
aesthetic   150, 153
Ahmadi   xix, 111, 114, 176
Ahmadiyya   xxii, 97, 172–73, 175, 177, 179, 182
Albania   97, 99, 184, 185, 187–89, 197, 199, 209
alcohol   22, 151, 218
Alevism   69, 73, 76, 81–82, 184–85
allochthonous   11
Alternative Dispute Resolution   v, xx, 24, 31, 33, 91–98, 100, 104, 106–108
American University of Beirut   xiii, xvi
angrezi shariat   32
Ankara   72, 74, 185, 192
Annotated Legal Documents on Islam in Europe   x, 109, 117n, 127
anti-discrimination   4
apostasy   viii, 172ff
al-'Arabi, Muhyi al-Din ibn (1165–1240)   174
Arkoun, Mohammed (1928–2010)   41, 48, 206, 216, 222n, 223
Armenia   71–72
asabiyya   40
assimilation   7, 9, 11, 14, 16, 18, 19, 27, 30, 59, 68, 72, 153, 216
asylum   101
AUB, *see* American University of Beirut
Austria   201, 217–18

Balkan   xxiii, 71, 74, 104n, 183n, 184–86, 193, 196–97, 199n, 206, 209–10, 212–13, 217–18, 221–23
Badr   132, 133
Bektashi   xix, xxii, 183ff
blasphemy   3, 145
Bosnian   viii, x, xix, xxii, xxiii, 46, 109, 184n, 198ff, 212ff
Bosnia-Herzegovina   46, 99n, 199–201, 206, 209n, 210, 218–221
Britain   xi, 23, 25, 28, 29, 31, 44, 49n, 91, 94, 97, 128, 140, *see also* United Kingdom

Caliphate   79, 140
Cartoon Crisis   xv, 46, 50, 143, 159–61
cathedral   57, 58

Catholic   5, 14, 40, 58, 59, 83, 85, 110, 112, 116, 119, 121, 125, 217, 220
Caucasus   71
Centre for European Islamic Thought   xv, 43n, 50, 164, 171, 215n
Centre for the Study of Islam and Christian-Muslim Relations   xiii, xiv, 159
Chaplaincy   59, 116, 118, 121, 162–64, 170
Christian-Muslim dialogue   xviii, 158m
Church of Denmark   54, 55, 60
churchification   vii, xx, 50ff
citizenship   12, 70, 72, 87
     citizenship, Danish   130
     citizenship, Dutch   7, 8, 9
     citizenship, French   4, 67, 72, 82, 86
     citizenship, German   70, 72
     citizenship, Turkish   67, 71
civil society   xiv, 40, 71
civilisation   12, 49n, 83, 132, 133, 137, 220
coexistence   xi, xxii, 158, 166, 213, 216
community   xi, xvii, xiv, 4, 11, 26, 27, 30, 33, 34, 46, 49, 64, 67ff, 92n, 97, 101n, 106, 142,143, 161, 167, 172n, 174–77, 193, 195, 196, 199, 201, 206–209
community, Islamic   44, 199, 201–205, 208, 209, 218, 219n, 220n
community, Muslim   xxi, 28, 41, 54, 57–62, 81, 97n, 109ff, 172n, 181, 199, 209
constitution   5, 6, 11, 15, 47, 54, 67, 70, 75, 97, 98n, 110–12, 118, 176
Constitutional Court   123, 125
conversion   60, 63, 190, 193, 196
convert   42, 113–16, 119–22, 124–25, 138, 153, 196, 216
cosmology   194
criminal   97–103, 106, 107, 165, 167
criminalisation   72, 81

Danish Institute in Damascus   xiv
demography   21, 32, 113, 115, 125
Denmark   xii, xiii, xiv, xxi, xxii, 31, 40, 49, 50, 54, 55, 59, 60, 128, 129, 141–145, 159–163, 166, 168–70, 176, 177, 224
Deobandi   46
Dervish   183–185, 188n, 189, 192

diaconia 161, 162, 166, 170

dialogue xii, xiii, xviii, xxii, 49n, 60n, 77, 157–61, 186n

diaspora 34, 68, 70, 74, 171

Disraeli, Benjamin (1804–1881) 128

DITIB, *see* Turkish-Islamic Union for Religious Affairs

diversity xv, xviii, xx, 6, 8, 10, 11, 14, 15, 17, 25, 44n, 45–48, 93, 97n, 98, 163, 164, 207n, 215, 223, 224

Diyanet, *see* Turkish-Islamic Union for Religious Affairs

dogma 37, 38, 49n, 150, 173

dogmatic 77, 150, 187, 197

domestication 4, 6, 19, 28

drug 99, 101, 106, 153

Egypt xiii, xxviii, 9, 99n, 115, 131, 132, 151, 177, 206, 208, 218

epistemology xix, 9, 16, 17, 49n

Erdoğan, Tayyip (1954 -) 70, 71, 80, 82

Erlangen Centre of Islam and Law in Europe (EZIRE) xix, 99

Euro-Islam 44n, 212, 213, 216, 224

European Council of Fatwa and Research 39, 205

European Union x, 65, 110

Evangelical Lutheran 54, 110, 162, 163

exceptionalism v, 3ff

Facebook 146, 149, 151

fatwa 3, 4, 39, 45, 129, 174n, 177, 180, 205, 209

foreign 4, 10, 16, 31, 42, 53, 61, 74, 75, 81, 83, 84, 120, 121, 144, 199, 200, 204, 208–10, 222

Friday prayer 114, 141, 147

fundamentalism 37, 40, 41, 74, 80, 94n, 152, 186n, 219

generation v, xx, 10, 26, 31, 42n, 43n, 45, 46, 67ff, 137, 142, 143, 201, 212, 215, 216

German Islam Conference 54, 92n

Germany v, xi, xx, 5, 49n, 50, 61, 65, 70, 73–75, 81, 84, 91ff, 210, 224

al-Ghazali, Abu Hamid Muhammad (1058–1111) 194, 205, 206, 209

ghetto 141, 149, 213

Gospel 190–193, 196

Greek 71, 110, 146

Gulf War xix, 3, 4, 16

Gülen, Fethullah (1941 -) 76n, 81, 205

hadith xxi, 25, 134, 136–40, 177, 178, 180–82, 187, 203n, 204

hagiography xxi, 137, 192, 193, 196

halal xvii, 117–119, 121, 139n, 204

headscarf xix, 16, 23, 63, 77, 222n, *see also* veil

heresy 153, 173, 182

hijab 117, 119, 121

Hinduism 5, 33, 65

Hudhaybiyya 133

Hungary 218

ideology 15, 45, 73–75, 78, 80, 212, 213, 221

imam 36, 39–41, 46, 51, 57–60, 64, 66, 68, 72, 75, 78, 83–85, 96n, 98, 100, 103–106, 117–21, 157n, 161, 165, 166, 168, 183, 187, 200, 201, 205–207, 219n

Imitatio Christi 192

immigrant xxiii, 3, 4, 6–8, 10, 15, 16, 31, 69, 71, 73–75, 77, 86, 93, 107, 113, 119, 121, 122, 124, 125, 141, 143, 144, 212, 213, 216, 217

individualisation 37, 40, 42, 87, 167, 168, 214

institutionalisation xx, 7, 18, 50, 51, 54, 55–57, 60–63, 65, 93, 97, 109, 185, 189, 190, 201, 221

integration xvii, xix, 4–16, 18, 28, 38, 42, 44, 50, 59, 60, 62, 64, 65, 73, 142, 161, 166, 196, 199, 201, 210, 212, 213, 215, 216, 219, 224

interdisciplinary xiv, xix, 22, 23, 26, 27, 199n

ISIS, *see* Islamic State in Iraq and Syria

Islam, European v, viii, xv, xvii, xix, xx, xxiii, 35ff, 66, 95n, 209n, 212ff

Islamic State in Iraq and Syria xviii, 23, 42, 59, 129, 140

Islamic thought 35, 41–45, 47, 48, 174n, 200, 204, 210

INDEX

Islamic-Christian Study Centre   xxii, 158, 162–69
Islamisation   9, 13, 17, 218, 219
Islamism   37, 74n, 151
islamophobia   xxii, 112, 112n, 182
isnad   136
isomorphism   56, 62–64
Israel   xiii, xiv, 131, 137, 180n

jahiliyya   130
Jain   30
Jama'at-i-Islami   176
Jamaat e-Tablighi   46
jihad   xix, xxi, 42, 129ff, 153, 174
jihadism   42n, 43n, 108, 128ff, 151, 186
Jordan   99n, 128, 129, 131, 140, 177
Judaism   83, 150, 188, 194, 216
jurisdiction   31, 91n, 96n

Kemalism   78–80
Khomeini, Ruhollah (1902–1989)   3, 78
kufr   130, 138, 178–79

laïcité   xxxvi, 66, 213
law
   law, civil   xxvii, 104, 117
   law, constitutional   54, 97
   law, customary   29, 93, 98n, 104
   law, German   100–108
   law, Islamic   xiii, xvii, xviii, xxi, 24, 33, 91, 93n, 98n, 105, 106, 109ff, 200, 204, 205
   law, marriage   30, 104, 105, 117, 120
   law, religious   29, 92n, 94n
Lebanon   xiii, xiv, xvi, 99n, 144, 166
liberal   xix, xxi, 5, 12, 17, 18, 37–41, 54, 55, 59, 60, 79, 129, 141, 149, 151–53, 213
literature   x, xiii, xxii, xxiii, 35, 94, 99, 132, 133, 138, 141, 143, 145, 153, 178, 181, 182, 198ff
literature, Islamic   xxii, xxiii, 153, 198ff
Lithuania   v, x, xxi, 109ff
Lutheran   x, 54, 59, 110, 159, 162, 163, 171
Lutheran World Foundation   159

madrasa   200, 204, 208
Makalat   xxii, 183ff
maqasid al-sharia   44

marriage   20, 27, 29, 30, 33, 87, 96, 98–101, 103–105, 107, 116, 117, 120, 200n, 207
   marriage, Muslim   27, 30, 31, 53
   marriage, Islamic   30, 104, 105, 117, 120, *see also nikah*
Marxist   73, 74
maslaha   44
messenger   134, 175, 178
millet   63, 67, 71
Millî Görüş   74–76, 78–85
Morocco   9, 10, 48, 99n, 129, 130, 139, 140
mosque   7, 30, 51–53, 57, 58, 64, 68, 74, 76–78, 83–85, 103, 104, 113, 114, 120, 144, 147, 149, 168, 176, 177, 198, 200, 201, 203n, 219
Mother Theresa (1910–1997)   183, 188
mufti   xxviii, 119, 120, 121, 138, 207–209
Muftiate   113, 114, 116, 123, 126, 219
multiculturalism   4, 8, 12, 14–16, 19, 31, 33, 48n, 86, 94n, 96n, 126
Muslim exceptionalism   3ff
Muslimophobia, *see also* Islamophobia
Muslims in Western Europe   xi, xvii, 3, 18, 34, 46, 59, 66, 223

Naqshbandi   76, 78
Netherlands, the   x, xix, 3ff, 49n, 84, 92
nikah   29–31, 117, 120, *see also* Islamic Marriage
Norway   x, 159, 210

One Law for All   22, 24
organisation   5, 7–11, 28, 46, 50ff, 69, 71, 73, 75–86, 92, 110, 112–114, 116, 122–25, 158–63, 166, 176, 185, 119, 203, 218, 219n, 221
orthodox   xxi, 40, 41, 86n, 110, 113, 152, 173, 182, 187, 188, 192, 196, 216, 217, 220, 222n
Ottoman   xviii, 67, 71, 183n, 184n, 185, 192n, 197n, 213, 218, 222n
Ottoman Empire   79, 184, 217

Pakistan   34n, 99n, 115, 129, 159, 172, 176, 177, 179, 180
Palestine   99, 129, 132, 142, 143n
parallel justice   v, 91, 95–99, 101, 103, 106, 107

pastoral care   161, 162

pluralism   xviii, xix, 20, 21, 25–27, 31, 33, 34, 36, 43, 44, 46, 48, 49, 63–65, 87, 91–94, 96, 126, 151, 186n, 187n, 201, 205, 206, 214, 217

plurilegal   21, 32

poetry   xxi, 142–44, 146, 148–50, 152, 204

post-Islamism   37, 42, 151n

priest   51, 57, 58, 60, 64, 121, 165

prison   xxii, 6, 59, 116, 121, 128, 129, 132, 141, 143, 157, 161–68, 208

privatisation   37

Protestant   5, 14, 58, 59, 83, 171

al-Qaradawi, Yusuf (1926 -)   204–206, 209

qibla   178

Qur'an   25, 43n, 130, 133, 140, 144–51, 153, 174n, 175, 177–82, 187, 193–95, 204, 208

Qur'anic   xxi, 77, 84, 133, 134, 138, 139, 146–52, 200, 202, 204

Qutb, Sayyid (1906–1966)   134, 138, 140, 205

rabbi   52, 58

radical   xxi, 42, 45, 70, 72, 80, 143, 151–53, 186, 200, 206, 207, 218

radicalisation   14, 152, 165, 166, 198, 200n

radicalism   17

Ramadan   39, 144

Ramadan, Tariq (1962 -)   36, 39, 40, 44, 47, 48, 152, 205, 216, 222n

recitation   xxi, 145–52

regulatory   20, 21

RELIGARE   xv, 91

religio-organisational   50, 57, 63, 66, 224

religion   xii, xiv, xv, xvi, 8, 10, 12, 16, 17, 19, 21, 22, 27, 35, 37, 38, 40, 41, 53, 54, 58, 59, 63, 64, 68–73, 76, 78–88, 91, 92, 108, 110, 117, 119, 120n, 130, 133, 135, 136, 148–50, 153, 158, 164, 170, 173, 175, 180–84, 188, 189, 193, 203, 207n, 212–14, 216–19

religion, freedom of   5, 6, 33, 97, 107, 172n, 174n, 208

religion, immigrant   6, 16

religion, traditional   35, 110, 122, 124

religion and culture   xvii, 8, 22, 53, 171, 209, 213, 221

religion and state   4, 48, 55, 57, 62, 64, 66, 93n, 110, 208n, 209n

revelation   48, 131, 179n, 188, 189, 194, 195

Rida, Rashid (1865–1935)   44

ritual   39, 119, 137, 144, 147, 149–51, 167, 183, 187, 189, 196, 200, 203, 205

Rome   36, 48n, 57, 131, 223n

Rushdie Affair, the   xix, 3, 4, 12, 15, 16, 23

Salafi   xii, 17, 37, 45, 100, 108, 114, 129, 198, 203, 205–207, 221

Salafism   104, 106, 186

Saudi Arabia   4, 208

School of Oriental and African Studies   xiii, xix, 25, 32

secular   xv, xvi, xvii, xxiii, 4, 18, 23, 30, 35, 39, 40, 53–55, 62, 99, 100, 104, 108, 118, 119, 122, 174, 185n, 208, 209n, 213–15, 217–22

secularism   27, 37, 39n, 40, 42, 54, 55, 59, 64, 82, 91, 171

secularisation   xxiii, 6, 36n, 37–42, 43n, 60, 125

securitisation   xxii, 14, 65, 198

September 11, 2001   xviii, 39, 159, 160

shahada   131, 133

sharia   xvii, xviii, xxi, 33, 40, 44, 45, 92n, 94–98, 103, 117, 119, 126, 138, 218n, 222

Sharia Councils   31, 97, 100, 218n

al-Shatibi (1320–1388)   44, 45

sheikh   76, 157, 184

Shia   78, 111, 115, 130, 174, 186n, 187, 196, 206

Sikh   29, 30

socio-cultural   20, 24, 32, 44, 103, 107

sociology   xv, xviii, 9, 27, 42, 54, 64, 66, 80

Soroush, Abdolhakim (1945 -)   41, 222

Spain   213

spiritual   xxii, 3, 73, 76, 110, 111, 113, 123–26, 151, 163, 164, 167, 168, 170, 185, 192n, 207

sufi   vi, xxii, 79, 151, 183ff, 203, 205–208

Sufism   114, 153, 186n, 196, 200, 204

Sunna   25, 178, 200, 204, 205

INDEX 229

sunni 69, 73, 74, 78, 81, 82, 110–20, 122–26, 172, 174, 175, 185, 193, 195, 197, 206, 207
survey vii, xi, 50, 67, 139, 207, 209, 214, 223
Süleymancı 74–79, 85
symbol 83, 88, 146, 189, 222n
symbolic 23, 27
syncretism 153, 186
Syria xiv, xviii, 99n, 129, 132, 140, 166, 177, 213

tafsir 134, 137–40
Tatar xix, 39, 111, 113–15, 119, 120, 122, 124, 125, 133, 199, 209, 212
terror xviii, 59, 141n
terrorism 27, 124, 128, 129, 132n, 139n, 140, 143n, 160, 165n
theology xii, xiii, xiv, xv, xvi, xix, xxii, 35–48, 50, 51, 54, 66, 84, 94, 145, 167, 168, 173, 175, 199n, 213, 222
Turkey xx, 9, 34, 67ff, 99, 104n, 131, 185, 199n, 218
Turkish xx, 67ff, 114, 189, 204, 211, 222n
Turkish-Islamic Union for Religious Affairs 74–76, 78, 79, 83–85, 114

Ukraine 109
ulama 58, 130, 133, 137, 176n, 219n
Union of Muslim Organisations 28

United Kingdom xiii, xvi, xxi, 20, 28–31, 91n, 92, 94, 100, 109, 128, 173, 176, *see also* Britain

Vatican 40
veil 23, 37, 39, 46, 133, *see also* headscarf
Velayetname xii, 183, 184, 186, 189, 190ff
violence 17, 42, 43n, 45, 46, 93, 96–98, 100n, 101, 103, 104, 106, 132n, 139n, 140, 141, 142, 172, 182

al-Wahhab, Muhammad Ibn Abd (1703–1792) 44, 199n
Wahhabi 45, 186, 199n, 206, 221
Weber, Max (1864–1920) 70, 87, 189
witness 4, 17, 25, 30, 45, 95, 96, 102–105, 128, 133, 143, 153, 157ff, 201
World Council of Churches xiii, 159, 187
World War, First 185
World War, Second x, 6

xenophobia 67, 160

YouTube 142n, 146, 149

al-Zarqawi, Abu Musaab (1966–2006) 132
Zayd, Nasr Hamid Abu (1943–2010) 41, 206, 222n